D1055556

INDIRA GANDHI

INDIRA GANDHI
A Profile in Courage

TREVOR DRIEBERG

VIKAS PUBLICATIONS
DELHI ✳ BOMBAY ✳ BANGALORE
KANPUR ✳ LONDON

VIKAS PUBLICATIONS

5 DARYAGANJ, ANSARI ROAD, DELHI-6
SAVOY CHAMBERS, 5 WALLACE STREET, BOMBAY-1
10 FIRST MAIN ROAD, GANDHI NAGAR, BANGALORE-9
80 CANNING ROAD, KANPUR
17-21 SUNBEAM ROAD, NORTH ACTON, LONDON N.W. 10

DS
481
·G23
D74
c.2

© TREVOR DRIEBERG, 1972

SBN 7069 0180 0

PRINTED IN INDIA
BY AROON PURIE AT THOMSON PRESS (INDIA) LIMITED, FARIDABAD,
HARYANA, AND PUBLISHED BY MRS SHARDA CHAWLA, VIKAS
PUBLICATIONS, 5 DARYAGANJ, ANSARI ROAD, DELHI-6

PREFACE

THE RESPONSIBILITY for this book falls squarely on a good friend attached to the publishing house which has brought it out. I disown any blame cast on me for it. We were sitting in the Press Club of India, New Delhi, discussing likely subjects for books one afternoon in November 1971 when I suggested that a political study of the Prime Minister, timed for release at the start of the general election the following March, might be topical.

My friend jumped at the idea. "Why don't you write it?" he asked. He didn't give me time to say yes or no, taking it for granted that I agreed. After that scarcely a day passed without at least one telephone call from him to find out how the book was going. I began to hate telephones, even extending my phobia to Alexander Graham Bell.

This book is the product of my friend's bullying and cajoling. I hope he likes it. Now that the task is over, I am very grateful to my publishers, who gave me the fullest encouragement to work on a subject which has fascinated me as a journalist who has spent long years trying to unravel the intricacies of Indian politics.

Of all the significant and absorbing things I have seen in 27 years of newspapering, the most fascinating is Indira Gandhi's rise to power. As I pored over documents of various kinds in my search for authentic material for this book—biography is too presumptuous a word to describe it—I realised more and more that here was a unique political phenomenon. This was not because the Prime Minister is a woman, for I do not subscribe to the comforting male theory of female inferiority, a theory concocted by men to maintain top place in what is still very much a man's world. This theory is unfortunately accepted without question by the great majority of women.

Mrs Gandhi has attained a position of political dominance far beyond that of most dictators through purely democratic, parliamentary means. She commands greater respect and wields greater power than the great majority, if not all, of those who hold similar

693573

office through unfettered elective processes. And, what is even more significant, she uses this almost unlimited power she has in India in a democratic manner to serve democratic ends. Under her guidance, India has a great role to play in bringing peace and rapid, orderly development to the Third World, which though legally free is still bound to its colonial past.

In conclusion, I am grateful to all those who helped me in this venture, which started as a chore and ended with a feeling of fulfilment. Among them are D.K. Joshi and Jag Mohan, who read through the manuscript and offered invaluable advice. Jag Mohan, Virender Mohan and Veenu Sandal were of great help in picking material from assorted sources—books, magazines, articles, old newspapers and official documents—to provide me with the basic ingredients of this book. Finally, I must thank M.V.S. Prasad for chaining himself to a typewriter for long hours daily for three weeks to type drafts and fair copies of the manuscript in spite of a broken ankle in plaster, the result of an encounter with a taxi while riding a bicycle.

I hope those who read this book will derive as much from it as I derived producing it.

New Delhi   TREVOR DRIEBERG

CONTENTS

Dedicated to the shirtless ones of India, whose hopes of a better life in which poverty and unemployment are banished centre on Indira Gandhi. Their votes have made her the unchallenged leader of India, and they will be the ultimate judges of her success as Prime Minister of the world's largest democracy

CHAPTER ONE

THE FLEDGLING YEARS

MANY YEARS AGO, a little girl sat on her grandfather's knee as millions of little girls have done and will do. But in this particular instance the place where it happened was unusual. The scene was an improvised courtroom in the jail at Allahabad, a provincial city in the eastern region of what was then known as the United Provinces, a part of the British Indian Empire. Allahabad's main claim to fame is that it stands at a point where three rivers, Ganga, Yamuna, and the mythical Saraswati, mingle. Hindus from all corners of India come to Sangam, as the meeting of the rivers is called, to cast the ashes of the dead into their waters or to purify their own souls.

But this was a far cry from the events in the jail on December 7, 1921. The grandfather was Motilal Nehru, one of the most successful advocates practising in Allahabad High Court, and, what was still more important, an outstanding leader of the movement for self-rule for India. The girl who sat on his knee was four-year-old Indira Priyadarshini Nehru, the only child of his only son Jawaharlal. She was known affectionately among the family as Indu.

Motilal Nehru was on trial for participating in a satyagraha, a movement of peaceful protest, organised throughout the country by the Indian National Congress. The aim of the satyagraha was to impress on the British rulers of the country, both in New Delhi and in distant London, that the great majority of the people of India stood squarely behind the Congress in its demand that colonial rule end and they be given the right to guide their own destinies.

Motilal, an imperious, quicktempered but lionhearted and generous man whose word few people, either in his close family circle or in the legal or political world, dared challenge, sat back in his chair and looked at the proceedings more like a disinterested spectator than its central figure. Not so his granddaughter, for whom this was the first encounter with the majesty and solemnity and impartiality and all the other paraphernalia of British justice. She watched it intently, her large, dark eyes, the most significant feature of her thin but finely chiselled face, taking in everything in what to her was a novel drama, the white man who sat in powdered wig and black gown on an elevated chair and listened, owl-like, to the arguments of prosecution and defence, and the obedient functionaries who bowed and scraped before this representative of the all-powerful British Raj. Her ears registered strange words that meant little to her then. For Indu, this experience was her "first baptism of fire in the political wars," according to her father's sister, the late Krishna Hutheesing.

Indira Nehru, who was later to become a world celebrity as Indira Gandhi, was thus initiated into politics. Many years later, she too was imprisoned, without trial, for the heinous crime of fighting in the nonviolent tradition of satyagraha for her country's freedom. Still later, 29 years more or less, she was to commit the even more heinous crime, in the eyes of some people who swear by liberty and democracy, of being instrumental in liberating another race living on the Indian subcontinent from a tyrannous military dictatorship.

But this was all in the future. In the early 1920s, she started her apprenticeship in politics at a time other children were playing nurse to dolls and making mudpies and skipping rope. Anand Bhavan, the Nehru mansion in Allahabad, was one of the centres of the Indian freedom movement. It was more like a political headquarters than a dwelling. People constantly came and went, always talking, arguing till the grey hours of the morning, drafting resolutions, issuing appeals to their countrymen to assert their right to rule themselves. The sole topic of conversation was *swaraj*—freedom. Among the frequent visitors to Anand Bhavan in those exciting days was Mohandas Karamchand Gandhi, the architect and foremost practitioner of nonviolent struggle, who was to have a lasting influence on Indira's political thinking and general outlook.

Rather a strange atmosphere for a little girl to be brought up in. These influences showed themselves in her activities even at this early, formative stage in her life. She used to round up the multitude of family retainers at Anand Bhavan and make speeches to them, exhorting them to strive for freedom the satyagraha way. While her elders talked, unconscious of the child sitting silent among them, she was absorbing ideas, half-formed, half-comprehended, that were later to be the foundation of her philosophy of life.

December 1921 was a sad month for the Nehru household. The heads of the family were in prison. Motilal and Jawaharlal had been sentenced to terms of imprisonment for refusing to pay the fine of Rs 500 imposed on each of them for their part in the satyagraha. Imprisonment did not, however, liquidate their obligations to pay the fines. The British-imposed laws demanded that the amounts be collected by seizing their movable property and selling it for whatever it would fetch until these sums were realised.

Policemen in uniform descended on Anand Bhavan, grabbed anything they could lay hands on and took it away. What they took was of much greater value than the Rs 1,000 that was due to their masters. To nobody at Anand Bhavan were these unwelcome visitors, little better than plunderers in the livery of enforcers of law and order, more repugnant than to Indu. How dare they invade the house of her grandfather and father in their absence and walk off with their property? Among the articles they made off with were carpets, silverware, and even the family motor car. She stormed at them in Hindi, ordering them to put down their loot and get out. When they ignored her and jeeringly went about their business with clumsy insolence, she shook her tiny fist at them, once even attacking one of them physically.

She described these incidents later in these words: "This continuous process of despoliation was irritating enough, but to watch it impotently was beyond the patience of a strongwilled child such as I was. I protested to the police and indicated my strong displeasure in every way I could, once nearly chopping off an officer's thumb with a bread-slicing gadget."

Many years later, that same fist, grown larger but still retaining its grace and softness, was to be clenched and raised at public meetings throughout the country to drive home a point to multitudes of her countrymen. It was destined to symbolise the indomitable courage and will of this woman who was to change the history of the Indian subcontinent in as decisive a manner as the older generations of freedom fighters to which Motilal and Jawaharlal Nehru belonged did when they won swaraj in 1947.

The Nehrus were highly respected in Allahabad. Motilal Nehru was a national hero, as his son and granddaughter were to become later. But in the centre of British power in New Delhi and among its local representatives they were considered a bad lot. They bred sedition, talked and acted in a way designed to bring disrepute to the British Raj, the self-proclaimed protector and benefactor of India's unlettered, starving millions. Of course, these bureaucrats would not admit that this illiteracy and starvation were the handiwork of their supposedly beneficent rule, and they objected when people like Mahatma Gandhi and the Nehrus and other Indian nationalists said so.

Jawaharlal had been educated in Britain and had qualified as a barrister there. He had even been permitted to school at Harrow, one of the most sacred institutions of the British establishment, and go on to Cambridge University in the hope that he would learn gentlemanly ways and practise them when he returned to his motherland. But alas, this was not to be. Were the Nehrus, father and son, grateful for these opportunities to learn to think and live like the British ruling class? Not at all. Like Caliban in *The Tempest,* who used the language Prospero taught him only to curse, they acquired the language of the masters of their country to spread subversion and rebellion. It was enough to send shooting upward the blood pressure of any imperial satrap or underling toiling manfully to shoulder the burden of empire in the uncongenial climate of the Gangetic Plain.

This was the atmosphere in which Indu grew up. She even transmitted it to her playthings. One day, while the nation was responding to Gandhi's call that it refuse to cooperate with the foreign government by withholding taxes and in other ways, Indu was playing with her dolls and tin soldiers. She lined them up in two opposing rows, one comprising unarmed satyagrahis and the other clubwielding policemen and British soldiers carrying rifles. She harangued the satyagrahis, explaining the great role they had to play and exhorting them to show no fear of the awesome enemy.

She stuck flags, cut out of paper and coloured with crayons, in the hands of the satyagrahis. Then the opposing forces moved against each other while the organiser of this political pageant shouted excitedly:

Bharat Mata ki jai (long live Mother India)
Hindu-Muslim Zindabad (long live Hindu-Muslim unity)
Mahatma Gandhi ki jai (long live Mahatma Gandhi).

The opposing forces met, and in the ensuing clash between the violent and the nonviolent the right cause prevailed.

These and similar events in the early life of Indira Gandhi assume historic significance today. One may well ask: Would she be what she is, and where she is, if her upbringing had been different? If, in her childhood and girlhood, she was not actually near a centre of power, she was near one with this potential, an alternative centre in which the aspirations and hopes of the Indian people were concentrated. She lived in an ambience in which the conquest of power to achieve national liberation was the most essential and vital element.

Politics is fundamentally the art of acquiring and keeping state power. A politician is a professional practitioner of this art. If he thinks differently, he is a misfit. He should not be in politics. Deep inside her, in the subterranean corridors of the unconscious, Indira Nehru must have at a very young age developed an urge for political power, not as an end in itself but as a means to achieve greater national ends. At the appropriate time, when circumstances combined to project her as India's third Prime Minister in 1966, the practical lessons she had learnt, more by chance than deliberately, over the years, starting with that chill December day in a tomblike, stonewalled room with barred windows in the prison house in Allahabad and continuing for 45 years, fitted her for the astounding role she was to play in the 1970s.

When George the III of Britain was still a child, his mother used to tell him : "George, be a king". Nobody told Indira in her childhood: "Indu, be a prime minister." But such were her surroundings that they inevitably stimulated in her those faculties necessary to wield power, to command men and lead nations. Thus, when the call came to her, she was prepared mentally for it. In seven swift years she soared from comparative immaturity and obscurity to accomplished statesmanship and to be numbered among the decisive leaders of Asia. Her apprenticeship was long and laborious, but when she finally arrived at the centre of the political stage it was with the force of an atomic explosion.

Many years later, Indira acknowledged the debt she owed Gandhi, who with her father and grandfather was a seminal influence on her in the most impressionable period of her life. She once wrote: "He forms part of my earliest memories, and as a very small child

I regarded him not as a great leader but more as an elder of the family to whom I went with difficulties and problems which he treated with the grave seriousness which was due to the large-eyed and solemn child I was." As she grew up, she studied his style of political work at close quarters and drew lessons from it. She learnt "how intimately he was in contact with the masses of our country, their thoughts, their ideals and aspirations. This contributed in no small measure to his greatness." It has also contributed greatly to Indira Gandhi's success as Prime Minister of India and undisputed leader of the Congress Party. She learnt too from the Mahatma that "religion and politics were not to be expounded, but to be put into practice by making them part of our daily lives and of our normal thinking."

Recollecting these early days in an article written in 1961 to commemorate the centenary of her grandfather's birth, Indira said he had bought in 1900 the house in Allahabad where she was born and spent her childhood. He named it Anand Bhavan, the Abode of Joy. She wrote: "In days of affluence or in days of hardship, the household was sternly governed by my grandfather—his awe-inspiring temper softened by quick forgiveness and infectious laughter, his strict discipline tempered by his love for his family and his enormous zest for life."

In February 1922, after violence had marred the civil disobedience movement Gandhi had launched the previous year, he called off the satyagraha, much to the surprise and displeasure of other senior Congress leaders like Motilal Nehru. Under Nehru's inspiration, some Congressmen decided to form a new group called the Swaraj Party to speed up the process of winning independence. Indira recalls that her grandfather issued a manifesto on behalf of the Swaraj Party from Anand Bhavan in 1923, warning the British Government that unless India was granted the status of a dominion within the British Empire immediately his party would adopt a policy of "uniform, continuous and consistent obstruction with a view to make government through the assembly [the Central Legislative Assembly in New Delhi] impossible." A conference of all Indian political parties was appointed to draft a new constitution for the proposed dominion of India and held its meetings at Anand Bhavan.

But the Nehru mansion was more than a place for political debate.

Its activities were many and varied. "It was home and a training ground not only to us who were born or brought up in it but also for many others, young and old; some came because they were far from home (one young man was from Ceylon) or simply because they found more inspiration or sympathy or understanding than in their own homes," says Indira.

It also functioned as an emergency hospital for the victims of police brutality in clashes with satyagrahis. Government hospitals often refused to treat Congress volunteers wounded by rifle fire or by charges with *lathis,* long canes tipped with iron at the striking end. In her own words: "One night several quite young boys were brought in with bullet wounds and in critical condition. My mother persuaded my grandfather to allow her to keep them in the house. So from September 1929 a part of the house was turned into a hospital. In the beginning doctors came only at dead of night and the women of the house, including myself, aged 12, were the nurses. Later, there was a good staff and suitable equipment."

Anand Bhavan, according to Charles F. Andrews, an Irishman who joined the Indian freedom movement and was a valued friend of Gandhi and the Nehrus, was like "one of the stately country houses in England owned by the high aristocracy." The style of living of the Nehrus did not, however, continue in this manner much longer. Motilal Nehru decided to hand the house over to the nation and built a smaller one in the same grounds. The family moved into this modest dwelling in 1928. It was also named Anand Bhavan.

The old mansion became Swaraj Bhavan and was turned into the headquarters of the Indian National Congress. It held this status until the Congress Party shifted its main office to Delhi in 1946. In 1948 the Congress Working Committee decided to turn Swaraj Bhavan into a home for children, and the Children's National Institute took it over in 1949.

The new Anand Bhavan has also been gifted to the nation by Mrs Gandhi. On November 1, 1970, she handed it over at a formal ceremony to the Jawaharlal Nehru Memorial Trust. With tears rolling down her cheeks and a catch in her throat, she said at the ceremony, to which she had invited 500 relatives, friends and former Congress colleagues of Allahabad: "Anand Bhavan was hardly ever my home in a real sense. I studied at different places, and wandered from place to place. I have memories only about this home. The police used to lathi-charge volunteers brutally, and the injured were brought to Swaraj Bhavan. Those days, because of fear, doctors refused to treat the wounded during the day. They would come in the darkness of the night to attend to them. Those were glorious days. Congressmen gallantly braved tremendous hardships because they knew that they were loyal soldiers in the struggle for India's freedom. People complain of their difficulties today, but what did those poor people get by participating in that struggle, I ask."

Mrs Gandhi recalled that her first quarrel with her father took place at Anand Bhavan in 1930. The civil disobedience movement was on, and one of its features was emphasis on *swadeshi*—using only Indian products. In observance of this directive from Mahatma Gandhi, the Nehru family made a bonfire of all their foreign clothes and knickknacks. Books, of course, were spared. Into the fire, lit on the terrace of the house, went dresses of costly fabrics and other personal wear of Indira, and her collection of foreign dolls. Indira wanted to go up to see the fire, but her father refused, saying it was past her bedtime. She appealed to her grandfather, who replied: "Yes, darling, I will take you." How her father reacted to this act of indiscipline she did not say.

Indira's formal education began when she entered St Cecilia's School, run by Roman Catholic nuns, in Allahabad in 1924. But throughout her girlhood and womanhood her real education in the many facets of life was to come through the world of politics into which she was inducted at Anand Bhavan when she was scarcely out of infancy. Her educators were the men and women who came there to frame plans for India's freedom in association with her father and grandfather, and others whom she met when she travelled with her father to Congress sessions in different parts of India. Later, her horizons widened as she was introduced to foreign statesmen, writers, and philosophers in the course of European tours undertaken with her parents. Her schooling was sporadic, often interrupted by change of place and by the upsets in the Nehru household caused by her father's frequent arrest in the years of freedom struggle that were climaxed by independence in 1947.

Indira had a liberal education in the true sense of the word.

She read what she wanted, concentrated her attention on subjects which interested her, and most of what she learnt was through the use of her own powers of observation and comprehension, which were sharpened in this process. Her mind matured earlier and faster than those of other Indian children of the same age and social standing who went through the grind of the sterile system of instruction that still continues long after it has outlasted its usefulness, if it was ever useful. Her own definition of education is: "Education in the widest sense of the word is the training of the mind and body, so as to produce a balanced personality which is capable of adjusting, without undue disturbance, to life's changing situations. This cannot be achieved through schools or book knowledge alone."

She roved freely through her father's wellstocked and wideranging library, reading Shakespeare and Shaw when other girls were nourished intellectually on a diet of fairy tales and nursery rhymes. It was in this library that she first read about Joan of Arc, the woman who created a sense of nationhood among the French and roused them to resist a foreign invader who, incidentally, belonged to the same nation as that which ruled India in the twentieth century.

The story of the Maid of Orleans made an indelible impression on her mind, as her father mentions in one of the letters he wrote to her from prison, starting in 1930, when they were cut off from one another for long spells. The passage from the letter reads: "You remember how fascinated you were when you first read the story of Jeanne d'Arc and how your ambition was to do something like her....One little test I shall ask you to apply whenever you are in doubt. Never do anything in secret or anything you wish to hide. For, the desire that you want to hide anything means that you are afraid, and fear is a bad thing and unworthy of you. Be brave, and all the rest follows."

This lesson was apparently well learnt, for not even the worst enemy of Indira Gandhi can accuse her of physical or moral fear. Like Joan, she has stirred the Indian people to new heights of national consciousness, imbued them with a feeling that a great destiny lies before them, and if she has not actually led them on the battlefield, her spirit has inspired them to a swift victory in war which has made their country the most powerful military-political force in the vast region bordering the Indian Ocean.

Perhaps of all the major educative influences on young Indu the most important was the letters her father penned in prison. Published in book form later as *Glimpses of World History*, they served to give her that wider historic perspective that divides the statesman from the mere politician. A sense of history, of conscious participation in making it, is an essential quality of statesmanship, which is basically political planning for the future, whether of a nation or of the international community.

Towards the end of 1925 Indu's mother became very ill. She was in hospital in Lucknow for many months. Her doctors advised that she be taken to Switzerland for further treatment. Jawaharlal welcomed the idea. He wanted an excuse to get out of India for a breath of fresh mental air after long years of political agitation which to his impatient spirit seemed to be taking the Congress no nearer its goal. "My mind was befogged," he writes in his autobiography, "and no clear path was visible; and I thought that, perhaps, if I was far from India I could see things in better perspective and lighten the dark corners of my mind."

Mother, father, and daughter sailed from Bombay for Venice at the beginning of March 1926. Nehru's sister Vijayalakshmi and her husband Ranjit Pandit accompanied them. The Nehrus planned to return to India by the end of the year at the latest. But their stay abroad lengthened to one year and nine months.

They visited several capitals of Western Europe besides other centres of culture. To Indira, the wealth and glitter of these countries, even though they were in the process of recovering from the First World War, was a revelation. They contrasted so strongly with the living conditions of most people in her own homeland. She asked her father the reason for this great disparity. He replied that the affluence of the Westerners depended on the riches they extracted from such colonial possessions as India. In order that some people in the West may be well-fed and well-housed and live in comparative security, millions of people in Asia and Africa had to make do with little or nothing. But even amid the plenty of the West there were pockets of poverty, he said, drawing her attention to the slums of London and Paris. The rulers of the West exploited their own countrymen as well as their colonial slaves.

As her parents travelled from one country to another, sightseeing and holidaying, meeting important people in different walks of life, Indira moved from one school to another. She attended three in this time, including the International School the League of Nations ran in Geneva. Whenever possible, she accompanied her father when he called on some eminent person whose personality and conversation might benefit her. In this way she was a silent listener while Nehru discussed world politics, the rise of fascism in Italy, and Indian independence with Romain Rolland in the villa of the French novelist and humanist at Villeneuve, Switzerland.

Among the numerous other people of consequence who impressed her at such meetings were Charlie Chaplin, Einstein, Bernard Shaw, and Ernst Toller. Each of them in his own way contributed to her understanding of life and human nature. She told a writer many years later: "I know I would have been a very different person if I had not met certain people in my life." But the four most important living influences on her character and thinking she listed were her grandfather Motilal, her father, Mahatma Gandhi and the most versatile man of letters of modern India, Rabindranath Tagore.

Another landmark in this crucial formative stage of her life was accompanying her father in 1929 to Lahore, where as newly elected president of the Indian National Congress he declared that its aim was nothing less than *purna swaraj*—complete freedom. Back in Anand Bhavan, she watched him drafting the Congress pledge of independence. When he had completed his task, he gave her the document to read aloud.

The Lahore session passed a resolution demanding independence and set January 26, 1930, as Purna Swaraj Day. On that day Congressmen throughout the country took the pledge Nehru had drafted and the Congress Working Committee had approved. "We believe," the declaration opened, "that it is the inalienable right of the Indian people, as of any other people, to have freedom and to enjoy the fruits of their toil and have the necessities of life, so that they may have full opportunities of growth. We believe also that if any government deprives a people of these rights and oppresses them the people have a further right to alter it or to abolish it. The British Government in India has not only deprived the Indian people of their freedom but has based itself on the exploitation of the masses, and has ruined India economically, politically, culturally, and spiritually. We believe, therefore, that India must

sever the British connection and attain purna swaraj, or complete
independence."

The declaration ended by calling on the people of India to end
this "fourfold disaster" to their country not through violence but
"by withdrawing, so far as we can, all voluntary association from
the British Government, and will prepare for civil disobedience,
including nonpayment of taxes. We are convinced that if we can
but withdraw our voluntary help and stop payment of taxes without
doing violence, even under provocation, the end of this inhuman
rule is assured. We therefore hereby solemnly resolve to carry out
the Congress instructions issued from time to time for the purpose
of establishing purna swaraj."

These were brave words and revealed confidence in the final
outcome of the struggle, but they were somewhat overoptimistic.
The satyagraha which Gandhi inaugurated in March 1930 drew
in thousands of passive resisters throughout India, and great deeds
of heroism were done in the cause of independence. But it took
many more years of struggle and a world war in which Britain
was greatly weakened to achieve this end and set off the process
of liquidating colonialism in Africa and Asia.

In 1930, after a spell of relative slack, the tempo of the struggle
for independence began to increase. Gandhi launched the second
mass civil disobedience movement with a march from Sabarmati
Ashram, his headquarters near the city of Ahmedabad, in Gujarat,
to Dandi, on the west coast, to defy the British Government's law
forbidding people to make salt. Manufacturing this common commodity of everyday consumption was a state monopoly. The country
was in a ferment after Gandhi's arrest and imprisonment. The
atmosphere at Anand Bhavan was electric. Indira, now a girl of
12, wanted to join the Congress and take part in the popular defiance
of the alien power which ruled India. But she was told she was
too young for political action. She would have to wait until she
was 18. She explained later to a biographer: "So I got mad and
said: 'I'll have my own organisation'. " Thus was born the
Monkey Brigade, a junior army of the Congress. It got its name
from an episode in Hindu mythology. Its recruits were the children
of neighbours with Congress sympathies.

The brigade swelled to several thousands as recruits came from
all parts of Allahabad. It soon began to attract the attention of

the local bureaucrats. Indira taught her followers to march and drill, because without discipline there could be no organised action. Their duties were many and included running off thousands of copies of party bulletins and propaganda sheets, distributing them unseen to watchful policemen and plainclothesmen, carrying messages to Congressmen who had gone underground to evade arrest, cooking food for volunteers posted at Swaraj Bhavan, supplying water to thirsty demonstrators in processions in the hot, dusty summer months, and giving first aid to the injured in police cane charges.

In Indira's words: "In their own way, the children also acted as an intelligence group, because frequently the policemen sitting in front of the police station would talk about what was going on, who was to be arrested, where there would be a raid and so on. And four or five children playing hopscotch outside would attract no one's attention. And they would deliver this news to the people in the movement."

Motilal and Jawaharlal Nehru were arrested and given prison sentences in June for their part in the national satyagraha. Jawaharlal was placed in Naini Central Jail, across the Yamuna from Allahabad. On New Year's Day 1931, Indu's mother Kamala was arrested for the first time. Nehru's reaction in jail was: "I was pleased, for she had so longed to follow many of her comrades to prison." When a newspaperman asked her for a statement soon after her arrest, she said: "I am happy beyond measure and proud to follow in the footsteps of my husband. I hope the people will keep the flag flying." Nehru's own comment on this was: "Probably she would not have said just that if she had thought over the matter, for she considered herself a champion of woman's rights against the tyranny of man!"

Indu's father ended his fifth spell of imprisonment on January 26, but relief at this was outweighed by anxiety over the grave condition of her grandfather. He died on February 6 in Lucknow. One of the earliest and most important influences on the mind of the growing girl was removed. Among her family, she would now lean more than before on her father as her guide and adviser in the increasingly complex business of living in a society in ferment, in which the contradiction between the old and the new was deepening, and fresh values were increasingly needed to cope with the

problems that this fission created. Her grandfather belonged to
the older school of thinking and behaviour. By modern standards
he was a conservative and a traditionalist, in spite of his deviation
from orthodoxy and zealous patriotism. Her father represented
a new liberal tradition, not only politically but socially and culturally. He was a man of the new world that was coming into being,
of which Soviet Russia was at that time the beacon light. It was
a world in which the scientist and the technologist were to come
to the fore and bring about startling, worldshaking changes which
heralded the birth of post-industrial society.

In his increasingly frequent spells in jail from 1930 onward,
Jawaharlal maintained intellectual contact with his daughter
through the letters he wrote her explaining the development of
mankind from the earliest stage and its history down to modern
times. The letters reveal the humanism of the writer and the broad
sweep of his mind. They made a powerful impact on their young
readers.

In the middle of September 1932 Jawaharlal was again in jail
and Indu was schooling in Poona. Gandhi was in Yeravda Jail,
near Poona, and decided to fast to death as a protest against British
Premier Ramsay MacDonald's "communal award" under which
members of the scheduled Hindu castes were given separate seats
in elections to the central and provincial legislatures, a provision
which continues till today. The whole country was astir at Gandhi's
decision. At this time, Indu visited the jail, where her aunt Vijaya-
lakshmi was also incarcerated, with her cousins. Gandhi saw her
with them and sent off a telegram to her father in which he said:
"Indu looked happy and in possession of more flesh. Doing very
well." The father was deeply touched by this characteristic
gesture.

The year 1933 was bad for the Nehrus. Motilal, whose big law
practice kept the household at Anand Bhavan going, was dead.
Jawaharlal was too immersed in the national struggle to give any
time to law. In any event, his frequent arrests and imprisonment
prevented his building up a steady income from this profession.
Besides, his mother and wife were ailing. Financially, he was in
a jam. The family had been spending more than they could afford,
and there seemed no obvious way of cutting down expenses. But
the muddle over money did not worry Nehru. On the contrary,

he writes in his autobiography: "I was not particularly anxious about making both ends meet. I almost looked forward to the time when I would have no money left. Money and possessions are useful enough in the modern world, but often they become a burden for one who wants to go on a long journey. It is very difficult for moneyed people to take part in undertakings which involve risk; they are always afraid of losing their goods and chattels."

Such was the attitude to personal economic problems of the man who was to have the most important role in shaping Indira's mind and thinking. It was a philosophy of nonattachment to material goods. There is such a thing as the servitude imposed by inanimate possessions on the possessor. The more one owns the more it enslaves one. It is a comforting thought that when people in the advanced countries are becoming more and more consumer goods-oriented, and these are bought not because of their utility but because they are status symbols whose possession confers social superiority on the possessor, and the advertisement executive dictates social preferences and choice on behalf of his client of the moment, the leader of the second most populous nation in the world was brought up in an atmosphere where money and material goods were not considered the most prized things in life.

Still, the Nehru family had to face the hard reality that money was needed urgently for their existence at the level they were accustomed to. To get it, they sold off Kamala Nehru's jewellery, the household silverware and cartloads of the odds and ends that usually cluttered up the dwellings of people who lived according to the standards of the British upper-middle class of the Victorian era. Nehru says in describing this episode: "Kamala did not like the idea of parting with her jewellery, although she had not worn any of it for a dozen years and it had lain in the bank. She had looked forward to handing it on to our daughter."

Indira's sixteenth year was greeted by the "not unusual occurrence" of her father's arrest. He sent a telegram saying "going to other home," which meant he had been given a prison sentence. Indira was studying for the matriculation examination. Her mother was ill. Indira was troubled and anxious. This was the end of her school career in India. It also brought about a fundamental change in her attitude to herself. She explains: "I had wanted to be a boy, but at 16 the delight of being a woman began to unfold itself, and almost overnight the longlegged tomboy in frocks changed into a saree-clad young lady."

At the start of 1934 Kamala's health began to cause anxiety again, and Nehru took her to Calcutta to be examined by specialists. The journey also served the purpose of arranging for Indira's entry into Viswa Bharati, the cultural university Tagore had founded at Santiniketan, some 100 miles from Calcutta in rural surroundings, after she matriculated in a few months. Her future education troubled her parents. "I was wholly against her joining the official or semi-official universities, for I disliked them," says Nehru. "The whole atmosphere that envelops them is official, oppressive, and authoritarian. They have no doubt produced fine men and women in the past, and they will continue to do so. But these few exceptions cannot save the universities from the charge of suppressing and deadening the fine instincts of youth." These "centres of higher learning" were, as they are today, mere degree factories which produced semi-literate babus to man the lower rungs of the British-created bureaucracy.

After leaving Pupils' Own School in Poona, Indira joined her mother in Calcutta, to be with her and "to share with her the unsatisfactory but greatly treasured 20–minute fortnightly interview with my father." Jawaharlal was doing his seventh stretch in prison, this time under a two-year sentence. Mother and daughter spent much of their leisure at the headquarters of the Ramakrishna Mission in the city by the Hooghly river. "Sitting peacefully by the riverside, a new world of thought and experience opened out to me."

Indira enrolled as a student at Santiniketan. This is how she describes the impact it made on her at first sight: "Although an essentially quiet and introvert person, I had lived all my life in an atmosphere of noise, emotional and physical strain and hectic rushing about. The quiet and peace of Santiniketan was an entirely new experience. At 73, Tagore's tall, broad frame was frail and bent, his voice rather highpitched. But yet, with his wavy hair falling softly to his shoulders and his flowing beard, his deepset and penetrating eyes and wide forehead, he was beautiful to look at—a perfect picture of the romantic poet."

From earliest childhood she had regarded Gandhi and other eminent friends and acquaintances and political helpers of her grandfather and father as members of her family. "Even important

foreign personages who visited our home seemed to get absorbed
in the family circle; such was the tempo and informality of our
life in Anand Bhavan."

Tagore was different. He was the first person whom she consciously regarded as a great man, "and being painfully shy with
strangers I was completely overawed by his magnificent presence."
In her first days at Santiniketan, she kept as far as possible from
Tagore, although her mother and she lodged in his house. One
day he saw Indira talking and laughing with some other girls.
When they saw him watching them, they fell silent and looked
embarrassed. Tagore asked: "Why do you stop laughing? Are
you afraid of me? Why don't you come to me some time? Perhaps
you will be bored visiting an old man."

After that, they visited him often. "Many were the evenings
when a small group of us sat at his feet and talked of diverse subjects
or silently watched him paint. Often he would recite or read aloud.
He insisted that our dancing lessons should take place (in his house)
so that he could watch and comment."

The meetings with this many-faceted genius "influenced me
profoundly and helped in moulding my personality," she writes.
"We had a glimpse of the universality of his spirit, the broadness
of his vision and his strong sense of purpose. These were moments
of serene joy, memories to be cherished forever."

Towards the end of July 1934 Indira's mother's health took
a big turn for the worse. Indira has come to Allahabad to be with
her. She found her, in Nehru's words, "frail and utterly weak,
a shadow of herself, struggling feebly with her illness." Kamala
was 17 when she married, her husband 26. She was little more than
a girl physically, without sophistication. Temperamentally, they
were far apart, and there were frequent tiffs and misunderstandings
in their early married days. It was hard for each to adjust to the
other. Twenty-one months after marriage, Indira, "our daughter
and only child," was born.

Kamala remained, after 18 years of married life, girlish and
virginal in appearance, according to her husband. But he, though
fit and supple in limb and muscle, was balding, and what was left
of the hair on his head was grey. His face was furrowed and dark,
semicircles had formed under his eyes. "Often, in these later years,"
he notes in his autobiography, "when Kamala and I had gone

out together in a strange place, she was mistaken, to my embarrassment, for my daughter. She and Indira looked like two sisters."

Nehru was serving another prison sentence and was out on parole
for a few days to see his sick wife. On the eleventh day, he was taken
back to Naini Jail. Kamala was moved to Bhowali in the Kumaon
Hills in the hope that the fresh mountain air would do her good,
and Nehru was shifted to Almora Jail to be close to her. In May
1935, accompanied by Indira, she went to Badenweiler, in South
Germany, for specialist treatment. This was not successful, and Nehru
was discharged from prison when her condition became critical
in September. He flew to join her. Soon after, she was removed
to Lausanne, in Switzerland, where she died on February 28, 1936,
of a tubercular infection.

Indira was in her nineteenth year. Her mother's prolonged illness
and death, and the long separation from her father, left her physically
and mentally exhausted. She went to Badminton School in Bristol,
in the West of England, to prepare for entry into Oxford University.
This was the period of the Popular Front against Fascism. Hitler
and Mussolini were making threatening noises and the uneasy
peace of Europe was soon to be disturbed by the civil war in Spain,
that last dying gasp of West European liberalism before it succumbed
to Hitlerian bluster, permitted him to swallow Austria and dis-
member Czechoslovakia, and thus lead on to the inevitable con-
flagration of World War II.

It was also the heyday of pseudo-revolutionary leftism in Britain,
when intellectuals joined the Left Book Club sponsored by the
publishing house of Victor Gollancz and fraternised with young
men and women from the colonies who had come to Britain for
higher studies and passed resolutions at meetings calling upon
the British Government, then headed by Stanley Baldwin, to give
the colonies freedom. It was the year when Britain was rocked
by a constitutional crisis because its monarch decided to marry
a commoner, and an American at that, and had to quit his throne.

Indira entered Somerville College, Oxford, and read history,
but ill health prevented her from completing the course. At Oxford
and in London she got to know many Indian students. Among
them were several who entered politics on their return to India,
with varying degrees of success. Among them were Bhupesh Gupta,
leader of the Communist Party of India in the Rajya Sabha, the

upper house of the Indian Parliament, Jyoti Basu, one of the big wheels of the rival Communist Party of India (Marxist) in West Bengal, Mohan Kumaramangalam, a former Communist who is now a Congressman and Minister of Steel and Mines in the Indian Cabinet, and Minoo Masani, once the bright hope of Indian socialism, then head of the public relations setup of the Bombay industrial house of Tatas, and later the forlorn hope of the conserva- tive Swatantra (Freedom) Party. He abandoned it after his defeat in the parliamentary election in March 1971.

Among the young Indian students was also Feroze Gandhi, a childhood friend of Indira whom she married later. A Parsee, he was no relation of Mahatma Gandhi. All these and many others gravitated round Krishna Menon, organiser of the India League, who persistently lobbied among Labour members of Parliament and other sympathisers of India for the speedy end of colonial rule.

Anti-colonialism, like anti-fascism, was strong in the foggy London atmosphere at that time. It meshed with the Communist cry for the end of "tyranny, oppression and exploitation," wherever they existed. Indira was active in enlisting sympathy and money for the progressive cause in Spain, doomed to defeat in advance because of massive German and Italian intervention and the nonintervention- ism preached and practised by the democracies of the West. It has been noted that Indira's contribution to the campaign was "not very vocal and demonstrative." She worked quietly and unostenta- tiously, selling programmes and tickets for fundraising shows. She attended debates on Spain and other burning political issues orga- nised by the Oxford Union and the Indian Majlis (Meeting).

In 1938 her father visited Europe, whose people were plagued by fears of war which came true a few months later. Indira accom- panied him to Paris, Prague, Munich, and Geneva, in the last of which the League of Nations was in its death throes. Hitler was preparing to march into Sudetenland, and Prime Minister Neville Chamberlain of Britain was getting ready to practise his umbrella diplomacy which came to be known as appeasement. Indira went with Jawaharlal when he called on various statesmen and diplomats, and she saw at close quarters the feeble, fumbling, halfhearted efforts they made to check the Führer's aggression against a virtually unarmed and peaceful neighbour. It was an educative experience which taught her that to give in to international bullies and black-mailers was fatal for any selfrespecting nation. She also learnt that in international politics principles and moral obligations and solemn promises went by the board when selfinterest was involved.

CHAPTER TWO

FREEDOM FIGHTER

IN 1938, INDIRA was back in Allahabad. Her studies at Oxford had been cut short by illness, and she had spent some time recuperating in a sanatorium. She was now 21. Her long-cherished wish to become a member of the Indian National Congress was fulfilled. She returned to Europe. This time her stay ended in 1941. The Second World War was raging, and Hitler had turned his Wehrmacht eastward against the Russians. The air blitz of Britain was at its worst.

Indira travelled by ship to India the long way round the Cape of Good Hope. Among her fellow-travellers were two Indian students she had known well in Britain, Bhupesh Gupta and Feroze Gandhi. The steamer called at Durban, centre of a thriving Indian business community. Nearly half a century earlier, Mahatma Gandhi had fought the racial discrimination of the white minority rulers of South Africa there before returning to India to lead the national movement for independence.

Jawaharlal Nehru was known and respected among these prosperous businessmen. They turned out in strength to honour his daughter on arrival with garlands, sweets, and gifts. But their enthusiasm melted away completely after her first and last public address in the city. This was the first time she had spoken at a large meeting on a political subject. Normally silent, even tongue-tied, accustomed to share her thoughts only with herself, she was stirred to this effort by what she saw as she drove through the city with her two friends.

Their tour included the black ghettos in which the Africans were herded. What a contrast with the opulence of the whites and the Indians. It was clear to her on whose side the Indians were in the war of races in South Africa. So when she arrived at the place where a public reception had been arranged for her she was seething with anger. The merchant prince presiding over the function sensed

trouble from a few preliminary remarks the chief guest had addressed to him in private.

After the conventional gestures of welcome he announced that
Miss Nehru would not deliver the speech they had come to hear.
But Miss Nehru was not to be done out of her right, and she was
on her feet while he was making his explanation and insisted on
speaking. The affluent, potbellied, selfsatisfied traders, bankers, and
government officials of Indian origin who had gathered to hear their
guest utter a few familiar platitudes on the freedom struggle in India,
a subject of no great interest to them, were horrified when she poured
out the indignation she had bottled up from the time she had seen
African slumland.

She condemned apartheid and compared the white man's oppression of the blacks with Hitler's persecution of the Jews. Africa belonged to the Africans, and one day they would regain their rightful
heritage. The white man would have to go, and what then would
be the fate of their Indian collaborators? Her audience one and all
turned against her, but from her point of view she had been a great
success. Her maiden speech to such a large gathering was oratorically
splendid. Indira Nehru had found herself. From then it was only
a matter of time and opportunity before she became a wholetime
politician and mass orator and distinguished herself in this role like
her grandfather and father.

Indira Nehru married Feroze Gandhi on March 26, 1942. She
was a Brahmin whose ancestors were originally from mountainous
Kashmir but had migrated southward and had settled in the North
Indian plains. He was a Parsee. His ancestors had come from Persia
many centuries before and had formed trading colonies along the
northwest coast of India. His ancestral religion was Zoroastrianism.
In India, even among the socially enlightened circles to which their
families belonged, such a union caused surprise and displeasure.
To the orthodox it was, of course, horrifying.

Kamala Nehru blessed this love match in her last days. Feroze
had helped Indira look after Kamala when mother and daughter
were on their own in Europe in that trying time and her father
was in prison in far away India. Some of Indira's close relatives were
unhappy at her choice. They felt she could have done better for
herself. But she stood firm, and she found a supporter in Mahatma
Gandhi.

Like Indira, Feroze belonged to the radical wing of the Congress. He believed in rapid, but democratic and peaceful, change to sweep away the accumulated rubbish of the past and build a forward-moving society in which such anachronisms as caste and religious bigotry and social injustice which condemned vast numbers of people to chronic poverty and starvation so that a few might be rich and overfed were abolished. Like Nehru and his daughter, he was a moderniser.

After their wedding they went in August, to Bombay where the All-India Committee of the Congress Party was meeting to serve notice on the British that they must hand over power immediately instead of making equivocal promises about doing so after the Allies had won their war against Hitler. Till then, the British expected unstinted Indian support for their exertions to make the world "safe for democracy."

Gandhi introduced the Quit India resolution at the session, and on August 9 the police swung into action and netted all the Congress leaders who had gathered in Bombay for the meeting. Among those arrested was Jawaharlal Nehru. He and other leaders were taken away to a fortress-prison at Ahmednagar, about 300 miles east of Bombay. Gandhi was held captive in the Aga Khan's palace in Poona, in the Western Ghats about 120 miles south of Bombay.

All over the country the police cracked down on Congressmen, and thousands were imprisoned without trial. Indira's aunt Vijaya-lakshmi Pandit was taken into custody on August 12, and Indira was now the seniormost member of the Nehru family at Anand Bhavan. This entailed on her a greater obligation to play an active part in the Quit India movement.

The old Nehru mansion, now named Swaraj Bhavan, was seized by the government on August 9. Soldiers were quartered there, and the house became the centre of operations to terrorise nationalists in the city and surrounding villages. Indira and other dwellers in the smaller Anand Bhavan by its side were constantly challenged at bayonet point by soldiers on guard duty.

Feroze decided after the roundup in Bombay to join the party underground and help run its propaganda machine. He grew a mustache and put on khaki. With his ruddy complexion he could pass for an Anglo-Indian. He travelled back to Allahabad in this outfit, but got off at a wayside halt a short distance from the city, fearing he might be recognised at its principal railway station. He hitched a ride to town in a truck full of British soldiers, but had great difficulty in getting off because his travelling companions feared the "damned natives" might chop him up if they caught him alone.

Feroze became one of the channels through which Indira could pass out money and propaganda literature to other underground workers who spread like a net over the northern region. They met secretly after dark for a few minutes in the homes of non-political friends. Although she tried to act as inconspicuously as possible, the police had their suspicions about Indira, and news came to her along the Congress grapevine that she was to be arrested. She had no intention of letting the police nab her easily. She quickly packed a bag with clothes and books and slipped out of Anand Bhavan to stay under cover with friends.

Whispers spread through the city that the Congress Party was organising a public meeting at five o'clock in the evening at a secret location. Indira was to address it in defiance of a government order banning public rallies and demonstrations. Policemen fanned out all over Allahabad to frustrate the Congress plan. Indira appeared at the meeting-place at the appointed hour. People who had assembled in shops and nearby houses hours before poured out to hear her. Indira had spoken scarcely 10 minutes when truckloads of British troops arrived and threw a cordon round speaker and audience.

Feroze was concealed and watching these developments through a shuttered window on the first floor of an adjoining building. But the sight of a rifle barrel barely a yard from Indira's head sent him rushing down head long and shouting to the gun-wielding sergeant not to shoot. The man lowered the weapon but took her arm to lead her to the prison van that waited to receive her. This was a signal to the crowd, the temper of which had risen to boiling-point. People surged forward to protect her from the *Feringhi,* as the British were commonly called. Then began a tussle for Indira's body. Some Congresswomen grabbed her other arm while the sergeant took a firm grip of the one he held.

Indira thought she would be torn in two as they struggled and dragged her with them here and there. In an article written in 1963 she recalled: "There was no firing though rifle butts were used and many were hurt. A large number of us, men and women, including my husband and [me] were arrested. The ride to the jail was rather an extraordinary one, for [the policemen] in my van were apparently so moved by my talking to them that they apologised, put their turbans at my feet and wept their sorrow because of what their job compelled them to do."

Indira had been familiar from as far back as she could remember with the grim, forbidding hellholes in which political offenders were locked up with those whom society termed common criminals. She had been taken to them to attend the trials of friends and relatives, including her father, or "for unsatisfactory but highly treasured 20-minute interviews" with persons under detention or serving sentences. A large number of her kinsfolk, both on her father's and mother's side, were imprisoned for the cause of freedom. Indira comments: "I do not know of any other family which was so involved in the freedom struggle and its hardships."

But this was the first time she herself was a prisoner. No charge had been laid against her, and she was to be held captive as long as the government thought fit. She herself did not expect to be released for at least seven years. Prison is a place where "each day is like a year, a year whose days are long," wrote Oscar Wilde, who spent several years in Reading Jail. Prison is where the days are wrapped in sameness, in spite and deliberate humiliation, and where the "essential fact in the life of the prisoner is that he takes a subhuman status," according to Lord Pethick-Lawrence, a British Labour leader who played a principal part in the negotiations a few years after Indira's arrest for the transfer of power to Indians.

She was an inmate of Naini Jail, which had received her father into its inhospitable caverns on several occasions. "The ground, the walls, everything around us was mudcoloured, and so became our jailwashed clothes," writes Indira. Even the food tasted gritty. Through the barred apertures of their cells the prisoners were exposed to the loo, the hot, deathdealing wind that sweeps across the Gangetic Plain in summer, duststorms, the monsoon downpour and the winter cold, when chill winds from the Himalayas cut like a knife.

Indira Gandhi received special attention from the jail authorities. "I was regarded as so dangerous," she told a newspaper interviewer in 1969, "that I wasn't even given normal prison facilities." Other political prisoners had the privilege of interviews with relatives or letters from outside once or twice a month. But she was denied these contacts with the world outside the stone walls that held her captive.

Feroze was in the men's section of the same prison, but only after persistent efforts were they permitted a short meeting. Soon after, he was moved to another jail. Reading and teaching the other women prisoners kept her busy. "I took over the entire care of a small baby whose mother I was coaching to enable her to earn her living on her release."

Indira was convinced that she would have to do her full term. She did not yearn for freedom, because all those she held dear were like her behind bars. "I was determined to bear all privations and insults smilingly." Public concern about the state of her health impelled the British governor of the United Provinces, Sir Maurice Hallett, to send the civil surgeon to examine her. The surgeon found her rundown and prescribed a tonic and a special diet containing high-protein foods. The surgeon had scarcely left when the jail superintendent tore up his prescription and flung the pieces on the ground. "If you think you are getting any of this, you are mistaken," he told Indira. She was not worried. She had not asked for them, not even for the surgeon's call.

Indira was released unexpectedly well before the long term she had resigned herself to was over. She had been 13 months in detention. Freedom was "like coming out of a dark passage—I was dazzled with the rush of life, the many hues and textures, the scale of sounds and the range of ideas. Just to touch and listen was a disturbing experience and it took a while to get adjusted to normal living."

In 1943, under persistent prodding from President Roosevelt, Premier Churchill reluctantly agreed to make some conciliatory gestures to India. The insensitive, unimaginative, and stiffnecked Lord Linlithgow was replaced as Viceroy late in the year by Lord Wavell, a valiant if not altogether successful field marshal of the British army who was not much better fitted than his predecessor for the dexterous operation entrusted to him. He released Mahatma Gandhi from detention on medical grounds in 1944. Nehru and the other detained Congress leaders were let out in June 1945.

From the time of Gandhi's release Congress political activity shifted from mass agitation to negotiations with the British, the Muslim League and other minority parties for a new constitutional setup which would ensure the smooth transfer of power. But, with the lifting of the irksome restrictions on any form of political protest, there was great mass pressure for the speedy conclusion of an agreement. The trial of officers of the Indian National Army organised by Netaji Subhas Chandra Bose in Malaya in wartime stirred the masses to new heights of nationalist fervour. In February 1946, ratings of the Royal Indian Navy revolted in Bombay and won much sympathy throughout the country from people, especially young men and women and students, for whom the departure of the British could not come too soon.

The revolt was a warning to the British and the Congress leaders to complete negotiations for handing over power without further delay. Wavell, who dragged his feet and seemed to be oversolicitous for the security of the Muslims and other minorities after independence, went and was replaced by the dynamic Lord Mountbatten. But the mischief Wavell had done could not be reversed. It was soon obvious to the Congress negotiators that freedom would involve the partition of India, much as they were against it. Wavell had allowed Mohammad Ali Jinnah, leader of the secessionist Muslim League, to have his way, and Pakistan became the heart's cry of the majority of Muslims in the country.

To Indira Gandhi, who had lived among Muslims from birth and whose family had close friends among neighbouring Muslim families in Allahabad and elsewhere, the thought of India's partition on a religious basis was repugnant. She had been brought up to accept people on their merits, whatever their religion, caste, colour or race. Although a fervent nationalist when it came to India's independence, Jawaharlal Nehru was also a confirmed internationalist who believed a time would come when all barriers between nations would be pulled down and there would be a just world social order. His daughter shared these views, and she had also worked in London with socialists and young nationalists from other colonial territories in Asia and Africa for the cause of anti-colonialism.

Thus, although she now had more time to relax and attend to family relationships, this period after the Second World War in which the fate of India was being decided through prolonged negotiations was also one of anxiety and sadness to her. Some older Congress leaders might be prepared to accept half a loaf as better than none, out of political expediency, and might argue that an India minus a large chunk of its Muslim population might be more manageable politically. But to younger idealists with a forward outlook like Feroze and Indira Gandhi this was a setback to the secular democracy they believed in. The voices of dissent were, however, drowned or ignored and the nation was divided in August 1947.

Independence brought no joy to the hearts of those who believed sincerely in the oneness of India. When this vivisection of a living integral social organism was performed, the blood of its people flowed freely. Refugees from Pakistan came into India with "harrowing tales of murder, rape and loot, which started off the nightmare of retaliation in Delhi and Punjab," in the words of Indira. In this insane holocaust, she returned to the line of duty, visiting refugee camps and seeing that the destitute and injured were looked after as was best in the circumstances, going to areas where mobs were rioting and killing and seeking to give what comfort and hope she could to the sufferers.

Although she had seen political mass movements at close hand and participated in them before, this was an altogether new experience. For the first time, she came in direct contact with human suffering and misery and evil hatred at its worst. Now she was closer than ever before to the common people, the people for whose betterment she pledged her political career in 1969 when she gave a new lead and new life to the moribund Congress Party.

The travail of the common man in this gigantic social upheaval also brought her for the first time "really close" to Mahatma Gandhi. "I was new in Delhi, I had a tiny baby and was far from well," she wrote in 1957, "but Gandhi sent for me to work in the terror-stricken Muslim areas of the city. It was dangerous work and calculated to bring the utmost unpopularity, and yet one could not say no to the plea: 'I trust you to see this work through. I have asked several others and they have replied "Yes, Bapu," but I know they are still hesitating.' For months I spent 12 hours a day in the worst trouble spots. Whenever possible I went to Bapu to report, and these visits gave me fresh strength; but on many days there just wasn't time. On these occasions he would send a message or a flower."

In the riots, Indira saved many lives, "only, alas, to earn the worst abuse from the victim as well as the attackers," Indira wrote in an article in 1957. "For months afterwards streams of refugees used to pour in. Every day, I sat stolidly and patiently in one place between 8 a.m. and 1.30 p.m. and sometimes again [throughout] the afternoon interviewing group after group. For the majority, there was not much one could do except listen to their tale of woe, but even this apparently gave peace of mind, and there were always just enough cases which were within one's power to help to keep up hope."

At last, "peace reigned again in the narrowest *gali* [alley] and Hindu-Muslim neighbours were shaking hands and visiting one another's homes. I was exhausted and on the verge of collapse. Gandhi packed me off to Lucknow for a rest, with the wonderful words: 'Now I know your education and your years abroad have not been wasted'."

This was another landmark in the political evolution of Indira Gandhi. She was now in her thirtieth year, a wife and mother. She was woman enough to believe that "motherhood is the highest fulfilment" for her sex. She could write: "To bring a new being into this world, to see its tiny perfection and to dream of its future greatness is the most moving of all experiences and fills one with wonder and exaltation." Her own childhood, she saw in retrospect, was abnormal, "full of loneliness and insecurity." That determined her to devote all her time to her children. But this was not to be.

When her father became Prime Minister and moved into the stately bungalow formerly occupied by the British commander-in-chief of the armed forces in India, he needed an official hostess at the prime ministerial residence. "At first," she says, "it was only a question of setting up a home for my father in New Delhi and coping with the social obligations of the Prime Minister's House. But gradually circumstances and my own intense interest in the path which the country was trying to follow drew me deeper into public affairs." Neither wifehood nor motherhood could keep her away from the career that destiny had picked for her. That was politics.

CHAPTER THREE

APPRENTICESHIP IN DELHI

FOR THE NEXT 17 years, from 1947 to the time of her father's death in May 1964, Indira played the role of stewardess of her father's household at No 3 Teen Murti Marg, New Delhi, and was gracious hostess to the stream of official and unofficial guests who flowed into New Delhi from all parts of the world to see India, new in freedom but very old in culture and tradition. Most of them were deeply interested in India's future from the point of view of how this would affect their own nations, and to talk with the man who was guiding the destinies of the young nation and who was already being looked upon as the future leader of resurgent Asia.

For Indira it was a big sacrifice on one hand. It meant subordinating her own family life and personal aspirations and desires to play an important, but still backstage, role in not just her father's but also her country's interest. Perhaps another woman would have regarded this as an ordinary chore, to be borne uncomplainingly for her father's sake. But on the other hand it was a glittering opportunity for Indira to continue her education in politics and the labyrinthine ways of life in general. Meeting world political leaders and a host of other people who were eminent in various spheres sharpened her insight into human psychology, the motive forces of action, the thinking behind such action, and individual reactions to persons and things and circumstances. And always there was her father to comment on these people, to explain the nuances of what they said or implied.

January 1949 presented one of these opportunities on a big scale. Hitherto, she had only travelled westward, seen at close quarters and talked with statesmen and politicians of the Western countries, urbane, sophisticated people most of them, but bred in an environment and style that was completely alien to the Indianness of India. They were mostly disillusioned men weary in body and spirit, who had lost faith in the future of Europe and only thought of conserving what they had.

Such men and women could hardly be inspiring to a politically alert young person from a country that was emerging from the prison of colonialism and had a vast, almost limitless, potential for economic growth, social change, and political influence before it. India, and with it Indira Gandhi and millions of the Indians of her generation, were starting on a long and exciting and hazardous journey into the unknown under her father's leadership while the world of these Westerners was shrinking and a big question-mark seemed to hang over their future.

But January 1949 saw the first meeting in modern times of the leaders of 19 Asian nations in an environment free from foreign domination. The conference met at Nehru's suggestion to protest against the attempt of the Netherlands to regain forcible control of its former colonies in the Indian Ocean east of the Straits of Malacca which, under another dynamic leader, Dr Sukarno, had banded together to form the Indonesian Republic. This was also Indira's first encounter with the leaders of the emerging nations of the East. She had already been with her father to one international meeting. This was the conference of Prime Ministers of Dominions of the British Commonwealth in London in October 1948. The meeting made Commonwealth history. For the first time, an Asian nation was represented in what had been till then an exclusive white man's club.

When the older members permitted the entry of the first non-whites, India, Pakistan, and Ceylon, they felt they were conferring a great favour on these ex-colonials. But the club grew in the next few years rapidly as many more Asian and African and Caribbean countries became independent. Soon, it was a black and brown man's club in which the whites were a tiny minority. And far from conferring favours on the newcomers, they were the favoured ones, for the international prestige of Britain and the other old members got a boost from the presence of the Africans and Asians. After the Second World War, Britain was no longer a front-rank power either economically or militarily. In the new alignment of international forces, the expanded Commonwealth helped it maintain a position of importance much out of proportion to its actual importance.

The following November, Indira heard her father address the

United Nations General Assembly in Paris. The next year she accompanied Nehru on his first state visit to the United States. Indeed, this was the first time he and his daughter were visiting the land of the Colossus of the Western world. It was a voyage of discovery for both of them. At that time Indian feelings for the US were warm, mainly because of the sympathy President Roosevelt and many other Americans, officials and more so nonofficials, had shown for the Indian struggle for independence and for its leaders, particularly Mahatma Gandhi, over many years. Roosevelt had been primarily responsible for pinning down Churchill to a promise of freedom for India after the defeat of the Axis Powers in the Second World War.

So it was in a spirit of friendship that the transatlantic mission was undertaken. Unfortunately, it was in quite different circumstances that Mrs Gandhi herself visited the US as the guest of President Nixon in November 1971 when she was head of government. Washington's attitude to New Delhi had by then somersaulted and cold suspicion prevailed in the White House, although the admiration of ordinary Americans as well as of leaders of public opinion for Mrs Gandhi surpassed that they had ever had for her father.

Indira also accompanied Nehru on most of his frequent tours of India, for she had had little opportunity to see very much of her own country before. This was the chance to study the diversity of peoples and customs and attitudes that went to make up this huge nation. She accompanied him when he went to inaugurate the "temples of tomorrow," the dams and power stations which were to provide the infrastructure for the new industrial India which he hoped to build as rapidly as possible in his lifetime. Nehru was a moderniser, and he saw that the cobwebs and junk of the past which littered Indian society and thinking and politics could only be swept away through modernisation of its economy.

When there was more cake to share among so many who were multiplying so fast, he hoped the struggle for existence would lose its sharpness and the antagonisms built on differences of language, caste, and religion would soften and the old India would give way to the new of his dreams, where social justice and sufficiency for all and tolerance would prevail. Indira shared this dream. She felt the same enthusiasm as he did about economic and social planning. She thrilled at the thought of giant steel mills and other plants that would fabricate the capital goods needed to establish a heavy industrial base to speed up modernisation.

Keeping house for Jawaharlal Nehru would have taxed the ingenuity and patience of the best-trained and most accomplished hostess. The guests who streamed in for breakfast, lunch, afternoon tea, or dinner had varied eating habits, and these had to be kept in mind in preparing to entertain them. There was a conference of Buddhist leaders from various countries in 1956 to celebrate the 2500th anniversary of Buddha's attaining Nirvana. Among the delegates was the Dalai Lama—this was before the revolt in Tibet and his flight for asylum in India—and many venerable bhikkus. They had been invited to lunch. Suddenly it struck Indira that the monks must est their last meal of the day before noon, but the other guests would not be free until half past one. So the kitchen staff had to work in top gear to have lunch ready for the monks at half past eleven, while 100 other guests had it at the appointed hour.

Nehru had a habit of collecting new recipes and details of customs for treating guests on his frequent tours of India and other countries. After attending a banquet at Buckingham Palace he decided that Prime Minister's House should follow the royal tradition of serving milk and sugar before coffee. This often bewildered guests, says Indira, and they looked round furtively to see whether they had forgotten to help themselves to coffee or had mislaid it.

On another foreign trip, he stayed at a country house where everybody served himself to breakfast. This suited the Teen Murti household because breakfast was a hurried meal. But it did not suit most guests, and in the end the hosts had to serve them.

Then there was the Prime Minister's private menagerie, which he was very fond of showing to distinguished visitors. It included dogs of good pedigree and mongrels picked off the streets, parrots, pigeons, squirrels and "practically every small creature common to the Indian scene," says Indira. To this was added a Red Himalayan panda acquired in Assam, "although we did not know what it was until we reached Agartala and were able to study the book of Indian animals in the commissioner's library."

Indira's sons Rajiv and Sanjay named the new addition Bhimsa (like Bhim, a strong man in Indian mythology). When he grew up he was presented with a wife named Pemma, which means lotus in Sikkimese. Nehru called on the pandas and their cubs regularly on his morning stroll through the grounds attached to his residence. The next and most exciting newcomers to the animal population of the house were three tiger cubs. They soon became prize attractions for visitors, and among the world's notables who petted them were Tito and U Nu. Tito wanted one of them and got it, and the other two were sent off to Lucknow Zoo when they got too big and created a domestic security problem.

In 1952, the first elections based on adult franchise were held in India. Millions of unlettered peasants and workers were voting for the first time. This was the biggest experiment in democracy in the world, and its outcome aroused much interest in India as well as abroad. Many pundits, Indian and foreign, doubted whether it would succeed. They felt that democracy could not function effectively in a country as poor as and as illiterate as India, where factors like caste and religion swayed popular decisions.

Even today, 20 years later, after the overwhelming victories of Mrs Gandhi in the parliamentary elections of March 1971 and the state legislature elections 12 months later, the doubters continue to doubt. They are ready to jump at complaints that the elections were rigged, the easiest explanation some parties can find for their shattering defeat. This attitude seems to stem from an inbuilt conviction that democratic values can be practised only by white people, and that too only by whites in the West and in countries elsewhere which are ethnically and culturally Western.

Even those pundits who measure Indian elections with slide rules and adding machines and talk about parameters and multiplier effects and other pseudo-scientific mumbo jumbo and write articles and books to prove that the voters should have acted differently have come round to admitting that democracy does seem to work in India. But they do so patronisingly and with amused surprise, as though they were talking about a monkey which could read the alphabet or eat with fork and knife.

The first general election was a test of Nehru's leadership. He carried the Congress election campaign on his shoulders. It was virtually a one-man affair. He traversed the country, addressing meetings of multitudes wherever he went. People had ears only for him. His party lieutenants in the states were left the task of organising the voters to go to the polls. He was 63 at the time, but he carried out this physically taxing job without any letup for weeks.

Indira went with him on most of his campaign tours, seeing that he
did not strain his energies overmuch. She had another role to play
too. Increasingly, Nehru was turning to her to help him solve his
his problems. When candidates had to be selected for parliamentary
seats, he often sought her opinion about the suitability of the men
seeking nomination.

Indira herself did not seek election although a nomination was
hers for the asking. Indeed, she was sounded about standing for
election to Parliament, but she refused. She felt she was not yet
ready to enter the parliamentary arena although she was active
in the Congress organisation. She had been requested, practically
ordered, by the party bosses in her home state, now renamed Uttar
Pradesh (Northern Province), to accept a seat in the Vidhan Sabha
(Legislative Assembly), but she had declined. Her father had neither
said yes or no when she asked his advice. He told her to make up
her mind on her own.

Top Congressmen came increasingly to see her and ask her advice
on matters about which they wished to consult her father. She was
also taking more active interest steadily in public affairs, especially
those connected with the welfare of women and children. Her
interest in education received concrete shape in a college for girls
she founded in Allahabad in memory of her mother.

Nehru took Indira with him to the crowning of Elizabeth II
in London in 1953. Among the notables she met was Churchill,
then Prime Minister for the second time. Nehru returned straight
to New Delhi after the ceremony, but Indira flew to Moscow. This
was a significant detour. It was her first visit to the Soviet Union,
which was still recovering from the enormous ravages of war and
which was to see the death of Stalin in a few months and
a complete change in policy towards the newly independent developing countries which had chosen to stay nonaligned in international
affairs. It was also a sort of reconnaissance for the trip Nehru planned
to that country. His visit came the following year and he wanted
to have her firsthand impressions of the Soviet leaders and the feel
of the atmosphere in Moscow.

On the way back to India she stopped over at Tashkent, capital
of the Uzbek Republic. She saw how this region, inhabited mainly
by people of Central Asian stock and Muslim by religion, had
caught up with modernity in a few decades. At the time of the

Bolshevik Revolution in 1917, Uzbekistan was a colonial backwater of the Czarist Empire, its people nomads living on the margin of starvation, a place where officials of Russian stock were sent as a punishment for administrative incompetence. It was also a place for political exiles.

Nehru went to China in 1954. Indira went with him. Premier Chou En-lai had earlier the same year visited New Delhi unexpectedly to discuss a peace settlement in Indo-China. The Indian visitors were impressed by the evident signs of progress under the new order in China. Nehru had visited Chungking alone on the eve of the Second World War and had met Generalissimo Chiang Kai-shek and other Kuomintang leaders there. In his autobiography he described Chiang as one "who embodies in himself the unity of China and her determination to be free." Madam Chiang, he observed, "has been a continuous source of inspiration to the nation."

Sitting in his island fortress across the Straits of Formosa and waiting for the day when, with US support, he could deliver mainland China from communism, the aging Generalissimo could not have been pleased at the praise Nehru had for the new regime in Peking. Chiang had come to India in February 1942, obviously under US sponsorship, to tell the Congress leaders to support the Allies in the war against fascism. The Viceroy, Linlithgow, was reluctant to let Madam Chiang and him meet the Congress chiefs, but they finally met Gandhi in Calcutta and Chiang later issued a statement backing Indian independence.

President Tito of Yugoslavia was the first leader of a socialist state in Eastern Europe to pay a state visit to India. He came late in 1954. Indira sat in on the talks he had with Nehru, a silent but keen observer and listener. This was to be her role from now on whenever world dignitaries came to see the Prime Minister. Sometimes, she would speak when her opinion was sought.

In a biographical study of her, Khwaja Ahmed Abbas, a left-leaning journalist and author of Bombay, says her father gave her the "most exhaustive political training that any young aspirant to high office could ever have." She was constantly at his side for 17 years "while he tackled the most crucial problems of his country and the world. Few prime ministers or presidents in the whole world have come to power with such a thorough lifelong preparation to play the leading role on the political stage." Looking back, Abbas observes that "one might say that this 'daughter of the Indian Revolution' was all along being groomed as the heiress-apparent to her father's kingsized position in the country."

Indira was also moving up in the party hierarchy. New responsibilities were given to her in 1955 when she was named a member of the Congress Working Committee, the highest executive authority in the party. Soon after she was nominated to the Central Parliamentary Board, which chooses candidates to run for Parliament, and the Central Election Committee, which vets lists of candidates for contests to the state legislatures. She has been a member of these three bodies continuously since she was appointed to them.

A big rise in the party hierarchy swept her to its apex in 1959. Indira Gandhi became President of the Congress, the third member of the Nehru family and the fourth woman to hold this key position in India's biggest national party. Her father was 40 when he presided over the Lahore session of the Congress in 1929. She was 42 when she became its head. Her election surprised Congressmen as well as the nation, for before the session it appeared that the party leaders had agreed S. Nijalingappa should be elected unanimously, as was the usual practice.

Nijalingappa was the party boss in the southern state of Mysore. He was on his way to Nagpur by train from Bangalore, the capital of Mysore, when the Congress President, U.N. Dhebar, summoned a meeting of the Working Committee in New Delhi. The subject of the meeting, much to the surprise of some of its members who thought the last word had been said on the subject, was the choice of Dhebar's successor. Lal Bahadur Shastri, who succeeded Nehru as Prime Minister in 1964, suggested informally that Indira Gandhi be chosen for this office. Nehru was present, and it was soon apparent to the other members that this move had his approval.

The problem that followed this decision was how to break the news to Nijalingappa. It was finally settled that the bosses of two other southern states, K. Kamaraj, of Tamil Nadu, and N. Sanjiva Reddy, of Andhra Pradesh, should handle this delicate and decidedly unpleasant job. They flew to Madras to meet Nijalingappa, and in the end all three of them issued a statement supporting Mrs Gandhi's candidature. These three men were to figure prominently in the tussle for control of the Congress Party in 1969 which ended in the victory of Mrs Gandhi over the so-called Syndicate of provincial warlords who teamed up to throw her out. They all joined the Syndicate against her.

This episode was seized upon by political observers in New Delhi, some of them not very friendly to Nehru, as evidence that he was building up his daughter as his successor. Nehru was now 70, and for quite some years the question had been asked discreetly in various circles in the capital: After Nehru, who? It was true Nehru showed no signs of failing health, and his mind was as agile as ever, but no man is eternal, and so the question who would succeed him became a matter of concern to people who wanted continuity of leadership of the country and the Congress Party as well as to those who had less noble aims. While no lobbies were as yet discernible in the party, certain inidividuals were projecting themselves, but not openly, as Nehru's successor when he was no more.

Nehru's detractors rumoured that he had picked Krishna Menon, then riding high as Defence Minister and apparently the Prime Minister's closest, or only, confidant in the Cabinet. But Durga Das, the capital's leading political columnist and no great favourite at Teen Murti Marg, thought differently. He wrote in his weekly Diary in the *Hindustan Times* in June 1957 that "if Mr Nehru is consciously building up anyone, he is building up his daughter." Durga Das says in his memoirs, published in London in 1969, that he had sensed this when Dhebar nominated her to the Working Committee two years earlier, and her elevation to the presidency of the party confirmed his suspicions.

Durga Das says his paragraph on Mrs Gandhi upset Nehru so much that he called Durga Das to see him twice and told him at the second meeting that what he had written might hurt his daughter. Durga Das assured him that such was not his intention in publishing this comment, and on the contrary it might prove helpful to her in the future. Apparently, Nehru was not the only prominent Congressman whom it upset. Some others who fancied themselves for the prime ministership when it became vacant, as they no doubt fervently hoped it would soon, thought he had taken leave of his senses.

In retrospect, was Nehru wrong or guilty of impropriety if, as was rumoured more and more strongly in political groupings hostile to the Nehru "dynasty," he deliberately groomed his daughter as his successor? The charge of impropriety may be dismissed without further argument. But was his judgment at fault if he did what he has been said to have done? There can only be one answer to this. Nehru's decision, if he made one as alleged, is justified by the happenings leading on from the meeting of the All-India Congress Committee in June 1969 when the first direct confrontation took place between Mrs Gandhi and the Syndicate. If, under the pressure of circumstances, she had not decided at that meeting to break with entrenched reaction and privilege, where would the Congress, where indeed would the Indian nation, be today?

Mrs Gandhi did not speak at the plenary Congress session at Nagpur. Instead, she addressed a youth rally. Few prominent Congressmen turned up to hear their new president. A youth leader and member of Parliament who had drifted in to the meeting walked out while she was speaking with this contemptuous remark to a journalist from Delhi: "What will this woman say?" Although other Congressmen were not so outspoken, this was the general attitude to the person to whom they were 11 years later to bow and scrape in response to even a casual glance.

Mrs Gandhi's election as party president backfired on me. I was deputy news editor of the *Hindustan Times* and was on night duty on the Sunday she spoke at the rally. Around 11 o'clock I received a phone call from one of the editorial highups. I was instructed to see that the report of Mrs Gandhi's speech was put on the back page because she should not get "too much publicity." I conveyed the order to the chief subeditor, who was aghast. In fact, the whole news desk froze in amazement for a few seconds. I then wrote a note to the news editor, explaining the circumstances in which Mrs Gandhi had been taken off the front page, and went home to sleep.

The next morning, I gathered when I went to office in the evening, hell broke loose in the staid, stuffy news room of the newspaper. Another highup tore into it in a mood to hang, draw and quarter the perpetrator of this act with his bare hands. My note gave the facts. The same evening I was told that my late-night caller would not instruct the news room in future on how stories should be handled.

In the state of the party's political health in 1959, accepting its presidency was no honour. It was a sticky, wearisome job and required much courage and patience to handle. The grand old party of Indian independence was in pretty bad shape, and being its president at this juncture was not exactly the right way to push one's way up the political ladder. The party was wobbling like a rudderless ship with a big leak, and the chances were that it would sink before it could be brought to port for repair. It had neither unity of action nor of purpose. Factionalism, one of its chronic ailments, had gone so far as to be apparently beyond cure. Another disease almost as deadly was linguism. With different groups pressing the demands of 14 or 15 languages, not to mention a few dialects which also had their champions, India seemed on the way to suffering the fate of the Tower of Babel.

Kerala had voted the Communists into office in 1957, and from portents on the political horizon it looked as though a few more states would do the same in 1962, when a general election was due. Why did Nehru see that his daughter was elected president at this critical phase in the life of the Congress? Did he have faith in her ability to find a cure for the divers diseases, including hardening of the arteries and softening of the brain, that had afflicted the Congress? Most, if not all, the Congress leaders were nearing the stage of political exhaustion, or had already reached it. They were extinct volcanoes. They had gone through the storm and stress of the struggle for independence, and they had, at least most of them, made real sacrifices and experienced great hardship. Now, as they were approaching the sixties and seventies, all they wanted was a quiet and secure life, with the assurance that they would not have to face want when they were put on the shelf. Others wanted to stay in politics and draw interest on their capital—their achievements for swaraj—till their last breath.

This was not the kind of leadership that could save the mortally sick Congress Party. These men were committed to preserving the status quo. They were too occupied with the present to realise that their actions were endangering their own future, for if the party foundered they too would surely founder with it. Mrs Gandhi was different. She belonged to a younger generation. She was forward-looking, while most of her colleagues at the top of the pyramid were steeped in the past. Those who called themselves Gandhians had only the outer vestments of Gandhism. Immaculately laundered khadi topis covered heads through which coursed the most un-Gandhian thoughts. Their acts were no less un-Gandhian.

It was with these pharisees as partners that Mrs Gandhi had

to shoulder her new responsibilities. She went to work with a will. She started well with a press conference at which she spoke out. She said: "The nation is in a hurry and we can't afford to lose time. My complaint against the Congress is that it is not going as fast as the people are advancing." Of course it was not. These tired, decrepit old men could not keep pace with the advance of the new nation. They had stopped thinking originally many years before, if they had ever been capable of original thought. They were absolutely unreceptive to new ideas and were a brake on the nation's progress. And they would continue like that until ruthless surgery was practised and they were chopped off. That was to come just about 10 years after Mrs Gandhi became party president. When it did, the howls and shrieks and imprecations of the victims of this operation without anesthetic of any kind rent Delhi's air for many months.

Indira's term of office was brief, extending only 12 months, but in it she showed a capacity for hard and sustained work, meticulous care and promptness in dealing with problems and correspondence and attending to details which were normally overlooked. At the sleepy, sloppy Congress headquarters at No 7 Jantar Mantar Road, New Delhi, the new broom swept vigorously and infused a sense of discipline where indiscipline was the standing rule. In the short period at her disposal and to the utmost extent possible in it, she tried to modernise this vital nerve centre of the party. She brought a few younger people into the Working Committee, but here she had to tread warily. The party bosses, the men who took the big decisions and kept the machine running and well oiled, were always quick to react against any move that seemed to threaten their interests.

Indira kept herself away from the petty intriguing and squabbling that surrounded her. She did not lean towards any side in the more serious factional and linguistic disputes which were the predominant themes of party politics in almost every state and Union territory. This year in office enabled her to study members of the higher echelons of the Congress hierarchy at close quarters. In her tours as president she also got to know provincial party men of the second and third rank and to size up their potential as leaders. Speaking at Congress rallies helped her get over the natural nervousness she felt when she had to address large gatherings. She developed her style of speaking, using Hindi that was easy to understand, and its delivery was simple, chatty, aimed at each individual in her audience and not at the mass.

The presidency was another important step in her training in political leadership. It was notable for two major initiatives Indira undertook. The richest and commercially and industrially most advanced state in India was Bombay, on the west coast. It had been spared in the reshuffle of state boundaries on the basis of language in the mid-1950s. But a powerful movement had developed among the Marathi speakers who lived in the southern part of the state for Samyukta (United) Maharashtra, and Bombay city had been engulfed in the worst riots in its history over this issue in 1956. Now the Gujarati speakers who inhabited the northern part also demanded a separate Mahagujarat (Greater Gujarat). The big textile city of Ahmedabad, where Mahatma Gandhi had many years before founded a trade union for mill workers which became the nucleus of moderate unionism in India, also witnessed a long period of rioting as violent as that earlier in Bombay in support of the demand.

For long, many senior Congressmen stood out against the demand that Bombay State be divided. They felt that linguism had gone far enough, and if allowed to go further might lead to secessionist movements that could break up the country. But Mrs Gandhi realised that while this was a speck on the horizon there were more immediate dangers arising from opposition to the two separatist demands. Maharashtra and Gujarat had always been political strongholds of the Congress Party. Under the stress of the emotions generated by New Delhi's coolness to the demands, regional parties were springing up and threatening to undermine the power of the Congress in Bombay. These new growths were backward-looking socially and politically, they appealed to past glories which tended to breed a parochial brand of chauvinism which were a more immediate threat to national solidarity and unity than those imagined by the opponents of dividing Bombay State on the basis of language.

After visiting the storm centres in the composite state and talking with the local Congress leaders, Mrs Gandhi took the initiative in raising the question of division before the Congress High Command in Delhi. She pointed to the dangers of ignoring what were undoubtedly popular demands, sanctioned by the Indian Constitution. Her point of view prevailed, and the new states of Maharashtra and Gujarat came into being on May 1, 1960.

This was a signal achievement, but the highlight of her term as president was toppling the Communist government of the south-western state of Kerala. This government, headed by E.M.S. Namboodiripad, was formed in 1957. It soon ran into head-on collision with the wealthy and influential Roman Catholics and the Nair community among the Hindus on the issue of state control of schools and colleges.

A mass anti-government drive was launched in which a Catholic priest, Father Vadakkan, played a leading role. Young Catholic men and women, called Christophers and dressed in white robes, paraded the towns of Kerala agitating for the overthrow of the godless Namboodiripad, who allegedly wanted to turn education institutions into hothouses for atheists who would one day hand India over to the Soviet Union.

The Congress president intervened in the confrontation beween the government and the militant Catholics and Nairs. She advised New Delhi to hold fresh elections in Kerala so that its people could show their confidence, or lack of it, in the Namboodiripad government. Since conditions in the state were greatly unsettled as a result of the agitation, fresh elections would naturally have to be preceded by a stretch of President's rule, under which the state would be administered directly by the Union Government. This would give time for emotions to cool. When Mrs Gandhi laid her proposal before the Congress high command in New Delhi, Nehru, Pant and many others shook their heads vigorously in disapproval. But she persisted, and she was backed by the mounting tempo of popular agitation in Kerala as well as by Congress rank and filers in the Indian capital. She got the government to agree to dismiss the Namboodiripad ministry and place Kerala under President's rule. So the Communists went out of office after 23 months, declaring Mrs Gandhi had done them dirty. A general election was held in Kerala in 1960 and an alliance of parties led by the Congress won a majority in the state legislature.

The Congress Party leaders in New Delhi came under much criticism throughout the country for teaming up with the Muslim League to win a majority. The critics said the Congress, wedded to secularism, had sullied its image by its link with an avowedly communal party, the very party which had worked for the division of India and the creation of Pakistan in British times. In defence

of this alliance, Mrs Gandhi reportedly told an American newspaperman: "I don't believe the Muslim League is any more communal
than anyone else in Kerala. Everything is run by the Nairs, the Nesto-
rians, the Namboodiris, or some other sects. You have to deal with
communal parties unless you want to forget about Kerala
entirely."

After this, the Muslim League became respectable in Kerala.
Even the Communists decided the League was not as communal
as its name implied and embraced it as a partner in electoral alliances and coalition governments. Today, the League is a partner in
a government headed by a member of the Communist Party of India
and including Congress ministers. The League has also become
acceptable in West Bengal, another state where it wields some influence, and both the Congress and the Communist Party of India
(Marxist) compete for its favours.

Some years later, an Indian writer asked Mrs Gandhi how she
would have reacted if the Communists had come out on top in the
1960 elections in Kerala. She replied: "I would have accepted
it as the verdict of the electorate." The significance of this episode
is that in a situation which called for initiative she acted boldly
and speedily. She showed that she knew her own mind and could
act with vigour to implement a decision once taken.

At the end of her year's term, she was pressed to continue another
year, as most other presidents did. She refused. She was unique
among Congress presidents in never having presided over an open
session of the organisation and in never having delivered a presidential address.

Mrs Gandhi was widowed in September 1960. Her husband died
after a second heart attack. A promising political career was cut
short. Feroze was an intelligent man with strong convictions, courageous and hardhitting in the Lok Sabha, the lower house of Parliament, of which he was a member. He was independent and was
not satisfied to be merely the son-in-law of the Prime Minister of
India. If he had been spared, he would have made his mark on
his own merits, not as the husband of Indira Gandhi.

The sixth decade of the twentieth century was a testing-time for
India and its leadership. While Pakistan continued unremittingly
hostile, for hostility to India was one of the inbuilt components of
that non-nation's ethos, the emotional sustenance necessary for its

survival as two different entities with practically no common interests, a new enemy appeared in the north. This was the People's Republic of China, the self-proclaimed champion of all the downtrodden of the world, the arch-foe of imperialism, neo-imperialism and every other ism which stood in the way of Peking's establishing political hegemony over the Third World.

China's hostility to India surfaced towards the end of the 1950s. It was a projection of the struggle for supremacy with the other Communist giant, the Soviet Union, in the developing, semicolonial half-world of Asia, Africa, and Latin America. It took the form of reviving claims to territories along the Himalayan border on the ground that in times past these territories came within the orbit of influence of the former Manchu Empire. The "revolutionaries" in Peking did not think it odd to make territorial claims based on commitments allegedly made to the imperial regime. When the Bolsheviks, on the other hand, seized power in 1917 under Lenin, one of the first acts of the new Soviet state was to publish all secret treaties entered into by the Czarist Empire, repudiate all unequal treaties and the claims of their predecessors to other nations' territories.

Under the pressures on India from across the northern border, there were eruptions of communal and other forms of disunity within. In 1962, serious riots broke out between Hindus and Muslims in Jabalpur, a city in the western region of Madhya Pradesh, a large, sprawling state in Central India where the extreme rightwing Jana Sangh, supported by feudal and princely groups which were strong in this economically and culturally backward area, was building up a challenge to the Congress. Mrs Gandhi, who had no official position at the time but was emerging as one of the more dynamic younger leaders of her party, went there on her own and sought through her individual efforts to restore peace between the two communities and help and protect those in need of it.

The war forced on India by Peking the same year entailed fresh responsibilities. The people had to be alerted to absorb this new shock, aimed at disrupting national unity. Nehru too had to be shielded from this blow, which he regarded as a gross betrayal by the men in Peking whom he had tried to befriend when the young republic was surrounded by a steel wall of hostility built by the United States, and whom he was instrumental in making acceptable to the developing nations of Africa and Asia. Among the many fresh commitments Mrs Gandhi undertook in this connection were membership of the National Defence Council, of the National Integration Council and of the executive committee of the National Defence Fund, and chairmanship of the Citizens' Central Council.

When the Chinese invaders cracked the Indian defences in the Northeast Frontier Agency, one of the territories they claimed, and moved swiftly towards the plains of the Brahmaputra Valley in Assam, Mrs Gandhi travelled by Indian Air Force plane to Tezpur, headquarters of the commander in this sector, Lt-Gen B.M. Kaul. She went among officers and soldiers, spoke to the wounded, tried to rouse the flagging spirits of those who were whole in body and give them the determination to stop the aggressive Chinese at all costs.

To Nehru, now 73, Peking's perfidy was a mortal blow. It shattered his dreams of building an area of peace and economic cooperation in which the developing nations would get their fair share of material goods and play an independent role in world affairs. Overnight, he had changed into a weary, disillusioned old man. He walked with a stoop, as though in pain, his face was sombre and lined deeply, his elan was irretrievably lost. Indira devoted much of her time to nursing him back to health. Her efforts were vain. Neither doctors nor nurse could heal the damage to his mind. In January 1964, Nehru had a stroke at a Congress session at Bhubaneswar, capital of the eastern seaboard state of Orissa. After that, his doctors ordered strict rest in bed. For four months, this dynamo which had never been idle physically or mentally for any stretch of time since anybody could remember, was immobilised. His daughter was constantly beside him, and through her filtered news of the world outside the sickroom.

Meanwhile, manoeuvring to step into the still living leader's shoes became more and more frenzied among his colleagues in the government and the party. Names were bandied to and fro, chief among them being that of Morarji Desai, the tallest Congress leader in his home state of Gujarat. Desai, known for his ascetic ways and acid tongue and almost fanatical commitment to prohibition, had been Nehru's Finance Minister until August 1963 and rated the second-highest-ranking minister after Nehru. Then Nehru had asked him and some other members of the Union Cabinet and chief ministers of states to step down voluntarily under the Kamaraj Plan.

K. Kamaraj, Congress president, was the boss of Tamil Nadu. A strapping man with a greying toothbrush mustache and small but very penetrating eyes, he hid a remarkably agile brain and ruthless will behind a curtain of ignorance of English and Hindi. When he communicated with the Delhi press, he spoke in Tamil and needed an interpreter. He liked to clown in the presence of reporters, but this was part of the disguise of this southern Machiavelli. In the ensuing power struggle after Nehru's death Kamaraj played the role of kingmaker, preferring it to that of king, which many of his supporters in the party and in the press urged him to confer on himself. Kamaraj held this pivotal position, which made him stronger than even the prime minister, from the struggle for the Nehru succession up to 1967, when, after he had helped Mrs Gandhi to a second term of office as head of government, he found his power gradually evaporating.

The Kamaraj Plan was essentially a bid to counter the waning popularity of the Congress by getting some of the top provincial leaders to quit ministerial posts and mastermind efforts to strengthen the party at the grassroots. Kamaraj shrewdly realised that if this was not done the party stood a good chance of being defeated in the general election in 1967, and his fears were partly fulfilled. Kamaraj had read the danger signal correctly in the results of the general election of March 1962 in Tamil Nadu, where a provincial party, the Dravida Munnetra Kazhagam, was building itself up on the demand for an independent Dravidian state in the south.

Durga Das, who retired as editor-in-chief of the *Hindustan Times*, its leading English newspaper, in 1959, chronicles in his memoirs that Nehru was sold on the proposal when Kamaraj presented it to him. He christened it the Kamaraj Plan and got the Congress Working Committee and the AICC to endorse a revised version of it under which all the central ministers and chief ministers would resign and leave Nehru to decide who should be retained and who go forth to toil in the Congress vineyard, which sadly needed expert care.

Nehru's motive, Durga Das says, was to clear the way for his daughter to succeed him, and the biggest hurdle in attaining this goal was Morarji Desai. On the face of it, this deduction seems somewhat farfetched, but if Nehru was entertaining any thoughts about who was to succeed him, as he had premonitions that his time was drawing near, he probably wanted Desai out of the running because he had reservations about Desai's undoubted conservatism in economic as well as social and political thinking, his authoritarian attitude to people, and his pronounced tilt towards the United States.

The crisis came on May 27. Nehru had another stroke, collapsed and did not recover consciousness. I recall the day clearly. I was then news editor of the *Indian Express*. The news came around two o'clock in the afternoon on the teleprinter. We had no time to react to it personally. The immediate task was to bring out a special supplement containing the news and put it on the streets before our rivals came out with theirs. The chief subeditor, who should have been on duty, had taken a few hours off to attend to some personal business and was late. He dashed in now, tears streaming down his cheeks, sobbing "O God, Nehru is dead." Work went on without letup until far at night. I recall Frank Moraes, editor-in-chief, sitting through it all, writing an editorial, a biographical note and a long article of personal appreciation for the editorial page on a man whom he admired probably more than anybody else he knew, and calmly and unobtrusively giving instructions or advice when it was sought.

It was only around midnight, when all the loose ends had been tied, that I sat back and breathed freely for the first time since the ill tidings had come. It was only then that the full impact of what had happened dawned on me. Nehru is dead, I repeated to myself. I shall never see Nehru again. It seemed unbelievable. Nehru was India. Nehru was universal. He represented all the basic decencies of human life. What now? And I thought of all the rats who were busy right at that moment sharpening their claws and preening their whiskers for the great race that would now begin. I bade my editor goodnight and went home.

CHAPTER FOUR

CABINET MINISTER

INTEREST IN THE prime ministerial stakes was intense in every corner of the country. In spite of having been unwillingly pushed down from the Olympian pinnacle of power in New Delhi a few months earlier, Morarji Desai was the raging favourite. The candidate himself oozed self-confidence. It was inconceivable that his party colleagues in Parliament would not pick him as Nehru's successor, for what worthier person there was he could not imagine. Besides, was he not well liked by the tycoons of Bombay, Calcutta and, nearer home base, Ahmedabad? Who could look after the interests of big business better than he could? Their interests certainly had to be looked after, for who put money into the Congress kitty when elections had to be fought?

Then there were the big farmers and moneylenders, the men who still ruled the village and who could be depended upon to roll up votes for the Congress Party. They too considered Desai the right man for the top spot in New Delhi. So did many other special interests and supporters of the status quo, including the bureaucrats, because Desai was a "safe" man. He would not upset their apple carts. And, to commend him further, was he not a Communist-hater of the purest water? He rated the same class as Edgar J. Hoover, the unchanging head of the US Federal Bureau of Investigation.

But Kamaraj, who was now all geared up to start his kingmaking role, had doubts about Desai. Indeed, he feared that the glowing testimonials produced on behalf of the strong man from Bulsar, his birthplace in Gujarat, were disqualifications. Kamaraj was thinking ahead of the 1967 elections, and he and other party chiefs felt that under Desai's leadership the party would surely suffer disaster. The Congress needed a new image. It had to be given a veneer of progressivism if it hoped to carry credibility with the electorate three years from then. Another compelling reason for not choosing Desai was that with his unshakable conviction of being always right and morally superior and his fads and fancies he was a difficult man to get on with and would make teamwork difficult. Once he got the bit beween his teeth, even Kamaraj the ringmaster might find him too difficult to handle.

Kamaraj chose Lal Bahadur Shastri. According to Durga Das, Shastri was really Nehru's choice. Apparently, he had indicated this to Kamaraj in his political will and testament. Durga Das narrates that when Nehru realised he would not live long enough to make the succession secure for Indira, he decided to put Shastri in the slot until she was ready to take over. In making this stopgap arrangement, Nehru presumably, by some miracle of foresight, knew Shastri would not live much longer than he would or that he would, out of gratitude to his patron, step down for Indira at the appropriate moment.

The first alternative may be dismissed, unless one is prepared to concede that Nehru was a crystal-ball gazer and knew that Shastri would die tragically at Tashkent in January 1966. The second may also be rejected out of hand because Nehru knew enough of history to realise that gratitude is not a highly valued commodity in politics, and once Shastri was firmly in the saddle he would not voluntarily get out again for Indira or for anybody else. Shastri had been known to the Nehrus from the time he had been a humble party worker in Allahabad. Humility was Shastri's greatest virtue. Each rung of the ladder on which he climbed to success was formed of it. It pleased him to pose before foreigners as a humble little barefoot boy from the backwoods. He was Nehru's Home Minister at the time the Kamaraj Plan was put into operation. To prove his loyalty to his leader, he offered to resign before any of his colleagues. His resignation was accepted.

Indira persuaded her father to bring him back to the Cabinet as Minister without Portfolio after Nehru fell ill at Bhubaneswar. He would sit quietly, making himself as unobtrusive as possible, in an anteroom in Nehru's house for as long as an hour until Indira was ready to see him and take whatever message he wished conveyed to Nehru. But this model of loyalty and humility had little time for Indira once he became Prime Minister. He even avoided seeing her, according to Durga Das, explaining that he had developed a feeling of inferiority in relation to her.

This was scarcely the way a person in whom Nehru reposed absolute trust and expected to honour an unwritten political commitment would behave. It is rather difficult to believe that Nehru was
such a Machiavellian that he pounced on the Kamaraj Plan as a
weapon to lever Shastri into the prime ministership as the first step
towards putting his daughter there. This was not Nehru's style.
Anyway, there are too many imponderables in this devious piece
of strategy to make it credible.

Shastri won, but only after he had made a gesture to Mrs Gandhi
by suggesting that she take her father's place. Shastri won through
the application of a principle new in Indian politics—consensus.
To avoid a contest between Shastri and Desai, which would have
revealed to the nation a picture of discord in the highest party echelons, Kamaraj went to work behind the scenes on Desai and his
supporters until Desai agreed to withdraw and support Shastri,
who thus became the Congress Parliamentary Party's unanimous
choice. Desai gave in when he realised that he would be defeated
on a vote as Kamaraj and his lieutenants had lined up the majority
of Congress members of Parliament behind them. A "loyal and disciplined soldier" of the Congress, Desai bowed out willingly, according to reports broadcast by his supporters. But those who enjoyed
his confidence knew he had done so very grudgingly and had spoken
bitterly about Nehru, holding him responsible for his humiliation.
The nation was to hear more about Desai's discipline and loyalty
and devotion to socialism in his further bids to wrest the prime
ministership and in his subsequent confrontation with Mrs Gandhi.

Shastri thought he had discharged his debt to the Nehrus by making Indira his Minister of Information and Broadcasting, with fourth
ranking in the Cabinet. This was regarded as one of the minor ministries by those who did not understand the importance of communication in shaping men's political thinking and other attitudes
in fast-changing present-day societies. Today, control of the mediums
of communication with the people is politically more important
than such portfolios as home and finance. Control of licences for
imports or for new industries is not more significant than control
of the instruments which influence minds and decisions.

Mrs Gandhi went about her first official assignment with characteristic methodical attention to detail. She tried to streamline and
modernise the ponderous, creaking governmental propaganda

machine, snarled like other government undertakings in miles and miles of redtape that nullified attempts to give it speed and efficiency and firm political direction. Her staff found her wide awake and receptive to new ideas, and also found she had a mind of her own, and her own ideas about how things should be done. She encouraged them to initiate change and assured them of her protection against political pressure if they took correct decisions that might be unpopular with people higher up. She took much of the starchy puritanism out of film censoring and made the development of television a priority. Files did not gather dust on her table, and decisions were taken and executed with refreshing promptitude.

In Moscow, there had been a big political shakeup in 1964. Khrushchev, the man who built a bridge between India and the Soviet Union and gave massive aid to create India's heavy industrial base and political and military support in the war with China, was out and a new team was in power, with Kosygin as Prime Minister and Brezhnev in the much more powerful position of general secretary of the Soviet Communist Party. New Delhi was somewhat worried. Would the new men be as uninhibitedly friendly to India as Khrushchev? Would they make up with China, whose enmity was one of the reasons for Khrushchev's ouster? There were also reports that the new men were planning to restructure Soviet policy towards the Indian subcontinent, which might mean that Moscow would stand nonaligned between New Delhi and Rawalpindi. At the same time, the Russians were watching political developments in New Delhi carefully. They doubted whether Shastri was as well-intentioned towards them as Nehru had been.

The Soviet leaders invited Mrs Gandhi to Moscow in 1965. They knew her well as she had visited Moscow on her own and with Nehru, and they trusted her. They wanted to gauge the new political climate in New Delhi by talking with her. Mrs Gandhi returned with the good news that fears of a chill in India-Soviet relations were unfounded.

Mrs Gandhi's tour took her also to Paris, London, and Belgrade. Her soundings of diplomatic opinion there convinced her that Soviet policies, "whether in the internal sphere or in the field of international relations, and the Soviet attitude towards India and China will remain unchanged," according to a report of what she told newsmen on returning to New Delhi. The Moscow-oriented newsmagazine *Link* of New Delhi said the tour "has confirmed the impression that her presence in the government lends it international prestige and is taken as a guarantee of continuation of the national policies associated with the name of Jawaharlal Nehru."

Mrs Gandhi was different from other ministers, most of whom allowed their departmental secretaries to run their ministries and signed whatever they were told on the dotted line. She criticised bureaucratic ways, and when she saw things going wrong she said so. She was willing to risk her political reputation to undertake tasks which she felt had to be done. One instance was the violent reaction in Tamil Nadu to Prime Minister Shastri's decision to enforce the constitutional deadline for making Hindi the official language of India. The date fixed was January 26, 1965, and the announcement of his decision in New Delhi touched off furious riots in Madras city.

Mrs Gandhi alone of all the Cabinet Ministers flew to Madras and tried to pacify the enraged Tamilians. Shastri and his Home Minister, Gulzarilal Nanda, who was mainly responsible for the order on the use of Hindi, had to retreat. But this injudicious action cooked the Congress goose in Tamil Nadu, which voted the Dravida Munnetra Kazhagam to power with a big majority in the general election in 1967. This action, taken without consulting the governments of the states where Hindi is not the spoken language, has set back by many years the possibility of its replacing English as the official medium of communication in India. The Union Government is now committed by legislation not to displace English so long as any state favours its retention. Today, two full-fledged states, Nagaland and Meghalaya (the Abode of the Clouds), both in the northeastern region, have chosen English as their official language.

Mrs Gandhi entered the Shastri government in June 1964, and found a seat in the Rajya Sabha, the upper house of Parliament, in August. She had been offered her father's vacant seat in the Lok Sabha, Phulpur in Allahabad district, but she preferred to wait before testing her popularity at the hustings. She stood for the Lok Sabha in the 1967 general election from Rae Bareli, her husband's former constituency in Uttar Pradesh. She sought re-election from there in March 1971 against a formidable rival, Raj Narain, a tub-thumping, mudslinging leader of the Socialist Party who often descended to the vocabulary of the gutter and who had sworn he would defeat her. In the event, she trounced him soundly.

The year 1965 was one of anxiety and much trouble for the Indian people. President Ayub Khan of Pakistan started making ugly noises across the border, and finally struck on April 9 in Kutch, a partly marshy, partly sandy wasteland between the Pakistani territory of Sind and Gujarat in India. When a ceasefire was negotiated in June after sporadic fighting, the Pakistanis had succeeded in grabbing some territory under Indian control. Subsequently, a three-member international tribunal was appointed to adjudicate. As a result of its ruling, by two votes to one, more than 300 square miles of territory passed from India to Pakistan, whose original demand was for more than ten times that area.

Pakistan's appetite was whetted. The Kutch action was a probe to test India's preparedness and fighting ability after two and half years of intensive expansion and re-equipping in the wake of the debacle in NEFA. Pakistani eyes focused greedily on Kashmir, which it had continued to claim from 1947 onward. Grabbing the Kashmir Valley had become a Pakistani fixation, and Pakistani propagandists told people in other countries that until Kashmir was "restored" to Pakistan the two neighbours on the Indian subcontinent would never live as friends. Unfortunately, many people who should have looked more carefully into this claim swallowed the Pakistani line blindly and blamed India for not giving Pakistan its due at the time of partition. These people have been misled further by the noise a rump of Kashmiri politicians in opposition, banded together in the Plebiscite Front and the Action Committee, make in the valley.

The fact is that hatred of India is the only force that holds Pakistan together. Even that ploy did not succeed in East Pakistan, now the People's Republic of Bangladesh. It seems to be losing its effectiveness in what is left of Pakistan in the west, but in 1965 it was still a powerful instrument in the hands of the military dictatorship when it wanted to create a war psychosis. Kashmir was the tangible object on which Pakistani ambitions and hates and fears were concentrated. If the Kashmir problem had not existed, it would have been necessary for the militarists in Rawalpindi to invent it. If the Kashmir Valley had fallen into their greedy hands as they wanted, they would have had to find some other cause of enmity towards India.

The return of Kashmir to its rightful owners, coupled with artificially created hysteria over imaginary threats of attack on Pakistan, have been the stock in trade of the rulers of this freak called Pakistan since it was delivered in 1947. This has served as a means for channelling internal discontent away from the real source of Pakistan's troubles, the oligarchy of feudal landowners and bureaucrats who rule the country through terror with the help of the army, most of whose officers belong to the feudal aristocracy of West Punjab and the Northwest Frontier. In September 1965, the Pakistani army struck at India again, and its objective as before was the Kashmir Valley.

The 21-day war ended in a stalemate, with both sides claiming victory. If the commanders at Army Headquarters in New Delhi had not dithered, military observers believe Indian troops would have been able to invest the key cities of Lahore and Sialkot in West Punjab. With Sialkot in their hands, the road to Rawalpindi would have been open. With this strategic advantage, a satisfactory political settlement might have been secured. But at the end of the fighting, in which both sides had pretty nearly reached exhaustion, Pakistan had failed in its main objective. The Kashmir Valley was safely in Indian hands.

What was Mrs Gandhi's part in the war? She showed she was a woman of almost limitless courage. While the fighting was at its bitterest, she visited the front line at Haji Pir, a strongpoint in that part of Kashmir the Pakistanis had grabbed in 1947 and had held on to from then, although India is its legal owner. A senior officer of the Indian Air Force forbade her making the trip from Srinagar because it was too dangerous. A helicopter was standing by. Full of resource, she got a member of her staff to engage the officer in conversation. Suddenly, scenting something wrong, the officer swung round and asked: "Where is Mrs Gandhi?" Where indeed was she? Up in the helicopter, on her way to the front.

A British newspaperwoman wrote in July 1969: "Many Indian Army officers and men have told me that, often, in the thick of the fighting, a slight, saree-clad figure would appear, and it would be Mrs Gandhi, anxious to check on the welfare of the troops and see how things were going."

Mrs Gandhi stayed only 19 months at the Ministry of Information and Broadcasting, not long enough to make more than a scratch on the surface of the problems in it. In January 1966, she was called upon to shoulder bigger burdens. Shastri had gone to Tashkent to

negotiate a peace settlement with Ayub Khan under the auspices
of Kosygin. This meeting was significant for several reasons. This
was the first time Moscow was undertaking a major peacemaking
role on the Asian continent singlehanded. Secondly, it was doing
this in respect of a quarrel between two members of the Commonwealth of Nations. The Commonwealth's seniormost partner, Britain,
was nowhere in the picture. But Harold Wilson, then British Prime
Minister, stood on the sidelines and did a little cheering for Pakistan.
This piece of gamesmanship evoked loud and angry protests from
India, and MPs belonging to different parties demanded that the
government pull out of the Commonwealth. In his autobiography,
published some years later, Wilson apologised, saying he had been
misled by pro-Pakistani bureaucrats in Whitehall. By committing
itself to seeing that both sides honoured the agreement, the Soviet
Union was staking a claim to a close, permanent interest in the affairs
of the Indian subcontinent.

Shastri died in Tashkent in the very early hours of January 11
after signing the agreement with Ayub Khan. The strain of the previous few days, of almost continuous high-pressure negotiations,
brought on a heart attack which killed him in bed. Once again,
in much less than two years, India had lost a Prime Minister through
sudden death. While Nehru's prolonged illness indicated that his
end might be near, Shastri's was quite unexpected, although he had
shown signs of overstrain some months before and had been advised
rest.

Shastri's body had barely arrived in New Delhi when the prime
ministerial stakes were on again. Once more Morarji Desai's spot-
lessly white and well-starched Gandhi topi was in the ring. This
disciplined and loyal soldier of the Congress could not be held back
from offering his services to the nation. It seemed that this time,
at any rate, nothing could prevent him for gaining his heart's desire.
In his anxiety to serve the nation, he forgot however, to consult
other members of the Congress high command before announcing
his candidature.

Jawaharlal Nehru and Indira Gandhi

← With her eldest grandchild Rah

...th her elder son Rajiv,
...s wife Sonia, and
...unger son Sanjay

→
...elcomes British Prime
...inister Edward Heath
at Delhi airport

↓ With Dr Henry
Kissinger

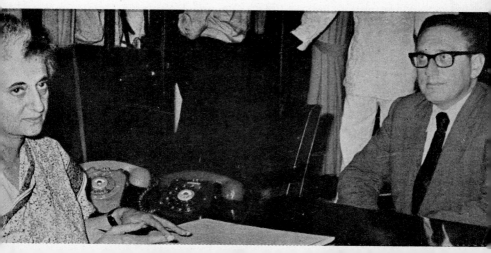

↑ With Marshal Tito and Madame Broz

Sheikh Mujibur Rahman arrives in New Delhi
from London

↑ Reception for President Nasser

ecting a guard of honour with Soviet Prime
ster Alexei Kosygin at Moscow airport

↑
With Sirimavo Bandaranaike at Colombo
airport

← Shaking hands with I
tennis captain Rama
Krishnan

↓ Garlands for the pe

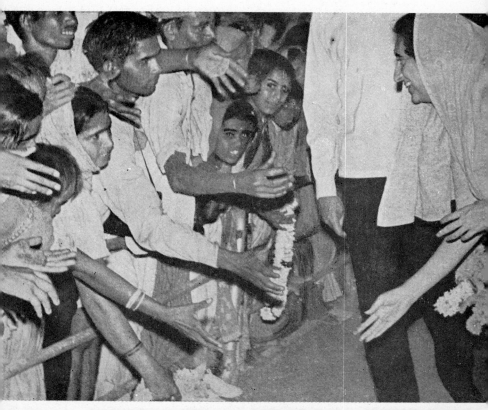

↓ Addressing a public meeting at Ramlila Grounds, New Delhi, on December 12, 1971

↓ Informal press conference after election as Prime Minister 1966

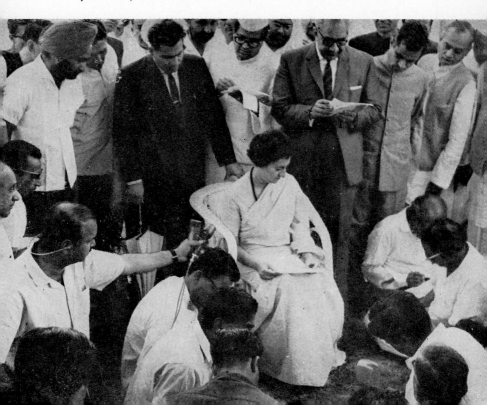

Meeting of Congress Party Parliamentary Board

Addressing an Election Meeting at the Boat Club, New Delhi

CHAPTER FIVE

HEAD OF GOVERNMENT

IN THE WHISPERING galleries of New Delhi, other names were also tossed around besides that of Desai. None of them had, unlike Desai, openly declared they were running. But the news got around that they would not say no if they were offered the post. Among them was Home Minister Nanda, who, as at the time of Nehru's death, was acting head of government. He had reportedly consulted his pet astrologer and had been asssured that this time he would not be cheated of his just due. Desai is said to have received the same assurance from his astrologer. Other names mentioned were Defence Minister Y.B. Chavan, S.K. Patil, Congress chieftain of Bombay and the party's chief fund-raiser, and Mrs Gandhi's aunt, Vijaya-lakshmi Pandit.

Nobody at this stage mentioned Mrs Gandhi as Shastri's successor. Chavan was the man on whom people were ready to lay their money. I was working with United News of India in New Delhi at the time. My guess was that Chavan, who had built up a reputation as a good administrator and able speaker in Parliament in his four years in charge first of defence and later home, should win on merit compared with others whose names were discussed in the press and the lobbies of Parliament. I checked with V.P. Rama-chandran, a senior correspondent of UNI who is now the agency's deputy general manager. He scoffed at me. "Indira Gandhi," he replied. For a moment I gaped unbelievingly. On sober reflection, the inevitability of Mrs Gandhi dawned on me. The provincial chief-tains, headed by Kamaraj, had secretly decided to get her nominated for the post. The chief ministers had blessed the move. These weighty endorsements guaranteed her victory.

Nanda never really had a chance as he had antagonised most of the chief ministers by various acts in his tenure as Home Minister. Chavan had been smeared by newspaper reports which identified him with big business interests in Bombay. His rating in the southern states was not good, and in the minds of most Congressmen he was associated too closely with his home state of Maharashtra. It was not difficult to conclude by a process of elimination that Mrs Gandhi was the only member of the party's top brass with a national aura after Nehru's death.

Only two candidates were left in the field, Mrs Gandhi, the official nominee, and Desai, who resolutely refused to pull out in spite of pressure from several directions. This time he was determined not to let what he considered his right elude him. The disciplined soldier of the Congress was ready to forget discipline temporarily to uphold a principle, though what that principle was few people outside the ranks of his committed supporters could discern.

The party strongmen wanted Mrs Gandhi for two compelling reasons. They knew there was a tough election battle ahead in 13 months. They calculated that some of the Nehru charisma had rubbed off on his daughter, and that she was a better votecatcher than anybody else they could think of. Besides, Mrs Gandhi had the reputation of being radical, even a socialist in the broad sense in which the term was used in Congress circles. And wedded to her satisfactory antecedents was the belief they held that she was, after all, only a woman and a novice in politics, and they, hardheaded, hornyhanded, politicians with the scars of many a battle to show as proof, knew how to handle her. They would give her a year or so in office, and after the elections had been won ... well, they knew exactly what had to be done. Indira Gandhi accepted the honour they offered her, with a becoming show of modesty and gratitude.

Desai was not lying idle while all this was going on at Kamaraj's house on Jantar Mantar Road which was within hailing distance of the Congress headquarters. He sent a written appeal to all Congress MPs, soliciting their support. In it he said he was offering himself to them on the basis of his good work for party and government in various capacities. The times were difficult, he noted, and whomever they picked as prime minister would have to shoulder heavy responsibilities, both in domestic and foreign affairs. He had therefore expected the party's policymakers to make a sincere effort to find a leader acceptable to all. The unwritten inference for all who could read between the lines was of course that Desai himself was the only person who fitted the bill.

"On the contrary," wrote Desai to his parliamentary colleagues, "those who, by virtue of their positions had a special responsibility to be above personal prejudices and animus, seem to have decided that the search for unanimity should mean the elimination of all those whom they did not like." He added: "I have been greatly distressed to see how all kinds of unhealthy precedents are being set up in the effort to claim unanimous support for the choice of a few people who are in positions of authority." In short, the group of overlords who were to become known three years later as the Syndicate had done the dirty on him by supplanting the man in whom party and people had faith with a nobody who had no support but theirs.

The upstart candidate's reply to Desai's insinuations and charges was: "I have served the country in my own humble way in various capacities and situations. It is for members to judge and decide. I can only say that I shall continue to serve the ideals we all cherish." Kamaraj refused to share with the press what he thought of Desai's charge against "those in positions of authority." But Atulya Ghosh, kingfish of the West Bengal Congress, and D.P. Mishra, Chief Minister of Madhya Pradesh and a staunch supporter of Mrs Gandhi, had a lot to say about Desai.

Ghosh, a member of the Congress Working Committee, said it was "highly undemocratic" for a senior member of the Parliamentary Board to announce his candidature without consulting other members of party high command. He said: "We all expected Mr Desai to [work] with others to solve this leadership question instead of soliciting support from individual members of the party for his own candidature."

Mishra commented to newsmen: "It is a reflection against MPs to suggest that they are being [pressured] by chief ministers. So far as my own state is concerned, the members met and were requested by me to decide freely. They all congratulated the chief ministers for having truly reflected the minds of members of Parliament from various states, and unanimously decided to vote for Mrs Indira Gandhi."

The next day, January 19, the Congress Parliamentary Party gathered in the Central Hall of Parliament to elect a new leader. Excitement was intense, for up to voting time Desai and his followers were predicting a victory for the people's candidate against the choice of the party bosses. When the ballots, cast in secret, were counted, the verdict was Indira Gandhi 355, Morarji Desai 169, invalid 2. Total number of votes: 526 out of 551 Congress MPs. This was a convincing victory for Mrs Gandhi. The loser was the first to congratulate her. He pledged his full cooperation to her "in whatever manner I can give consistent with my self-respect and the interests of the country," insinuating that these interests might not be quite safe in her hands. Then came a venomous blast: "I do not want to refer to the election, which is now over, because one should not go into any postmortem. It does not help us. But I hope and pray that in future, at any rate, the atmosphere of fearlessness will be cultivated in the party and in the country, because this party has the greatest responsibility in the matter of creating fearlessness in the country." In other words, Desai had lost because his fellow MPs had been bulldozed into voting for his rival.

Indira Gandhi became Prime Minister of India on January 24, when she was sworn in before President Radhakrishnan in Rashtrapati Bhavan. She declared her policy in a broadcast over All India Radio two days later on Republic Day. She pledged herself to follow the policies of her father—democracy and secularism, planned economic and social advance, and promoting friendship among nations. She undertook to implement, in letter and spirit, the Tashkent Declaration, an expression of the desire to maintain the friendliest relations with neighbours and to resolve all disputes peacefully. She focused national attention on the food problem caused by drought in several parts of the country and said her government's first duty would be to distribute grain to those who needed it urgently.

She said: "While peace is our aim, I am keenly aware of the responsibility of the government to preserve the freedom and territorial integrity of the country. We must therefore be alert and keep constant vigil, strengthening our defences as necessary. The valour, determination, courage and sacrifice of our fighting forces have set a shining example."

She sought the cooperation of all sections of Indians to build a dynamic and progressive society and a just social order. That could be done only through hard work, cooperation, and unity of purpose. The government would continue to encourage and help private enterprise. She approached the vast problems facing the country with humility. The tradition of Mahatma Gandhi and her father "and my unbounded faith in the people of India give me strength and confidence." India had often given proof of an indomitable spirit, and in recent years, as in the past, "it has shown unmistakable courage and capacity for meeting new challenges. There is a firm base of Indianness which will withstand any trial."

She got down to business right away. Kerala faced a great shortage of food. She urgently appealed to the rice-growing states of the south to send stocks to Kerala immediately. She announced she was flying to the state to see that everything was done to meet the crisis. She was advised not to do so, but she went. She was advised again on arriving in Trivandrum, the state capital, not to speak in public as the Communists, who had not forgotten her role in the downfall of the Namboodiripad ministry in 1959, would make trouble for her. But she insisted on going to a meeting convened for her. She was greeted with slogans and shouting. When the clamour diminished, she called for quiet so that she might speak. She was suffering from severe food poisoning at the time.

Next she flew to the Mizo Hills in Assam, where a section of tribesmen was threatening armed revolt. They wanted an independent state of Mizoram. She reasoned with them instead of threatening military action. But this became necessary a few months later when the Mizos rose up and tried to get what they wanted by force.

West Bengal was also short of rice. Prices were shooting up, hoarding and blackmarketing were rampant in the city. Leftist party leaders threatened a *bandh* (complete stoppage of all activity) in Calcutta if something was not done immediately. Mrs Gandhi went to Calcutta to talk over the problem with the leftist leaders, but the state government arrested them before she could do so. She went back to New Delhi and had talks with the opposition leaders there. She then persuaded the West Bengal Government to let the leftists take out a silent procession of protest against lack of food and rising prices.

Mrs Gandhi set off in March on her first foreign tour after becoming Prime Minister. She visited Paris, London, Moscow, and Washington officially. The trip was undertaken to acquaint the governments of these countries with her policies and to assure them that no changes would be made in the principles of foreign policy Nehru had laid down. She was the first woman head of government to visit Washington. She was an object of curiosity to Americans, who, with all their claims to modernity, could not believe that a female could direct the affairs of a nation of 500 million.

Vice-President Hubert Humphrey had visited India a little earlier. He went back to Washington and told people there that Mrs Gandhi was "quite a politician . . . a politician of considerable magnitude." She also impressed President Johnson when he played host to her at the White House. He discovered that "behind the sophisticated look there was also a sophisticated mind which had been trained over the years to deal with political problems and political situations," according to one newspaper report. She did "a million-dollar public relations job," it said. She intended to remain what she was, a moderate-minded, undoctrinaire leader of India, "not in our pocket of course, but also not at our national throat." *Time* newsmagazine said: "Johnson found her a fiercely independent ruler with a determination equal to his own."

Mrs Gandhi met some of New York's leading bankers, industrialists, and financiers from Wall Street at dinner on March 30. She told them that India needed more capital from abroad. She said: "The aid which we have received hitherto has been on a generous scale in absolute terms. But relative to other countries it has been somewhere at the end of the list on a per capita basis." She told the industrialised countries of the West to open up their markets "much more than they have been prepared to do so far." She added: "In this country you have always believed in pushing back your frontiers. In the last century you tamed the Wild West. My appeal to you today is that in the next few decades you should allow yourselves to be tamed by the developing East."

Mrs Gandhi addressed a gathering of 1,000 friends of India at a banquet in her honour in New York on March 31. The subject of her talk was the twin threats to India's security and integrity—China and Pakistan. She warned nations that were friendly to India against "unrealistic political and military assumptions or an artificial balance of power that merely aggravates tensions."

In the most forthright speech of her stay in the US, she explained to her distinguished audience, which included United Nations Secretary-General U Thant, that the decisions of the Security Council and the General Assembly on Kashmir in the late 1940s and early 1950s now had only an academic value. This was parti-

cularly so after Pakistan's invasion of India in 1965. China's hostility towards India and encouragement of Pakistan's warlike designs
were new factors which had altered the Kashmir issue materially.
Showing concern at Chinese supplies of military material to strengthen Pakistan's already menacing war machine, she said Peking's
spreading influence in Asia could be dammed only by helping non-
communist Asian nations to establish popular, progressive, and
nationalist governments dedicated to fulfilling the aspirations of
their peoples.

She called for continuing friendship between India and the US.
She asked the Americans not to be "irritated by misunderstandings
or diverted by difficulties." She explained: "Indo-Pakistani relations
all too often are equated with Kashmir. Now Kashmir is not the
cause but rather a consequence of Indo-Pakistani differences. There
was no Kashmir problem on August 15, 1947, when India and Pakistan became independent. The problem, as it is called, arose some
months later with the invasion of the State of Jammu and Kashmir
by Pakistan. This is the UN finding and the basic fact.

"India agreed to, and indeed suggested, a plebiscite at the time,
but on condition that the state was first cleared of the invader and
peace returned. The UN endorsed this condition. Since this basic
condition was never fulfilled by Pakistan, there could be no question
of a plebiscite, which was categorically defined as the very last stage
of a clearly defined sequence of events. It is now too late to talk of
a plebiscite. The second invasion of Kashmir by Pakistan last autumn
has destroyed whatever marginal or academic value the old UN
resolutions might have had. Kashmir is also vital now to the defence
of India in Ladakh against China.

"Any plebiscite today would definitely amount to questioning
the integrity of India. It would raise the issue of secession—an issue
on which the United States fought a civil war not so very long ago.
We cannot and will not tolerate a second partition of India on religious grounds. It would destroy the very basis of the Indian state.

"China's hostility to India and her courtship of Pakistan has also
introduced a material change in the situation. China is almost the
only country to have denounced the Tashkent agreement. And now
we read of Chinese military supplies being given to Pakistan. We
are concerned about these developments, specially against the background of China's desire to stir up trouble wherever it can."

This is India's final answer to Pakistan's repeated claims to Kashmir. President Bhutto has revived the demand indirectly by saying that the right of the people of Kashmir to self-determination must be conceded. Mrs Gandhi's arguments against disinterring the Kashmir question are reinforced by Pakistan's third major war of aggression against India in December 1971. They derive still more force from Chinese replenishments of arms and armour, reportedly to re-equip several divisions, to compensate for the Pakistani losses of material in the 14-day war.

Against whom is China arming Pakistan? The question answers itself. When John Foster Dulles decided to make massive gifts of weapons to Pakistan and train its military manpower, in spite of strong Indian protests, in 1954 under a mutual defence pact, the reason he gave was that Pakistan must become a bastion of the "free world" against atheistic communism. Dulles was a great believer in God. In fact, there were times when he imagined he was God himself. His self-imposed mission was to rid the world of communism and make it safe for the godly.

But this was only the overt purpose of sharpening Pakistan's teeth and claws. Its real aim was to pose a constant threat to India. A haunting fear of Western statesman was that, like China, India would become an Asian power. With its growing economic and military might, it would then be the political focus of the developing nations in the Third World. Thus Western influence among these nations would lessen, and probably vanish altogether some day. So what better way was there of preventing this dreadful development than keeping India economically weak, and this could be done by using Pakistan as a pistol constantly pointed at its head and making it divert its capital resources from economic and social investment to military spending to counter the Pakistani threat. China is following the same Dullesian policy today. Peking wants leadership of the Third World and is bending all its efforts to see that New Delhi does not become a competing centre of attraction for the nations which belong to it.

Mrs Gandhi told the banqueters in New York: "China is taking great care to avoid direct military involvement in Vietnam. But China's shadow does fall across Southeast Asia. The real threat from China is, however, less military than political. But Chinese influence will be diminished if its neighbours in Asia and nations of the developing world can build around popular and forward-looking nationalist governments dedicated to fulfilling the aspirations of their people. They would also be greatly strengthened in this purpose were they to see a strong and viable alternative model to Peking." This model was India.

Soon after her return to New Delhi, the government devalued the rupee by a whopping 57 per cent. In taking this momentous decision Mrs Gandhi relied heavily on the advice of her Planning Minister, Asoka Mehta, who was thought highly of as an economic theorist. He had been for many years a leading light of the Socialist Party and was one of the founders of the Hind Mazdoor Sabha, a Socialist-controlled federation of industrial labour unions. He was not very popular among the Socialists, who thought he had betrayed them for office, nor among his new Congress comrades, who regarded him as an interloper. Inimical Congressmen started a drive against Mehta, accusing him of deliberately misleading the Prime Minister at the prompting of Washington.

After devaluation Mehta's reputation as an economic pundit declined in government circles. He was an unhappy man, as his advice was no longer prized. He resigned in 1968, putting forward his dissatisfaction with the government's stand on the events in Czechoslovakia, culminating in the removal of Communist Party secretary Dubcek from office and the dismissal of the Czech government, as his reason for doing so. Devaluation raised a great controversy, with economic experts divided into two camps, one supporting and the other condemning the government. Kamaraj was very angry, saying he had not been consulted beforehand. Morarji Desai also came out against it. Some Congress leaders feared that the inflationary effect of such a drastic dose of devaluation on the internal price structure would set back still further the party's chances of success in the general election due early in 1967.

Broadcasting to the nation on June 10, Mrs Gandhi said price rises of goods which did not contain any imported materials were unjustified. She stressed the need for a suitable system for distributing essential consumer goods to check runaway prices. Denying the charge that the rupee had been devalued under foreign pressure, she said there was a time in the history of every nation when its future depended on its capacity for bold decisions and resolute action.

A combination of circumstances had almost halted the country's economic growth.

It was important to correct the distortions in the economy, increase the profitability of exports and encourage the substitution of Indian materials for imports in industrial production. It was possible to achieve self-generating growth within 10 years by aiming at a three-fold rise in export earnings by diversifying exports and an intensive search for new foreign markets as well as selling more traditional products.

The government was acting immediately to relieve serious shortages of commodities and avert further layoffs and shutdowns. The administration must be overhauled to enable it to take quick decisions and make it more responsive to national needs. The Rs 20,000 million invested in industrial and other business undertakings in the public sector must yield adequate returns. India could not afford deficit financing. She promised to write to the chief ministers to stop wasteful spending.

The picture Mrs Gandhi painted of the economy was far from reassuring. It was undoubtedly very sick. Falling production was sending prices up, and the value of the rupee was sinking. A few years before the rupee was at a premium in other Asian countries. Nobody wanted it now. It was true that the World Bank had advised the government to devalue the rupee as the first step in carrying out a thorough cleanup of the economic mess and had hinted that further aid might not be forthcoming from the bank, its affiliates and the consortium of advanced countries it had set up to help India meet its requirements of foreign credits to import capital and maintenance goods until this was done.

Devaluation was an inevitable step at this juncture. It meant recognising the truth about the economy and making the necessary preparations to remedy its ailments. But certain advance steps should have been taken to cushion the domestic economy against the impact of this massive reduction in the value of the rupee. This was where the bureaucrats and economic experts of the government failed. The immediate effects of devaluation staggered the consumer, forced him to take in his belt a few notches further, and this certainly did not make the government any more popular. Ineptly managed, this measure, with promising long-term possibilities, had a very adverse effect immediately on the economy.

In July, Mrs Gandhi took the initiative in trying to end the fighting in Vietnam. She appealed to Britain and the Soviet Union, cochairmen of the Geneva Conference of 1954 which brought about a peace settlement in Indo-China after the defeat of French colonialism at Dien Bien Phu, to reconvene the conference immediately to consider the grave state of Vietnam as a result of US military intervention on a huge scale in cooperation with its allies in Southeast Asia and Australasia. She called on President Johnson to stop bombing North Vietnam. This should be followed soon by a complete stoppage of hostilities on both sides in observance of the Geneva Agreement.

Mrs Gandhi said: "It is necessary to secure the withdrawal of all foreign forces from Vietnam and to insulate that unhappy country from every foreign interference so that the people of Vietnam determine their own future free of external pressures." Unless this was done, it would be very difficult to summon a meeting of the nations which participated in the conference of 1954. She made a seven-point proposal for ending the war, suggesting among other things that: the International Control Commission, comprising India as chairman and Canada and Poland as members, safeguard standstill arrangements after a ceasefire; India undertake whatever additional responsibilities this might entail; the Geneva Conference guarantee the integrity and independence of a neutral Vietnam and of Laos and Cambodia as envisaged in the 1954 agreement; and the Geneva powers underwrite a plan to rehabilitate and develop the three war-ravaged states of Indo-China.

Rumbles of disapproval were heard in Washington. Johnson was angered at the "ingratitude" of one who had only recently enjoyed his hospitality at the White House. "Why does Mrs Gandhi meddle with what is not her business?" an American diplomat asked me irritably in New Delhi. "If she wants aid from the United States, she shouldn't say things which upset the President." Washington assumed that what was happening in Vietnam was the concern only of the US and other crusaders against communism. They were busy saving India and other countries in South and Southeast Asia from the communist monster by a policy of organised massacres of civilians, spraying napalm on villages and chemicals on plants to defoliate them, and thus causing irretrievable harm to the country and people whose saviours they claimed to be. The American "liberation" of Vietnam will count among the greatest crimes in human history, just as Washington's clients in Pakistan were to emulate this feat in attempting to protect their brethren in East Pakistan from "conquest" by Indian "imperialism" in 1971.

At a press conference in New Delhi on July 19, Mrs Gandhi allayed lingering fears that Soviet relations with India had cooled somewhat since Tashkent. On the contrary, she said she had been assured by Kosygin on her recent visit to Moscow that he was very keen on continuing the dialogue with India and that this should lead to less tension on the Indian subcontinent, which the Russians always refer to as the Hindustan Peninsula. India, she said, was on its part ready for talks with Pakistan at any level to facilitate the full implementation of the Tashkent Agreement.

She said Kosygin had made clear in their talks that the Soviet Union had neither supplied arms to Pakistan nor had signed a pact for this purpose. The "basic position" of the Soviet Union on important issues of special interest to India had not changed. This was true too of its stand on Kashmir.

In a statement on her foreign tour, she defined India-Soviet friendship as a positive relationship aimed at no other nation. It did not come in the way of either India or the Soviet Union making friends with other countries. She mentioned this in the context of the Soviet desire to improve its relations with Pakistan and India's to maintain close economic links with the West.

As the year drew to a close, trouble and dissension dogged the government. The Sikhs, under the leadership of the Shiromani Akali Dal, a militant semi-religious, semi-political body, were pressing for the breakup of the strategic western state of Punjab to separate the districts with Punjabi-speaking majorities from those where Hindi was generally spoken. The Akali leaders calculated that such a state, with a Sikh majority, would enable them to wrest power from the Congress and give them a permanent place on the political map of India.

The Hindu minority opposed this demand vehemently, and turned to the Jana Sangh to fight their battle. The opposition to division of Punjab came not only from those Hindus whose mother-tongue was Hindi but also from those who spoke Punjabi. The Jana Sangh warned the Union Government that the Akalis were really working for a Sikh-dominated state, under the guise of wanting a Punjabi state in which Hindus and Sikhs would have fair shares.

Mrs Gandhi decided to concede the Sikh demand. The result was an orgy of rioting in the Hindu-majority areas of Punjab in which the organising brain was said to be the Jana Sangh. While violence was stepping up in that state, several thousand demonstrators marched on Parliament House in New Delhi on November 7. Naked sadhus brandishing spears were in the vanguard, I saw from the Parliament corridor. The demonstration had as its ostensible aim pressuring the government to ban the killing of cow for meat. When the crowd which had gathered outside the bolted and padlocked gates leading to the building tried to break a cordon of policemen and scale the surrounding boundary wall, the police fired to disperse them.

This was the first instance of firing to counter violence so near Parliament. Several demonstrators were killed, and the mob retaliated by smashing and burning property in the complex of government buildings on Parliament Street. Firm action restored peace and order in a matter of hours in the city. The demonstration was intended to intimidate the government, and some leading Congressmen who had no liking for Mrs Gandhi were suspected of having a hand in it. Their aim was to bring about Nanda's removal from the cabinet and thus weaken Mrs Gandhi, who would then be more vulnerable to direct attack.

Home Minister Nanda lost his portfolio, for there was evidence that he had been informed of the trouble brewing in Delhi some days earlier but had not taken proper care to squelch it. He was asked to resign, and Defence Minister Chavan took his place. Nanda made a long statement on his resignation to the press—although he should have first made it in Parliament as convention demanded—in which he reeled off a string of charges against the Prime Minister. Mrs Gandhi retorted that they were "astonishing, extraordinary and regrettable."

The division of Punjab into two states was taken in hand. One, where the Sikhs had a slight edge over the Hindus in numbers, continued to be known as Punjab. Punjabi, written in the Gurumukhi script used by the Sikhs, became the state language. The districts where Hindus speaking Hindi formed the bulk of the population became Haryana. Both states have their capital in the same city,

Chandigarh, in the design of which the French architect Le Cor-
busier had a big part.

Mrs Gandhi told Parliament in a debate on the November 7
incidents that it was her privilege as Prime Minister to take
certain decisions. She would choose her cabinet as she pleased,
and if any minister disapproved of anything she did the door
was open to him to get out. People who had thought she would
be putty in the hands of the provincial barons who had helped
her to office were learning the hard way that Indira Gandhi was
a woman who could not be twisted and turned to suit anybody's
whims or interests.

She advised those who were anxious to protect Mother Cow
from the butcher's knife to direct some of their attention, energies
and funds to saving thousands of cattle which were starving to
death in the drought-stricken regions of Bihar and Uttar Pradesh.
Such advice fell on deaf ears. None of those who were ready to prance
and yelp against cow slaughter in the streets of Delhi and make
rabble-rousing speeches on the same theme in Parliament had time
for practical efforts in this direction. For them, the cow was much
more a political than a sacred animal, to be exploited as election
time drew near. As for devoting some of their time to succouring
hungry human beings, they would have considered such a
suggestion outrageous. Cows were politically more valuable than
humans in their inverted scale of values.

A broadcast on November 16 on the drought in these two states
emphasised the difference between Mrs Gandhi's thinking and that
of the professional friends of the cow. She appealed for a truce in
politics to speed up relief work in the affected areas, where conditions were worsening daily. The food and livelihood, the well-being,
the very survival of millions of inhabitants of the areas of drought
should remain above politics. Appealing for the utmost austerity,
she said preparing and observing the strict discipline of a national
food budget was immediately necessary. The government would
try to import grain on a large scale, but at the same time the people
must learn to share the regional surpluses available within the country fairly. She announced the establishment of a new national fund
for famine relief.

The year 1966 had begun badly with Shastri's death. It was also
ending on a sombre note, with a shortage of food that threatened

to turn into a famine which might take away millions of lives. But this fearful possibility, played up widely in the foreign press, was not realised, thanks to the vigorous and well-directed efforts of the government, backed by the United Nations and private social welfare organisations in India and abroad. The teams of movie and television cameramen who came posthaste to India to film heaps of corpses and carcasses of the victims of famine were cheated. India had proved it could cope with a calamity of such enormous dimensions. But the worst of the problem was not overcome until several months later.

In this new, onerous assignment, probably one of the most difficult of its kind in any country which practised the parliamentary system of democracy, what had Indira Gandhi to say for herself? Her replies to questions shot at her by a Bombay journalist are revealing. Asked what the significance of her election was, she said: "Perhaps it ensures some kind of continuity—continuity of policy, and also perhaps continuity of personality." This statement reveals how closely she identified herself with Jawaharlal Nehru. She looked upon herself as a projection of him, not only in politics but also as a person.

She was asked whether her election had deep sociological and ideological implications for the development of India as a country upholding certain values and ideals associated with Nehru. She agreed with the first part of the question, but said that the values and ideals involved were not Nehru's "personal legacy" but those of India.

She said she believed in socialism, "but not in a dogmatic way." She believed that all forms of exploitation must end. This undoubtedly had to be achieved through socialism, "for a large number of people are economically weak, and the economically stronger elements ride roughshod over them." She added: "I believe in the people's right to a better life—not only materially but also mentally and spiritually. I have been lucky to have had a rich life of the mind, and it hurts me to see people steeped in such poverty that they are rendered incapable of appreciating culture and the arts. I would like conditions to be created where all the people would be able to enjoy and appreciate these finer values of life."

She believed that young people had a special role to play in building the new India of her dream. She told her interviewer:

"Young people today have a lot of dynamic energy and vision, a desire to do things, and these must be tapped in the national interest. In every sphere of activity, youth must be inspired with a sense of involvement with national development. Young people must be trained to take up positions of responsibility in all departments of national life."

In the campaigning which preceded the fourth general election in February 1967, Mrs Gandhi fulfilled the role that had fallen to her father in three previous elections. She toured the country making speeches to an electorate which in many states was plainly hostile to the Congress. This time the going was proving much tougher than in previous elections. Kamaraj had been right when he foresaw trouble and wanted to give the party a new image. Mrs Gandhi stressed the need in her speeches for a strong centre in New Delhi, "abridging the autonomy of the states. Such a centre would coordinate the activities of the states and look at their individual problems in the national context. India's stability could not be sustained if the country is Balkanised."

Ironically, Indira Gandhi was responsible in the first six years of her prime ministership for creating half a dozen new states, most of them out of what were former territories directly under the central government. But the effect was the opposite of Balkanisation. By satisfying the aspirations of the inhabitants of these territories for a bigger say in the management of their own affairs, these moves have strengthened national unity.

Mrs Gandhi's courage in the face of danger had another test in the campaign. She was speaking at an open-air meeting at Bhubaneswar on February 8 when stones were thrown at her. Orissa Chief Minister Biju Patnaik and Mrs Gandhi's security staff beckoned her to move back from the microphone in front of which she was standing till she was out of reach of the stone-throwers. She brushed them off and continued speaking in a hail of stones. One of them struck her face, cutting her upper lip and fracturing and displacing the bone in her nose. She was flown back to New Delhi and operated on to put the bone back in place. As soon as her doctors said she could move, she was back in the election battle, barnstorming with undimmed vigour.

When the election results were in, the picture was much worse than the most pessimistic fears of the Congress leaders. The party lost around 100 seats in the Lok Sabha, but it still had a majority of about 40. Some of its tallest poppies had been beheaded, including Kamaraj, Atulya Ghosh, and Patil. Kamaraj, to make the humiliation still greater, had lost to a student leader, an outsider who challenged the kingmaker in his own stronghold in Nagercoil district in the far south for a seat in the Tamil Nadu legislature. Mrs Gandhi, on the other hand, won comfortably.

The picture in the states was darker than in parliament. The Congress has lost out in several states, and there was no prospect of its forming governments in them even in coalition with opposition parties. For, having tasted blood, the oppositionists decided to form coalitions of their own, so bent were they on keeping the Congress out of office. These coalitions were strange amalgams in which Communists mated with the Jana Sangh and other conservative formations like the Swatantra Party. There was not the slightest chance of these parties agreeing on any common policies and programmes, and thus a period of nerve-racking political instability was ushered in. At one time, it was possible to travel through the Gangetic Plain, the most populous part of India, from Amritsar in Punjab on the West Pakistan border, to Calcutta in the east without passing through a single state under Congress rule.

The shift in the policy of the CPI towards the Congress was instructive. It had till then propagated support for the progressive forces in the ruling party against the forces of reaction and for the progressive national bourgeoisie against big business and the agents of foreign capital. After the Congress reverses in the elections it shifted ground. The Communist leaders met in Calcutta and decided that "the period of relative stability for the path of capitalist development and the exclusive role of the national bourgeoisie has come to an end. A new period of sharp confrontation between the forces of progress and reaction has begun. The country has clearly entered a period of instability and uncertainties."

Did the CPI leaders believe that the proletarian revolution was round the corner? Their subsequent actions seem to indicate that they thought a pre-revolutionary stage had been reached in which its task was to cement alliances with all and sundry against the Congress Party with the ultimate aim of mobilising the progressive intelligentsia and the workers and peasants for the final thrust for power. This "flexible" approach resulted in its chief spokesman in the Rajya Sabha, Bhupesh Gupta, suggesting that the Jana Sangh's mass base was growing, mainly because of its attraction for large numbers of the urban petty bourgeoisie who were disillusioned because the morrow on which the Congress had repeatedly promised jam in return for their votes never seemed to dawn. Gupta said "this mass base cannot but have its impact on the [Jana Sangh] leadership and give rise to differentiation within the Jana Sangh. Even the RSS [Rashtriya Swayamsevak Sangh, the organisation of storm troopers of the Jana Sangh] is feeling its impact."

Rajeshwar Rao, CPI general secretary, characterised the Swatan-tra Party unit in his home state, Andhra Pradesh, as a "poor peasants' party." Even the Marxist "deviationists" lost their untouchability temporarily as a result of the euphoric mood of the Communist theoreticians and strategists. But a minority, led by a former general secretary, P.C. Joshi, took a different view. Joshi, a consistent propagandist for a policy of simultaneous "collabora-tion and confrontation" with the Congress for many years, criticised his colleagues' "softness" towards the rightist parties. He called this attitude a new form of nihilism. He said the party position in 1948, when it advocated peasant guerilla war, which led to an abortive uprising in the Telengana region of the present Andhra Pradesh, was the "ultra-revolutionary" expression of the nihilism, while the position it had adopted after the 1967 elections was its "constitu-tional parliamentary" expression.

The danger arising from the instability of these misalliances to the unity of the country was real. Conditions became near-chaotic as one coalition after another fell after a few months, only to be suc-ceeded by others of even shorter duration. When fresh combinations were not possible, there were spells of President's rule in several states, and then came fresh elections, with results scarcely any more satisfactory. This was the crazy pattern of politics in India until the next general election in March 1971.

The reason for the Congress drubbing was not far to seek. It was not due to the failure of the Nehru magic embodied in his daughter to work on the electorate. A combination of events after the 1962 elections turned the tide of popular opinion against the Congress. The most important of them were the humiliation of the Chinese invasion in 1962; Nehru's death when the bewildered, frustrated nation needed his comfort and guidance most; the incidents in Kutch and the subsequent largescale India-Pakistan war, in which many people suspected India had not done as well as Congress and government spokesmen claimed; a widespread monsoon failure which brought with it privation and suffering to millions and the lowering threat of famine; and finally, the rise in living costs resulting from the hamhanded manner in which devaluation of the rupee was undertaken.

"In the circumstances," the British journalist John Grigg wrote in 1971, "it was not at all surprising that Congress lost ground in 1967. Under any other leader it must have lost power." The Syndicate should have thanked Mrs Gandhi for saving the party from total rout at the polls instead of trying to pin the blame for its humiliation on her.

But the election results had other lessons for those who cared to study them. It was more than anything else a feeling of disillusionment with the Congress for not fulfilling its promises of economic and social betterment that led to its discomfiture. More and more, the Congress was coming to be identified in the minds of the urban and rural poor and middle classes with privilege and inequality and unashamed self-interest. The average Congress leader was more concerned with getting a licence to start an industry or wangling a wellpaid job for his son in the public or private sector of industry than with the problems of development in the country. This was particularly pronounced after Nehru's death, when Congressmen in positions of power felt the deluge was coming and set about making the most of the opportunities they had. This behaviour only hastened the day of retribution.

The main beneficiaries from the anger of large sections of voters with the Congress were two extreme parties, the Jana Sangh and the Marxist Communists. The Jana Sangh was able to form coalition governments in Bihar and Uttar Pradesh, the second Mrs Gandhi's home state, in which they played senior partner. It emerged as the most influential party in the Hindi-speaking belt of North India, the traditional stronghold of the Congress.

If the Jana Sangh had been able to consolidate its gains, this would have meant the end of the Congress in the north. It might also have force because of its peculiar brand of communal politics. Its dominance in the Hindi belt stretching from Rajasthan in the west to Bihar in the east would have gradually alienated the non-Hindi-speaking states in other parts of the country, and centrifugal tendencies would have developed within a few years. That this did not happen and the trend towards it was reversed, and that India is more united today than what it was before February 1967, is due largely, if not solely, to Indira Gandhi.

CHAPTER SIX

SECOND INNINGS

AT FIRST SIGHT, the election results gave the impression that the Indian voter had gone haywire and had taken it into his head to scuttle the democratic system in India. On closer scrutiny, it appeared that there was method in his madness. The vote against the Congress was one of protest, an expression of mass resentment at the cavalier manner in which the Congress leaders had treated the voter in the past years, dangling carrots before his eyes at election time and then completely neglecting him. This time the intelligent voter was determined to teach his masters a lesson. He voted for any opposition candidate whom he gave a chance of winning. This resulted in atomisation, with no party getting enough seats to form a stable government on its own in most states.

Millions of voters, acting individually on this principle, had smashed the Congress monopoly of power. They had dragged it down from its high pedestal as the only national party, in fact as well as in name, and reduced it to one of many parties competing for their votes. They had deliberately broken up the old power pattern centring on the supremacy of the party and created conditions for the construction of a new pattern more receptive to their collective will. They had thus struck a blow for democracy, for the Congress, if it wished to survive the shock, must democratise itself and seriously set about fulfilling its pledges to the nation. This election was a sign of the growing maturity of Indian democracy. The voter had cleared the way for modernising the political system to meet the new demands of planned socio-economic growth and doing away with the old spoils system which served special interests.

The answer to the voter's protest was obvious. The Congress must cleanse itself of anti-democratic elements which had antagonised the Indian masses by working against their interests. The Congress in 1967 was still more a movement than a party with a clearly defined policy and programme. The test of a good Congressman was the khadi he wore and not what he thought and how he acted. The Congress was a hangover of the pre-independence era and was still trying to cash in on the claim that it had brought India independence. To the new generation which had grown up after independence this meant nothing. It judged the party on its present showing, not on the somewhat faded and tattered glories of the past.

While horsetrading oportunism rode high in most state capitals, what was going on in New Delhi? The Congress Parliamentary Party had to elect a new leader, and the Syndicate had gathered to take counsel and choose a person whom they would commend to the MPs. Mrs Gandhi was seeking re-election, and Morarji Desai was taking his third tilt at the prime ministership. He seemed determined to prove to the world the truth of the saying that you connot keep a good man down. This time the attitude of the Syndicate towards the contenders had changed. They had read the writing on the wall. They felt the central government needed a strongman at its head, not a weak woman who, they felt, had let them down in the elections.

Mrs Gandhi had also read the writing. But she interpreted it differently from the bosses. She believed that the Congress Party was doomed to extinction in the not very distant future if it did not make a serious effort to square its practice with its professions. The party must prove what it claimed to be, the party of the common man, bent on banishing the terrible poverty that still haunted millions of lives in spite of the achievements of economic and social planning, on reducing the vast gap between rich and poor, and all the other noble and laudable aims the Congress had listed in its manifestoes in successive elections.

To do this, Mrs Gandhi knew the Old Guard had to go. They were the biggest obstacle to moving in the direction in which it was necessary to take the nation if progress and the prosperity of all were its most desirable goals. She knew she would carry most of the younger party cadres with her if she challenged the men at the top. The bosses knew this too. Kamaraj would have liked to pull the rug from under her feet, but in the absence of a more suitable candidate who could defeat Desai in the event of a contest he decided to support her. Further, his eyes and ears in the other camp had reported that Mrs Gandhi might not take his move meekly.

If her fighting spirit was aroused, and there were people who vouched that she had plenty of fight in her, there was just a chance that she might quit the party and set up a rival Congress. If she did, the Syndicate might find that the majority of Congressmen in Parliament would follow her. At the best, from the bosses' point of view, she might be able to take only a section of the MPs with her, but without them the loyalists would not be able to form a government unless they brought the Swatantra Party into it.

Some members of the Syndicate favoured such a course, but Kamaraj was not prepared to go that far to the right. By Congress standards, he was a progressive. He had risen to power in Tamil Nadu as the spokesman of the downtrodden, and his image of progressivism would be badly smudged if he consorted with the unabashed representatives of big business and the remnants of the princelings who still dabbled in politics. In any event, a closer look at the list of Congress MPs seemed to rule out such a course. A majority of them were left of centre or centre and would be more likely to go with Mrs Gandhi if she decided to part company with the Old Guard.

The prospects before the bosses were not pleasant. They were used to leading, to having their commands obeyed unquestioningly, and here they were being led by the nose. They would have to go along with Mrs Gandhi, whether they liked or not. That meant choosing her for a second term as Prime Minister and going to work once more on Desai to produce a consensus. The role of mediator was played by two Congress veterans, D.P. Mishra, Chief Minister of Madhya Pradesh, and C.B. Gupta, Chief Minister of Uttar Pradesh. They jointly persuaded Desai to accept second position in the government without laying down any conditions. A contest at this time, in the party's greatly weakened state, might have been fatal to its unity. At first Desai resisted, but he was obviously the weaker of the two candidates and had to go to the wall. The provincial bosses had no choice, for if they disapproved of Mrs Gandhi they liked Desai still less. He was unexcelled in the art of making enemies.

He was willing to concede the party leadership in Parliament to Mrs Gandhi provided she was willing to give him a status in her cabinet that would have virtually made him joint premier. Mrs Gandhi refused. You couldn't have two people at the tiller without rocking the boat, especially when they were as diametrically different in political and social personality as Mrs Gandhi and Desai.

A bargain was finally struck. Desai, who at one stage appeared as adamant as granite, agreed to be Deputy Prime Minister, provided the finance portfolio went with it.

Gupta, whose sympathies lay with Desai, and Mishra were entrusted with the task of persuading Mrs Gandhi to accept Desai's terms for withdrawing from the contest that seemed at one time inevitable. So she became Prime Minister for the second time without having to go through an election, while Desai, denied the crown he had set his heart on for the third, and possibly last, time had to accept the consolation prize. Desai attempted to stipulate what his powers and functions as deputy prime minister should be. Mrs Gandhi swiftly made it known that she considered the post a mere ornament. She would certainly not share her authority as Prime Minister with anybody. The last deputy premier was Vallabhbhai Patel, who held this position from 1947 till his death in 1950. Desai liked to regard himself as a *chela* (pupil) of the Sardar. They were both from Gujarat. There the similarity ended.

The new cabinet contained almost all the same familiar faces as the last. Mrs Gandhi had won her first confrontation with the Syndicate. But it was a brush, a skirmish compared with what was to follow in a little more than two years. But the bosses had seen enough of her in action to know they had grossly underrated her fighting potential. She was dangerous, they agreed, and they would be better prepared for the next round, which they knew would come sooner or later. Mrs Gandhi had lost a stout prop among the high-ups in Kamaraj, who from now on was to become increasingly hostile to her. On the other hand, she knew the majority of Congress MPs, especially the younger ones and the old Nehruites, were solidly with her, and that gave her strength for the battles ahead which she too knew were inevitable.

The general election had shown that the Congress was very sick. The sickness was organic. It was not a unified party with a clearcut philosophy and a well-defined programme to give practical shape to that philosophy. It consisted of pressure groups formed on different bases—religion, language, region, caste—struggling to get their snouts into the public trough. That had to end if the party was to get a new lease of life, and only somebody who was above these special interests could perform this act of resuscitation. There was only one person in the topmost echelons of the Congress Party who had this qualification. That was Indira Gandhi.

Another big test was to come soon. This test involved India's proud claim that it was secular, or to be more correct a society where there was freedom of worship for all and a state power which taught citizens tolerance and came down heavily on discrimination against religious minorities. A new President had to be elected in May for a term of five years. When the first President of the Republic, Dr Rajendra Prasad, ended his second term of office in 1962, the Congress Party backed the Vice-President, Dr Radhakrishnan, for the post. Now Radhakrishnan was due to retire, and Dr Zakir Husain was Vice-President. If what had happened in 1962 was to be taken as a precedent, the choice should have been Husain without any question. Mrs Gandhi thought so. But some of her colleagues in the Congress Parliamentary Party, and even in her Council of Ministers, disagreed.

Husain was a brilliant scholar and educationist. He had completed his academic studies in Germany and had joined Mahatma Gandhi as a young man to put into practice the Mahatma's theories on education. He had founded the Jamia Milia Islamia in Delhi, a Muslim national university where Hindus were as welcome as Muslims. I first saw Husain, who was Governor of Bihar, at the inaugural meeting of the National Integration Conference at Vigyan Bhavan, New Delhi, in September 1961. Nehru, who was presiding, was not himself. He seemed weary, more in spirit than in body, and he was drowned in his own thoughts. Mrs Gandhi read out a piece in a monotone, without carrying much conviction.

Several other distinguished figures spoke on the subject. The only one who impressed me was Husain. He spoke forcefully, with great conviction. You felt the man meant every word of what he said. He revitalised this torpid gathering briefly. He blamed the Congress Party squarely for encouraging discrimination based on religion and caste. To substantiate his charge, he said the party chose Muslim candidates to stand for national elections from constituencies where Muslims formed a majority or a sizable section of the voters. He also noted that some ministers in the Nehru Government employed only persons of their own caste as their personal staff. At a break in the session Kuldip Nayar, then an information officer of the Government of India and now resident editor of the *Statesman*, New Delhi, asked me in the corridor who among the speechmakers had impressed me. I replied: "Only Husain." Kuldip said: "I think he will rise very high."

But Husain's record of public service did not impress some Congressmen. They thought he professed the wrong faith for a President of India. Husain was a Muslim. The Jana Sangh too thought this debarred him from the presidency. The other secular national parties were split on the issue, though the opposition parties had jointly decided to sponsor former Chief Justice Subba Rao of the Supreme Court of India, who had resigned to contest Husain. Mrs Gandhi stood firm. Husain's election was a matter of principle to her. The Jana Sangh had turned the presidential election into a contest between a Hindu and a Muslim, and she would prove that a Muslim could be elected head of state in a country whose people were about 85 per cent Hindu. The Congress Parliamentary Board approved Husain by five votes to four.

Mrs Gandhi's belief in her countrymen's tolerance of faiths besides Hinduism was vindicated. Husain was elected by a sizable majority of more than 108,000 votes. After a series of disheartening setbacks in her first term as Prime Minister, Mrs Gandhi could now chalk up a significant gain. It was a victory on a fundamental issue which was of supreme importance to India's future, as great a blow in its way for secular democracy as the liberation of Bangladesh four and a half years later. It needed great courage for her to take this step, especially when her standing with an influential group of her party leaders was low. Had Husain lost the election, they would have demanded her resignation, and being a believer in democracy she would have had no choice but to accept their verdict.

Four years later, John Grigg was to write of her: "This is the woman who has outsmarted the toughest and most experienced politicians in India. And made many foreign critics look ridiculous. Like Queen Elizabeth I [of England], she belongs to a great political dynasty and has the heart of a king, combined with a woman's political finesse. But unlike Elizabeth she is a democratic leader, dependent on the electorate...

"She lacks her father's wideranging philosophic intellect, but in at least one respect her equipment for statecraft is superior to his. She is more realistic in her judgment of people and more ruthless in dealing with anyone who fails to make the grade or who shows signs of becoming an embarrassment to her.

"Nature and experience have made her a 'secret' person, very good at concealing her intention, always much readier to listen than to talk. But she knows how to take decisions and when to take them. The compressed force of her character can be traced to her childhood, which was exceptionally privileged but also in a sense deprived."

But in May 1967 all this was in the womb of time. Indira Gandhi was still struggling to find her feet, politically speaking. As for the ruthlessness Grigg mentions, it was used for strictly political purposes. Ruthless realism is one of the essential ingredients of a politician, and Mrs Gandhi was very much a politician, just keeping her head above water. She was to graduate to statesmanship later, when she had decimated the opposition to her within her own party and in other parties and a foreign foe who had one aim—to bring about the disintegration of her country. Outside politics, she was charming, considerate, and kind. In the Byzantine atmosphere of Congress politics in the national capital in the late 1960s, keeping one's counsel and listening rather than talking were necessary for survival.

The year 1967 saw two significant developments. The drought continued in the areas of great scarcity in northern India. While government and voluntary relief workers strove to save the starving in Bihar, in neighbouring West Bengal a new political force was emerging. This was the Communist Party of India (Marxist), which had broken away from the CPI in 1964. The drought posed a serious economic threat, the Marxists a political menace to the Congress. The drought was a more immediate problem which had to be tackled on a war footing.

The magnitude of the crisis may be gauged from the fact that India had asked its foreign friends for 10 million tons of grain in 1967 to pull the nation through the period of difficulty. The bulk of these supplies were from the US under Public Law 480. At the moment they were of inestimable value. Later, they were to cause worries because of the enormous accumulation of rupee funds to the credit of the American Embassy in New Delhi. The charge was to be made frequently in Parliament and from other forums that these funds were being used to finance undercover political activities harmful to India.

In 1967, ships were loading night and day at American ports with surplus food stocks to be carried to India as fast as possible.

And without them, there is no doubt that famine would have swept large parts of eastern Uttar Pradesh, northeastern Madhya Pradesh and southern and central Bihar. Opening a conference of Chief Ministers in New Delhi in April, Mrs Gandhi warned them of acute food shortage in the coming months. This, in combination with falling industrial production and largescale deficit financing by the Centre and the state governments the previous year, would send the price of essentials shooting up in the coming months. "This will not be an easy situation and there will be no soft options," she told them.

Several of the Chief Ministers she addressed belonged to parties unfriendly to the Congress. She told them that the general election which had brought them to power had generated a peaceful political transformation which had few parallels in the world since the Second World War. This was an important achievement, and the nation should draw strength from it. She foresaw disagreement between the Centre and the states under opposition party coalitions. She said: "These do exist in a democratic, changing, free society, but they need not lead to conflict. We can and should resolve our differences and disagreements through consultation, discussion and persuasion." Those critics of Mrs Gandhi, in India as well as abroad, who fear she will misuse her unchallenged authority as the supreme, and only leader, of India after the general election in 1972 to assume dictatorial powers might take what comfort they can from this statement.

She told the Chief Ministers that no new or special problem had arisen merely because the central and state governments had different political complexions. Centre-state relations were inherent in a federal setup. Local and regional interests and problems would also naturally exist in any large, diverse, developing country like India with a federal system of government. This was a built-in factor which did not necessarily have anything to do with the emergence of non-Congress governments in some states.

In the first half of 1967, scare stories of an impending famine which would be the most horrible in world history were appearing in the foreign press. A Roman Catholic priest of American nationality operating from Patna, capital of Bihar, was quoted as estimating the number of possible deaths at 10 million.

I set out at the end of April on a three-week tour of the worst-hit districts of Uttar Pradesh and Bihar. I travelled several hundred miles by jeep, going over unmetalled roads and cart tracks to remote villages inhabited by tribal people. I spoke to many of the sufferers, as well to state government ministers and other politicians, officials from departmental secretaries to *gram sevaks* (village workers), and Indian and foreign representatives of social welfare organisations and United Nations agencies.

I saw villagers engaged in relief work, which included excavating large tanks to hold rainwater, when it came, and queuing up in thousands for dry rations or cooked food at centres run by government or voluntary bodies. I saw teams of technicians using high-speed rigs to drill tubewells, as well as thirsty villagers digging shallow pits in the beds of dried-up rivers to get a few pitchers of water.

One of the positive results of the great drought was the discovery of large reserves of groundwater a few feet below the surface in chronically drought-ridden areas like Palamau and Hazaribagh districts of Bihar. The overall picture I took away with me at the end of the tour was that there would be no famine. Several factors contributed to this, starting with the prompt dispatch of grain, milk powder, high-protein foods and vitamins from foreign countries. All this material moved speedily to the points where it was needed with little or no waste because of the excellent delivery system organised by the state and central governments in association with UN organisations and private welfare groups.

The creation of this efficient feeder organisation was perhaps the key factor in staving off famine. United Nations observers told me that government officers, especially at the lower levels, had responded magnificently to the call for emergency action and had worked practically round the clock to keep the lines of transport moving at full steam. They got no money rewards for this extra work, and indeed no amount of money could have adequately recompensed them for their efforts.

Far from commendation and rewards, some of these men had to answer charges of allowing villagers to die of starvation through their negligence. I met one harassed and overworked deputy commissioner who had to put aside supervision of relief operations to travel to a village several miles from the nearest road to investigate a charge by an opposition member of Parliament that two persons had starved to death there. In another instance, I accompanied an assistant district magistrate and a doctor over hill and valley to look into a similar complaint in another village. Inquiries revealed that a woman had died in it, but she was over 70 years old and the cause of death was the natural feebleness of extreme age.

A further feature of this gigantic operation, involving the protection of a total population of about 40 million to 50 million and about a fifth of that number of cattle, was that it was organised and executed almost entirely by Indians. Some foreigners were present to see how the programme was working, and foreign welfare agencies sent helpers from abroad, but the main burden fell on Indians. The success of the undertaking belied the fears expressed in some newspapers in other countries that international direction was necessary if the programme was to succeed. In private, one heard foreign newspapermen say that Indians were incapable of handling it, and that a good part of the material aid coming from abroad would be diverted to the blackmarket. I was to hear similar remarks about the operations for the relief of millions of refugees who poured into India from former East Pakistan to escape President Yahya Khan's campaign of mass extermination of Bengalis in 1971.

But there was an even more important outgrowth of the near-famine, which gradually tapered off as the monsoon came with bountiful showers after two meagre seasons. The food crisis created by the drought resulted in postponing the start of the Fourth Five-Year Plan by two years. The Union Government realised that the fundamental task in planning was to put Indian agriculture on its feet, and this meant switching from primitive methods of production which yielded most farmers just about enough for their own subsistence to commercialised, sophisticated techniques which would create a marketable surplus to generate capital for investment in industry. The farmer had to be guided expertly from a subsistence economy to a market economy. The upshot of this thinking was the introduction in irrigated areas of high-yielding varieties of seed, more fertilisers, better implements, and other inputs. Once they were convinced of the benefits the new techniques conferred, farmers adopted them rapidly.

The Indian farmer was generally pictured, within the country as well as abroad, as ignorant, even stupid, lethargic, opposed to new ideas. There was no use trying to change his ways because he

would not listen to advice, wiseacres said. All that has been trans-
formed in the few years since the great famine that never was. A
new class of farmer is developing in most parts of India where the
"green revolution" is under way. Most of these men have been
farming all their lives, but now they are scientific farmers, and Indian
agricultural researchers and technologists cannot work fast enough
to cope with their demands for improved methods of cultivation
and animal husbandry.

If one wants to see real economic advance the right place to look
for it is the Indian village. Plough and bullock are giving way to
tractors, mechanical threshers and harvester combines. The Persian
wheel has been discarded for tubewells worked by electric or diesel
motors. Radios, refrigerators, sewing machines, and motor bicycles
are not rarities any more. India today produces more wheat than
it needs to feed its people. But there is a lag in other grains and in
commercial crops.

Protein is also deficient, and one of the great problems facing
the country's planners and administrators in the present decade
is overcoming the nutrition crisis. This problem cannot be solved
by producing unconventional foods in factories at prices far beyond
the reach of the protein-hungry millions but by giving them enough
of the average Indian diet, which has all the proteins needed by
child or adult. Rice or wheat and *dal* (pulses) and milk can meet
the protein requirements of 550 million Indians, provided there
is enough of these to go round. The great drought from 1965
to 1967 set the farm revolution going and its extension to cover all
types of major crops and the areas where dry farming is practised
must be one of the prime nationbuilding tasks in the 1970s.

The rise of the Marxists as a political force was another significant
feature of 1967. The electoral united front they headed in Kerala
enabled them to win 53 of the 59 seats they contested in the 133-
member state legislature. They also won all nine parliamentary
seats for which their men stood, out of the 19 allotted to the state.
They were the leading partners in the coalition government formed
with their man E.M.S. Namboodiripad as its head. But this gain was
comparatively less important than their advance in West Bengal.
Kerala was a political backwater, flanked on one side by the Ara-
bian Sea and on the land side by two states, Tamil Nadu and Mysore,
where the Communist movement was not politically important.

West Bengal was different. It was the connecting corridor between
the Gangetic Plain and the rest of peninsular India and the strategic
and sensitive northeastern region. It was flanked in the south by
East Pakistan, and to the north were three Himalayan kingdoms,
Bhutan, Nepal, and Sikkim. The neck of territory connecting the
northernmost part of the state with the northeastern region was a bare
10 miles wide. West Bengal was a powder keg which was ready to
ignite any moment, and had it gone up in flames it would probably
have taken the entire northeastern region of the subcontinent with it.

Of the 280 seats in the state Legislative Assembly, the Marxists
contested 135 and won only 43 against 127 secured by the Congress,
but the witches' brew of parties and splinter groups which consti-
tuted the Marxist-led united front harvested sufficient seats among
them to form a ramshackle government which showed signs of collapse from the moment it was formed. The results were not a true indication of the relative strength of the Communists and the Congress
as the left forces were split into two rival fronts. They came together
after the elections to form a government, the sole binding force
of which was opposition to the Congress.

As in other states where coalitions were formed, such a negative
base could not lead to positive results. No common policies were
possible, and a race started among the allies to grab as much of the
loaves and fishes as were available for themselves, their relatives
and their party following. The manner in which some ministers in
West Bengal as well as elsewhere openly took money or anything
else that was going caused even hardened Congress operators, now
sitting in opposition, to blush. The coalitionists knew that time was
flying and they must work fast. Most of their Congress rivals had
been in this business for two decades or more. They, on the other
hand, had only months to go. The bubble of being in office might
burst in their faces any moment.

The Marxist programme for building socialism in India envisaged
setting up a people's democracy and a government of the working
class based on a worker-peasant alliance as the first stage. The
people's democratic revolution would be anti-feudal, anti-imperia-
list, anti-monopolist and anti-revisionist, the last anti meaning that
it would oppose what they regarded as the pernicious collaborationist
policies of Moscow and its supporters in the rest of the world. The
Marxists emphasised radical land and other rural reforms to streng-

then the small peasant and the landless labourer economically. Foreign monopoly capital was to be hoofed out without compensation, thus freeing India's economic, social and political life from its "disastrous" influence. Bank nationalisation, reduced taxes on the essentials of life and greater powers for the states were among their immediate objectives.

If the Marxists broke with the Moscow Communists on the ground that they had strayed from the path of social revolution to the less thornier one of reformism and could not be distinguished from social democrats, some of their own party men strongly disagreed with their leaders on the question of contesting elections and participating in the activities of Parliament and the state assemblies. These extremists accused their leaders of sowing "bourgeois illusions" among the peasantry and working class and took their stand on the little red book enshrining the thoughts of Mao Tse-tung. They split from the new party and formed the Communist Party of India (Marxist-Leninist). They did not believe in constitutional methods of attaining their political goals. They operated underground, conspiratorially, with gun, pistol, bomb and knife.

Few of the Marxist-Leninists besides their leaders Charu Mazumdar and Kanu Sanyal had read Mao's thoughts or, if they had, were able to understand them. Fewer still had read Marx or Lenin. They were mostly disoriented young men and women of the middle class who were attracted to the new grouping because it seemed to offer a shortcut to social change and had elevated violence to a cult. They were social dropouts, materially or emotionally deprived or both, and the new creed appeared to give them an opportunity for ego-building which other parties did not. In the atmosphere of social decay that pervaded Calcutta it was easy enough to find thousands of young people who felt society had treated them shabbily and were ready recruits for the movement that was soon to be become known throughout the world as Naxalism.

Naxalbari was a sleepy little tribal village set in a forest in the narrow neck in the northern region of West Bengal. The Marxist-Leninists decided to make a laboratory experiment in revolution here. They organised the tribesmen against the *jotedars* (landlords) who hired their labour to work on their land or permitted them to sharecrop it. The tribesmen were little better than serfs, and when the message of revolt spread among them they readily seized on it as a way out of their miserable existence. A few jotedars were killed when they attempted to protect their land from expropriation. This happened when a united front of left and centre parties, spearheaded by a supposedly revolutionary party, was in power. The government put down the uprising, the commune which the Marxist-Leninists set up to manage the "liberated" territory dissolved with the arrest or flight of its leaders. The Naxalbari episode was soon forgotten, but it added a new word to the political dictionary of India.

Naxalbari deserves to be remembered because it was a crucial test of the professions of the Marxists to fight for a better deal for the sharecropper and the landless labourer in the countryside. When an opportunity came to prove them, the Marxists sided with those forces that were intent on suppressing them. Had the Marxists been true to their convictions, they should have logically quit the government and thrown their weight behind the rebels. The Marxist leaders showed by their action that they were ready to scuttle the programme of social change they were committed to in order to cling to power. These pinchbeck Lenins showed that when the chips were down they were also revisionists and opportunists, terms of abuse they bestowed on their Moscow-backed rivals.

An important issue concerning India's security from foreign aggression arose in July. The Lok Sabha debated a proposal that India accept a nuclear shield to be provided by the superpowers against attack by another nuclear power. The unnamed attacker was China, the maverick threshold world power which rejected any kind of control over nuclear striking capability. Mrs Gandhi explained her goverment's stand on the subject, saying that it would like a guarantee from all or some nuclear nations that if such weapons were used against a nation which could not retaliate in similar fashion they would rally to its support. She said such a guarantee would be a deterrent to any nuclear power with aggressive ambitions. In the final analysis, however, the effectiveness of a nuclear shield would depend not on the spirit in which the protected powers accepted it but on the national and vital interests of the giver. She noted that President Johnson had volunteered to provide such protection on his own without similar guarantees from other powers, meaning the Soviet Union, and the Indian Government had welcomed his statement.

India would like all nuclear powers, or as many of them as possible, belonging to different power blocs, to assure the safety of non-nuclear nations from nuclear strikes. That should lead to a ban on the use of nuclear weapons against countries which did not possess them, just as poison gas had been declared unlawful. She said India was against more nations going nuclear, but preventing proliferation was not an end in itself. The ultimate goal was total disarmament. The proposed treaty against proliferation aimed at freezing the nuclear weapons race at a given point, but that would not help so long as China did not subscribe to it.

These arguments have an academic ring today, five years after they were uttered. The world power balance has changed sharply. The United States, which was keen on offering a shield, is building a bridge between Washington and Peking and intent on quarantining the Soviet Union politically. Since India on the other hand is bound to the Soviet Union by a treaty of peace, friendship, and co-operation which commits each country to support the other in the event of an attack by a third country and is virtually a defensive alliance, it is a stumbling-block in the way of achieving this American objective.

Thus, instead of confirming Johnson's offer of a shield and trying to curb China's atomic potential, his successor President Nixon is likely to move in the reverse direction. He will probably use China's growing missile capability to pose a constant threat to India, thereby preventing India from taking any initiatives in South and Southeast Asia and also deterring it from developing its own nuclear weapons. Once China has built a sizable stock of missiles it will be able to use them to blackmail New Delhi not to go nuclear should it feel that India's security demands such a step. This would mean that India will have to depend in the future, as it does now, on a Soviet nuclear shield. But would this shield be available once the Chinese have missiles with a range long enough to pose a danger to the main industrial centres in the Soviet Union?

On February 19, 1968, the international tribunal appointed to adjudicate on the dispute between India and Pakistan over the Rann of Kutch announced its award. Pakistan had argued before it that the international boundary in this region ran roughly along the 24th parallel of latitude. This claim was rejected. Its acceptance would have meant a loss of 3,300 square miles to India. Mrs Gandhi told Parliament the next day that the tribunal had "by and large"

upheld India. "We had contended that the entire Rann was part
of India and the boundary lay roughly along the northern edge of
the Rann." She added: "One member of the tribunal [Ales Bebler
of Yugoslavia] upheld our claim, while the other two members upheld it with modifications in some sectors of the boundary. By a
majority, the tribunal has held that about 3000 square miles lie on
our side of the boundary, while about 300 square miles of the territory claimed by Pakistan lies on the Pakistani side of the boundary."

At a meeting of the Congress Parliamentary Party the same day,
she expressed surprise at certain remarks of the tribunal's chairman,
Gunnar Lagergren. It was evident from them that the award was
not based only on the documents and other material both sides produced before it but also on political considerations. She said Lagergren's remarks, with political overtones, were "strange". Their
implication must be studied fully. How could a judicial body take
political considerations into account? But the award was binding
on India under the agreement it had signed in 1965.

In his book *Confrontation with Pakistan,* Lt-Gen B.M. Kaul says
there was conclusive evidence to prove that the entire territory Pakistan had claimed was India's. The loss of 300 square miles of Indian
territory "is the price one has to pay when one keeps appealing to
foreign organisations or powers to adjudicate." He wrote: "The
new border in the Kutch area gives a great advantage to Pakistan,
which obtained a number of bets [pieces of high ground] while our
side is mostly swampy and lowlying. Patrolling by us in this area is
therefore difficult."

In the context of India's firm support of the Palestinian Arabs
cause against Israel, which has been misinterpreted in some quarters as enmity towards Israel and the Jews, Mrs Gandhi's views
published in the American magazine *Look* in April 1968 make inter-
esting reading. She denied India was hostile to the Jews, pointing
out that the Congress Party supported them when Hitler persecuted
them in the 1930s. She told *Look:* "I personally was secretary of
a committee set up to condemn atrocities aginst the Jews in Europe.
We do not have diplomatic relations with Israel because it would
only create unnecessary political problems for us at home and with
some neighbours—and we have enough problems already. But
there is an Israeli Consul-General in India—we are not anti-Israel
in any way."

On India's support to the Arabs in the long-drawn out UN debate since the Six-day War in June 1967, she said: "India has always been consistent in its position, based on long friendship with the Arab world and especially with the United Arab Republic. Yet India has accepted the existence of Israel from the very start." She added: "If Israel is to live in peace, she can only do so in friendship with her neighbours. She cannot do so with the help of a country far away. That is the point."

The National Integration Council was reborn in Srinagar in June 1968. After the big conference in New Delhi in 1961, the first council had been allowed to die a natural death. Presiding over the three-day meeting in Srinagar, Mrs Gandhi referred to the older body and said it was "unfortunate that we were lulled into a sense of complacency because of the tremendous upsurge of unity at the time of the Chinese attack in 1962." She hoped the new council would live longer and serve the nation usefully. The council had been reconstituted in the wake of serious Hindu-Muslim riots in in different parts of the country.

These riots could be traced to tensions created by the weakening of Congress power throughout the country. Fanatical organisations of both communities seized this opportunity to become more aggressive towards the other community. This raised fears in the government and among leaders of Hindus and Muslims that the country was heading for the type of confrontation between them that developed in the last years of British rule. Some leaders thought they saw a foreign hand in this trend, for if it was not checked through political, as opposed to police, action it could encourage separatist tendencies which would further weaken the central authority in New Delhi. This would have suited the policies of certain nations which were not well disposed towards India.

Mrs Gandhi said the "great menace which our country faces today is that of communalism." This was to be a recurring theme in her speeches in the election campaigns that followed in 1971 and 1972. The barbed comments she made in them were usually directed at the Jana Sangh, which she sought to identify with national disintegration. She said: "After 20 years of independence and at a time when we had thought that this problem was more or less solved, once again communal clashes are occurring in different parts of the country." She pinpointed "provincialism or regionalism or parochialism" as the second menace. "I believe this is evoked by the same sentiments which are behind communalism," she continued, "In fact, it is an extension of the same sort of feeling.

"Another serious danger to national integration and perhaps one of the causes of the other menaces which I mentioned is the persistence of inequalities. In law and theory, the ancient discriminations have been abolished, but opportunities have not been growing as fast as the aspirations of backward classes and tribes and minorities and other such groups. Another factor which can unite us or create barriers is ... language. Divisive forces and tendencies existed in India even during the years of the struggle for freedom, but the mainstream of nationalism was powerful enough to sidetrack them and also to fight them, and thus we were able to march ahead."

Mrs Gandhi said "the struggle for national integration, the ideals and aspirations embodied in our Constitution, has to be waged ceaselessly and tenaciously. I do not think a time can ever come when these forces will not want to raise their head. But it should be our endeavour to create an atmosphere and to create conditions in which this will not be possible and in which the whole of society will react against them." In ending, she called for a many-pronged attack on the forces of disintegration. "Merely to say that if we overcome economic disparities and attain a degree of affluence we shall solve our problems is not enough. And since every problem ultimately has its origin in the mind of man, we have to ensure that our educational processes, the books we read, the radio we hear, the films we see, do not distort the Indian mind but lead it towards integration and solidarity."

The members of the council applauded the Prime Minister's speech warmly, and at the end of the first session adjourned to the Shalimar Gardens for lunch as guests of Kashmir Chief Minister G.M. Sadiq. Srinagar is not a pleasant place in June. It is warm and dusty and smelly. The gardens were a delightful contrast. In its coolness, with water cascading along canals lined with flowering plants and with thickleaved trees to ward off the sun, distinguished people from all parts of the country, representing its intellectual, political and administrative elite, and a sizable number of journalists feasted royally. After that banquet in such inviting surroundings, the natural thing to do seemed to be to lie under a tree and have a siesta. Probably many council members felt the same as I did.

At the end of three days of deliberations the conference produced a resolution and its participants dispersed to their various destinations. In an article entitled "The Economics of Disintegration" I wrote shortly afterwards for *Now*, a manysided weekly of Calcutta which Humayun Kabir—who attended the council meeting as a member—had founded, I said: "A cynic may be pardoned for concluding that no ineffectual angel flapped its wings more futilely in a void than did the members of the National Integration Council perform their intellectual capers for three days in Srinagar. But, studying the proceedings more closely, one may discern some glimmerings of positive achievements amidst the platitudes and pious wishes and public posturings that are inevitable on such occasions."

If the outcome of the meeting disappointed many observers, they were to blame for expecting too much. "The council could really do little more than highlight the danger to national unity, attempt to analyse the problem, appeal for public cooperation to combat it and make some proposals for administrative action, all of which it did in different degrees. The editorial writers and columnists who have made fun of the meeting should realise that a three-day pow-wow of eminent politicians and public figures could not effect what only a social and economic revolution would be able to.

"The declaration of objectives with which the council wound up its activities is a statement of pious wishes with which nobody who prizes the integrity of the Indian Union can quarrel. Whether it required three days of earnest deliberation in the not-so-cool weather prevailing in Srinagar to produce it is another matter." I said that if "cynically coldblooded political calculations deepen the antagonisms that cut at the root of national oneness, the stunted growth of the economy despite three full plans and a fourth whose gestation is greatly delayed is the soil which gives rise to them. It does no good telling people to discourage communal ill-will and regional animosities and to wean 'misguided elements from paths of violence' if all the time powerful inanimate economic forces are pushing the nation in the opposite direction and the government is apparently unable to reverse the process.

"The growing tide of unemployment and underemployment, the mounting anger over frustrated hopes of better living conditions and opportunities for fulfilling individual and collective aspirations, the backlash of rising expectations and diminishing achievements are the basic causes of the crisis of disintegration India faces today." I said it was necessary to distinguish between exploiting differences of religion, caste and region and fighting for due recognition of the rights of religious minorities and submerged castes and creation of a favourable climate for the growth of regional cultures. One point which was successfully stressed at the conference was the possibility of developing these cultures, not at the cost of national unity but as a means of strengthening it.

"The cultural diversity of India is an inescapable fact, and if there is a movement for the creation of regional identities, this should be encouraged as part of the democratic process ushered in by independence," I ended.

Statehood for Meghalaya, separation of Mizoram from Assam, renaming the Northeast Frontier Agency Arunachal Pradesh as the first step towards giving the region a more tangible identity, and a Punjabi-speaking state in the west are moves in this direction.

A foreign policy issue which was vitally important for India's security and was to assume increasing importance with the passage of years was the expected change in the strategic pattern in Southeast Asia when Britain withdrew its military forces from the region in the early 1970s. The governments of neighbouring countries and the Western press speculated how the "power vacuum" they thought would be created by the departure of the British could be filled. The Indian Government took the view, however, that no such vacuum would develop. But it was anxious that the ocean should not turn into an area of great-power rivalry, as seemed likely with both the United States and the Soviet Union seeking to establish their naval presence in it.

On a visit to Australia and New Zealand, where much concern was being shown at the possibility that the absence of British naval units to police the Indian Ocean would make their sea links with Western Europe vulnerable to any unfriendly power, Mrs Gandhi said: "It is our experience that wherever there is any kind of outside force it encourages other groups also to try and have a foothold, and this creates tension. In a way, you could say that when the British left India, they left a tremendous vacuum, but the Indian people filled it themselves." India was against military alliances for security. If there was any threat to countries in Southeast Asia, this was through subversion and infiltration, not from military confrontation.

Mrs Gandhi said she favoured economic cooperation among the countries in the Indian Ocean region as the best form of defence for a country was a healthy, expanding economy. Speaking at a state banquet in Kuala Lumpur, she said India was ready to "participate in and support" a broad regional association in Southeast Asia on the basis of "equality and mutual benefit." She said the end of the war in Vietnam would inject dynamism into Southeast Asia. She added: "We must resist the temptation to introduce a cold-war atmosphere by forming antagonistic blocs in the region. India believes that the answer to the threat of subversion lies in strengthening the economic and political stability of the region and not through the formation of military alliances, which may lead to counter-military alliances."

In September, Mrs Gandhi set out on a 21-day tour which took her to Latin America, the Caribbean, the US, Britain, and West Germany. With its completion, she could claim to be the most-travelled head of government in the world. Each tour she undertook had a specific purpose: to build understanding and sympathy for India in every continent. She herself said in a statement that she was going "halfway round the world on the wings of friendship." She hailed "the bridge of goodwill and friendship built across the mighty oceans" by her visit and described her journey as "a mission of understanding—to know and to learn" and to give the people and leaders of these countires some idea of India and to discover "areas in which they could work closer together."

She went to New York on the way back from the Caribbean to address the UN General Assembly. She told it of her disappointment because, for all the loud talk in the UN about international economic and political cooperation, little progress was visible. She regretted that the trends towards a more peaceful and cooperative world, which Nehru had strongly advocated, had "received a severe jolt."

On New Year's Day, 1969, Mrs Gandhi held a press conference, her third in three years as Prime Minister. Nehru met the press once a month. In reporting the conference, I said it was noteworthy, apart from its news content, for the manner in which she carried it off in the face of more than 200 newsmen. I said she had revealed a self-confidence and poise which had been lacking in most of her public appearances since she became Prime Minister. At the start, she was obviously tense, as most people would be before such a gathering. But her initial anxiety wore off, presumably as she realised that the newspaper tigers in front of her were not so formidable, individually or collectively, as she had feared.

"In fact," I wrote, "after the first few questions anybody should have realised that the gentlemen of the press were not to be taken seriously. Indeed, most of them did not seem to take themselves seriously, and the conference degenerated into a fun fair in which the participants seemed to enjoy a brief moment of glory by turning the spotlight on themselves." I said Mrs Gandhi proved more than a match for her inquisitors. She was quick and terse in her replies, and her wit was much more spontaneous and had more bite in it than that emanating from the other side of the bright lights in the conference chamber.

I said the press conference was a very good exercise in public relations and did much credit to Mrs Gandhi's image-building. Her two flashes of temper were, "whether natural or carefully stage-managed, very effective. There was more than a touch of the old Nehru fire about them. The Prime Minister still lives very much under the shadow of her illustrious father, as her references to him in the course of her replies showed."

The most important points she made related to the Commonwealth, China, and Pakistan. On the first, she made it clear that her government did not intend pulling out of this organisation, nor had it considered this possibility recently. Such action would only be taken after consulting the other nonwhite members. But, I added, India "will have to find a new point of attraction" before taking such a decisive step, "and this is nowhere visible at the moment."

On China, she refused to be drawn into a categorical statement that New Delhi would not insist on Peking's falling in line with the Colombo proposals, made by a group of nonaligned nations to prepare the ground for peace talks between India and China after the war in 1962. But this was clearly implied when she said it was foolish to adopt rigid stances in such matters. "This is in keeping with the new theory of flexibility in foreign affairs about which so much was heard at the recent meeting here of India's envoys in South and Southeast Asia," I commented.

On Pakistan, I said Mrs Gandhi might have been more precise in defining her government's response to President Ayub Khan's latest offer of a no-war pact. What kind of diplomatic machinery did she envisage for settling disputes between the two countries? Was Kashmir one of the issues to be submitted to its scruting? I said that "the time for a no-war pact and setting up such machinery was before signing the Tashkent Agreement. To be more exact, before Indian troops withdrew from the vicinity of Lahore and Sialkot."

The meeting with the press was a good note on which to start the new year. At that time, how many people had an inkling of the tremendous political drama that would unfold in New Delhi later in the year? Indian politics, and society, was to be shaken to the roots, and a new pattern was to emerge after a series of inconceivably breath-taking events. I had noted that at the conference Mrs Gandhi was still under the shadow of her father. But before the year was out she was to emerge from it and take her place as the unchallenged leader of the Congress Party in her own right. That again was only a stepping-stone to unchallenged leadership of the nation.

CHAPTER SEVEN

THE GREAT DIVIDE

THE YEAR 1969 will go down in Indian history as that of the rebirth of the Congress Party after a purificatory purge of great severity. That purge was designed to remove the stigma that the Congress was a party of the elite, the political wing of the establishment which had taken over from the British and which treated the country as though it was its private property, to be run for the profit of a microscopic section of the nation. The Congress could only revive as India's largest and most powerful national party if it ousted entrenched privilege from its ranks, and the biggest vested interest in it was the Syndicate comprising provincial bosses grouped round the party president, 67-year-old Siddavvanshalli Nijalingappa. The other leading figures in the group were also in their sixties or seventies, men who had served the Congress from their youth. Among them were Morarji Desai, 73, S.K. Patil, 69, K. Kamaraj, 66, and Atulya Ghosh, 64, all members of the highest decision-making bodies of the party.

The ease with which the Syndicate was worsted before the end of the year and its members pushed out of the party to form a rump Congress of their own—although they claimed to have expelled Mrs Gandhi and her close followers and to be the legitimate inheritors of the Congress traditions—showed that they were mere creatures of circumstances, not the men of destiny they fancied they were. These sawdust Machiavellis were greedy old men, without any social or economic perspectives, who clung to power for power's sake, for the benefits it brought them personally or to those who were near them. They had no thought for the future except how to ensure their political survival. So far as they represented anybody or anything, it was the special interests of the privileged. They were, in spite of their loud professions of socialism, basically anti-people. The exception was Kamaraj, a down-to-earth character with deep roots among the masses whose association with the original members of the Syndicate was more a marriage of convenience than genuine conviction of the rightness of its policies.

Gappa, rotund, completely bald and bespectacled, had the physical appearance of Mr Pickwick. But people who knew him well in Bangalore said his nature was the opposite of that immortal character's. It was never his practice to help lame dogs over stiles like Pickwick, and they said he never forgot or forgave what he considered an injury. It was thus scarcely likely that he did not remember that Mrs Gandhi had indirectly caused his humiliation in Nagpur ten years before, when the mantle of party presidency was snatched away as it was descending on his plump shoulders.

Morarji Desai was a plaster saint whose high opinion of himself found few takers. He often mistook stubborn adherence to provenly wrong views as a sign of unbending allegiance to high principles. He had a rigid mind, and his selfrighteousness and biting remarks made him little loved outside his small circle of devotees. I cannot recollect ever having seen Ghosh, who was party treasurer and an MP, without his dark glasses. With them on, he appeared to have more affinity with the Mafia than with a nonviolent, middle-of-the-road political party the emblem on whose flag was a harmless *charkha* (hand-operated spinning wheel). A national who's who noted he was "a voracious reader" but did not say what he read. Desai plied the charkha every morning to exhibit his devotion to Gandhian ideals, but there is no record that any of his colleagues in the Syndicate performed this exercise regularly although they were pledged to take the party back to the path of the Mahatma, from which they said it had strayed.

Indian womanhood was represented in this distinguished group by Sucheta Kripalani, former Congress Chief Minister of Uttar Pradesh and Tarakeshwari Sinha, a member of the Lok Sabha from Bihar who had served as Minister of Revenue under Nehru. Mrs Sinha had cast herself in the role of La Passionaria, with the difference that one was the symbol of Spanish democratic protest against fascism while Mrs Sinha was the torch-singer of the "counter-revolution" within the Congress. She was addicted to reeling off Urdu couplets to embellish her fervent oratory.

Who could take these people seriously, especially tubby little Gappa, who dropped malapropisms whenever he opened his mouth—which was often, when it would have been wiser to keep it shut—to the newsmen who gathered daily at sundown on the lawn of No 6, Janapath, the government-owned house he occupied in New Delhi? Kamaraj's buffoonery in dealing with the press was a mask to conceal the thoughts that coursed through his very agile mind. In Nijalingappa, this behaviour was an unconscious manifestation of a cerebral vacuum. Only Kamaraj and Patil deserved respect among these men for their intellectual calibre. It was a pity that Kamaraj had got into the wrong boat, where he was an ideological and temperamental misfit. He had a sense of humour, another quality he shared with Patil, and in relaxed moments of contemplation he probably laughted to himself at the incongruity of his new political posture.

But at the beginning of 1969 the Congress Party still presented a smooth, placid surface to the outsider. The first rumbles of the storm that was to follow were visible only in April, when the party met at Faridabad, some 18 miles from Delhi in the state of Haryana. Meanwhile, Mrs Gandhi carried out a reshuffle of her Council of Ministers, in which there were few changes at the top but considerable adjustments at the lower levels. These moves had no political significance like those she was to undertake in the following months. The reshuffle was in February, the month when fresh elections were held to the West Bengal Legislative Assembly after the United Front Government had been dismissed by presidential order on the advice of the Union Government. The Congress went to the polls confident of a workable majority. Mrs Gandhi had campaigned on its behalf, and according to observers in Calcutta she had drawn larger crowds than ever before in her political career, larger even than those which had flocked to hear her father.

But when the election results were in, the United Front's share of the 280 seats in the legislature had soared to 210 while that of the Congress had fallen to a miserable 55 againt 127 in the dissolved house. The Congress losses were heavy in the areas Mrs Gandhi had visited. One reason given for this setback was that the state Congress organisation was still controlled by Ghosh and other men whose standing among the people of the state was very low. Commenting on the disconcerting results, *Now* wrote editorially: "The crucial fact of the West Bengal election is that the people wanted change. They had given the Congress a stern warning in 1967. They had at the same time indicated that if the Congress failed the people would create an alternative out of discordant elements. The Congress did not learn the lesson. Everything went on as before."

West Bengal was another warning to Mrs Gandhi to get on with the housecleaning of the party which was long overdue. The warning was reinforced by the results of the elections held in three other states at the same time as in West Bengal. In Punjab, the Akalis won more seats than the Congress and formed a government with its inveterate enemy, the Jana Sangh. In Uttar Pradesh, Mrs Gandhi could find some consolation in the fact that the party bettered its performance in 1967, largely because of her campaigning, but fell short of the absolute majority it needed to form a government. The party line was not to form coalitions in states where it lacked sufficient seats to form a stable government on its own.

In March, a Congress member of the Rajya Sabha made charges against Desai at a meeting of the Congress Parliamentary Party's Executive Committee which cast grave doubts on the integrity in public affairs Desai was so proud of. The member, Chandra Sekhar, was once a Socialist and now led a group of radical Congressmen whom the Delhi press had named Young Turks. They made more noise in Parliament than was proportionate to their numbers, but they acted as a brake on opposition parties as well as Congress groups which lobbied for big industrial concerns. Chandra Sekhar accused Desai of favouring certain firms with which his son was associated. In addition to his business connections, Desai Junior was also his father's private secretary.

In an editorial captioned Mrs Gandhi's Government, *Now* wrote that "a government where the mistrust among its major components is as deep as the discussion in the Congress Parliamentay executive has revealed has no right to exist. That it has not crumbled yet is a measure of the cupidity of the ministers and the tenacity with which they cling to power.... If there is to be a Congress government that will govern it is clear that it will have to be one without Mr Morarji Desai or without Mrs Gandhi. A government having both of them in leading positions must necessarily be a government of no movement and no decisions....That the Congress government at the Centre has had its day is now accepted by the Congress leaders themselves. What keeps them together is not confidence in the future but the fear of it." It soon became obvious, however, to the supporters of Mrs Gandhi and those of the Syndicate that they could survive only if they parted company, and this could be effected by one group throwing the other out.

In the course of an address to the Federation of Indian Chambers of Commerce and Industry, New Delhi, Mrs Gandhi spelt out the industrial policy of her government. She said its aim was to "infuse social purpose at strategic points in decision-making while avoiding cumbersome and unnecessary intervention." In a society where affluence and power are "tiny specks in the vast sea of poverty, it is not unnatural that monopoly should attract strong hostility." The problem of concentration of economic power would have to be dealt with by getting financial institutions to adopt suitable policies. "It is reasonable to expect that large industrial groups should raise a substantially larger part of the finance required for projects than is feasible in the case of smaller groups."

She said that although the rate of economic growth was important, this was not the only yardstick for progress. Real advance should be judged more by the composition of the national product and by the nature of the social forces development generated. More vigorous action would have to be taken to remove regional economic disparities. She explained that her government did not think in terms of one state being less developed than another but of the economic level of particular regions. She told industrialists to depend more on Indian technology instead of choosing "the easy path of importing established know-how." If know-how had to be imported, this should be done as cheaply as possible. She said the government was interested in centralising the purchase of know-how from abroad. When several units were to be set up in an industry about the same time, "the possibilities of saving foreign exchange by unified purchase of know-how should be explored."

The Congress session at Faridabad in April was notable for bringing into the open the sharp differences between Mrs Gandhi's supporters and those of the Syndicate on industrial policy. In his presidential address, Nijalingappa deplored the heavy losses the public-sector undertakings were incurring. He said they were badly managed and "there is a case for reviewing this public-sector attempt at establishing large-scale industries." With this sentence he raised doubts about the basic validity of state participation in industrial growth, one of the principles of planned development in India.

Mrs Gandhi took up the challenge. In a fighting speech, she said heavy industries had to be set up in the public sector not only because private businessmen were not interested in projects which called for large investments of capital and took a long time to yield profits but also because key industries—the commanding heights of the economy—should not be entrusted to individuals or small groups. She asked him whether an inquiry into the affairs of private-sector projects, which were not accountable to the public or to Parliament, would lead to "flattering conclusions."

Two days before this clash, a fire destroyed the hall in which the Congress delegates were meeting. I reported that many out-siders as well as Congressmen took this as a warning of the fate that would befall the party in the general election due in 1972. Ghosh tried to console them by recalling that this was the third incident of its kind at a session of the All-India Congress Committee. The fire should not therefore be regarded as a sign of divine displeasure, he said.

A subject of hot debate in the open session of the committee was a report C. Subramaniam, a member of the Working Committee and one of Mrs Gandhi's brains-trusters, had recently prepared on the party's political health. He had attempted to present an honest, objective analysis of the plight the party was in and to suggest a reasonable way of ensuring its survival as a serious force in national politics. He was assailed from all sides at the meeting.

I commented at that time: "The sense of realism and urgency which Mr Subramaniam sought to inject into the party was spurned at Faridabad, the timeworn shibboleths were paraded as if they represented the ultimate verities, and the Congress voted to go on being what it has been for the last two decades—all things to all men . . . In spite of the wishes of its leaders, the party itself is being polarised under the pressure of external forces which the leaders cannot suppress. The time has come when Young Turk and Old Gandhian can no longer hang together—even if the alternative is hanging separately. If they refuse to polarise, as they should, they face a much worse fate—total atomisation."

A few days after the Faridabad session, President Zakir Husain died of a heart attack. To him secularism was more than a moral conviction or an intellectual principle. It was a part of his persona-lity, arising spontaneously from his refinement and humanism. His election as President was both a recognition of his invaluable services to his country and the vindication of India's belief in tolerance and a multi-religious society. Politically, his death was a big blow to Mrs Gandhi. It presented the Syndicate with an opportunity to carry out the coup its members were planning to oust the Prime Minister. If they could not make a frontal attack on her, they could get their way indirectly by seeing that their nominee was elected Husain's successor. Thus they could make conditions so difficult for Mrs Gandhi that she might throw in her hand and leave the field open to them.

The Syndicate got a shot in the arm a few days later when Patil was elected to the Lok Sabha in a byelection. Kamaraj had already entered it in similar fashion, and Mrs Gandhi had offered him a place in her cabinet as a way of detaching him from the bad company he had fallen into. No such offer was made to Patil, who on arriving in New Delhi to take his seat declared war on fellow Congressmen who did not view the party's policies in the same light as he did. Patil unfolded his theory of "internal polarisation" of the Congress and advised those members who did not agree with him to get out or be thrown out if they refused to conform. The rightwingers, who had been on the defensive for some months, hailed Patil's return with the fervour usually accorded a liberator or a messiah.

But the Syndicate's joy was shortlived. Within a few hours of Patil's raising the banner of war against Mrs Gandhi, though he did not name her, the Congress Parliamentary Party showed what it thought of these moves. In electing its Executive Committee, members reaffirmed their faith in Mrs Gandhi's leadership. The first ten winning candidates were all her supporters, and nine of them were newcomers to the executive in keeping with Mrs Gandhi's policy of infusing new blood into the clogged arteries of the party. Only one of her candidates was defeated, and all the key elective posts in the executive went to her people. These results showed clearly on whose side the bulk of the Congress MPs were.

About the time Patil returned to New Delhi breathing fire and brimstone, Mrs Gandhi made a crucial alliance with Home Minister Chavan and Agriculture Minister Jagjivan Ram. This was the pivot on which she planned to organise her resistance to the plot that was hatching against her. I commented at the time that Patil's "brave words after his comeback looked very much like throwing the gauntlet at the Prime Minister." It appeared as though the Old

Guard was preparing for a showdown. But I noted that "after the parliamentary party elections it is clear that this ultimatum misfired. Instead of serving as a catalytic agent, it had the opposite effect of drawing the threatened groups together under the prime ministerial umbrella. Mr Chavan, for instance, is one of those who stands to lose everything as a result of Mr Patil's return to the political arena in New Delhi.

"Now, if there is any quitting of the Congress on the ground of disagreement on policies and programme, as Mr Patil demanded in his declaration of war on his detractors, it looks as though he and other likeminded Congressmen will have to pack their ideological baggage and depart."

The Syndicate was not idling while Mrs Gandhi was marshalling her forces against it. It made a secret deal with Desai under which he was offered the prime ministership until the fifth general election in 1972. Chavan, one of her props, was lured away by offering him the deputy prime ministership until Desai stepped down after the elections, when he would succeed him. Chavan's defection was a big blow to Mrs Gandhi, for it meant the loss of the votes of the Congress MPs and state legislators from Maharashtra to her presidential candidate.

The attention of the nation now centred on the Congress choice of a presidential candidate. Vice-President V.V. Giri, 75, let it be known that he would seek election as an independent when his expectations that Mrs Gandhi would sponsor his candidature faded. The Syndicate's choice was N. Sanjiva Reddy, 56, a member of its inner circle, former boss of Andhra Pradesh and Speaker of the Lok Sabha. This office was the compensation he received from Mrs Gandhi when she dropped him from her cabinet in 1967. He had been party president from 1960 to 1962. Reddy had a grievance against Mrs Gandhi for leaving him out of her cabinet after her election as parliamentary party leader for the second time. The Syndicate had bypassed Giri because he was suspected of secretly favouring Mrs Gandhi. Their strategy demanded that they install in Rashtrapati Bhavan a man whom they could trust completely. Sanjiva Reddy had no outstanding qualities to commend him for the highest office in the Indian Republic except his proclaimed loyalty to the group to which he belonged.

The issue at stake in this choice of candidates was not who should be President but Mrs Gandhi's political future. The bosses were determined to see her out of the prime ministership, and with so much at stake it was difficult to see how a compromise could be evolved to prevent the two rival groups within the Congress from putting up different candidates. It did not need much political perception to realise that without such a compromise the party was heading for a split. Veteran members who had gone through the struggle for independence thought this would be the beginning of the end of the grand old party. On the other hand, the enthusiastic younger generation of members who stood behind Mrs Gandhi felt that a split was the only way to ensure the party's survival as a vital force in Indian politics.

Meanwhile, Mrs Gandhi was not tipping her hand, but she was obviously not happy at the Syndicate's choice, which it was trying to foist on the parliamentary party. Other names were tossed around for the presidency, among them Jagjivan Ram and Defence Minister Swaran Singh. The more the issue was clouded the better for Mrs Gandhi. It gave her more time to prepare the ground for her candidate, whom she would name at the right time. The best guess was that it would be Giri, and soon newspapers which had written him off as too old suddenly discovered virtues in him which demanded that he be chosen to succeed Husain in accordance with precedent.

It was obvious that the Syndicate was trying to make it difficult for Mrs Gandhi to function as Prime Minister. The bosses were bent on enforcing a new principle in the relations between government and ruling party in a democratic, parliamentary setup. Under this system the Prime Minister, who leads the majority in Parliament, also leads the ruling party outside it. The bosses wanted to throw this accepted principle out of the window and substitute its opposite, that the Prime Minister must follow the line laid down by the party executive, in this case the Working Committee. To the Prime Minister this politically untenable doctrine, which would have subordinated her will to that of the executive, was anathema. She had obtained her mandate from the Indian people, and she was accountable only to the people who had elected her and not to the bosses, particularly when they represented only a small section of the people, those microscopic groups who thought they were more equal than others and wanted things to remain that way.

The All-India Congress Committee met in Bangalore, Nijalingappa's stamping ground before he was wafted to New Delhi. The Congress Parliamentary Board was also to meet there to pick the party candidate for Union President. Its seven members were Mrs Gandhi, Chavan, Desai, Jagjivan Ram, Kamaraj, Nijalingappa, and Patil. The proceedings of these two bodies in the pleasant climate of Bangalore were to see the start of the battle between the modernisers, led by Mrs Gandhi, and the supporters of the status quo which culminated in the final break the following November. It was a period of agonising suspense for the nation as well as for most of the antagonists in this relentless struggle for the body and soul of India.

Mrs Gandhi opened the attack with a long-distance missile fired from New Delhi. She sent a note to the committee on economic policy, describing it in what were to become historic words. She said she had "jotted down a few stray thoughts in a hurry" for the committee's consideration. Never before probably have such random jottings caused so much consternation and anger at a top-level meeting of Congressmen. Its author followed a few hours later to participate in the session, the delay in her arrival enabling her to reach Bangalore at a suitable time to study the note's fallout.

The note started with a general statement: "The time has come to restate our economic policy and set the direction in which we have to achieve our social goal. This has become all the more necessary in view of doubts that have been raised with regard to our intentions and our willingness to take the hard and difficult steps which are necessary." In the interests of "the weaker sections, minorities and underprivileged," whose cause the Congress had "always championed," she then listed a number of measures to be implemented.

They included a limit on the "unproductive expenditure and conspicuous consumption of corporate bodies"; a change in the test for creditworthiness incorporated in the lending policies of nationalised financial institutions; special efforts to develop backward regions of the country; shutting out big business from consumer industries wherever possible to encourage the cooperative and small sectors; barring foreign capital from industries where Indian know-how was available; establishment of service cooperatives in villages; reform of the agrarian laws to prevent landlords from taking away their tenants' holdings, and to permit tenants to mortgage the land they tilled to get credit for their farm operations; restricting the sale of land by economically and culturally backward groups; and strict enforcement of the limits on individual holding.

To the defenders of big financial and industrial interests in the cities and the landlord-moneylender class in the villages, this was almost like Red revolution. Three years earlier, in June 1966, the AICC had adopted a 10-point programme which proposed among other things social control of banks, nationalisation of general insurance, increasing state takeover of exports and imports and internal trading in grain, and the abolition of the privy purses and privileges of the former princes of India as they were "incongruous to the concept and practice of democracy." This was bad enough but now, according to the defenders of property, Mrs Gandhi had flung moderation to the winds and teamed up with the Communists and the wild radicals in the Congress Party.

Desai was particularly loud in his criticism of the implied move towards nationalising banks, taking it as a personal affront. He complained that social control of these institutions had not been given a fair trial. Industrial Development Minister Fakhruddin Ali Ahmed, a trusted lieutenant of Mrs Gandhi, reported Desai as saying: "As long as I am Finance Minister, this cannot be implemented. If the Prime Minister wants to do it, she will have to change her Finance Minister." Desai never expected the Prime Minister to take him at his word, and so soon after he had challenged her to do so.

Mrs Gandhi had tossed the apple of discord among the members of the Syndicate. She had raised an issue on which they could not duck confronting her if they wanted to maintain their influence in the party and among the privileged groups which backed them. Further, it drove a wedge through the Syndicate because Kamaraj among the hard core of the group and Chavan, who was wavering between the two camps, could not oppose it without blemishing their images as progressives. At lower party levels too bank nationalisation was a catalytic agent. It drove a dividing line between the sheep who supported Mrs Gandhi and the goats who were with the bosses. It was also a warning to the big business interests backing the bosses of what was in store for them if they encouraged attempts to topple her.

In the Working Committee, the majority sided with Mrs Gandhi, and it included, besides Kamaraj and Chavan, Ahmed, Jagjivan

Ram, D. Sanjivayya, who was to become president of the Congress in 1971 after the Syndicate had been routed, and Swaran Singh, at that time Defence Minister.

On July 11, the day after Mrs Gandhi's missile exploded in the Working Committee, Chavan, who felt uncomfortable in his exposed position and hesitated to make up his mind, turned up before the Working Committee in the role of peacemaker. He proposed a compromise which the AICC adopted, thinking thereby that the widening rift between the changers and the no-changers would close. Its members obviously did not realise that division at this stage was the only way to save the party from the disintegration they feared.

But if they thought they could paper over the cracks with this resolution welcoming the Prime Minister's note and commending it to the central and state governments, their wishfulness was negatived by the Parliamentary Board, which selected Sanjiva Reddy as the official candidate for the presidency. Five votes were cast for him, while two went to Mrs Gandhi's nominee, Jagjivan Ram. Chavan, Desai, Kamaraj, Nijalingappa and Patil voted for the Syndicate's choice, Ahmed and Mrs Gandhi for Jagjivan Ram, who, himself a member of the board, did not vote.

Mrs Gandhi confided in the press the next day. She had first suggested Giri, who had filled the vacant presidential chair, and when the bosses turned him down she proposed Jagjivan Ram. She said she was not so much distressed by the choice they had made—she had nothing against Sanjiva Reddy personally—but its manner. She was following a principle, that of a national consensus, and the consensus favoured Giri. Further, was it right for the bosses to drag the office of Speaker and its holder into politics by nominating Sanjiva Reddy? She said it was against the spirit, if not the letter, of the Constitution and the principles of parliamentary democracy to involve the Speaker in a political issue. Besides, the board decision was a "calculated" attempt to humiliate her personally and challenge her authority as Prime Minister. Mrs Gandhi faced two alternatives: she must either fight the Syndicate and change its decision to conform with her wishes or quit.

It was clear from her remarks that she would not accept defeat. She would show the bosses that she could fight them with their own weapons, and much more skilfully. If necessary, she was prepared to place the issue before the nation and let it choose between her and the bosses. There was no question that once the challenge had been made she had to counter it if she did not want to see power passing from her hands into those of the pillars of the status quo. There was now no question of retreat and hardly any chance of compromise. The chips were down and the tussle had to go on until the Syndicate was liquidated politically. This was the Indian version of the cultural revolution, and its political implications were as deep-going as those of the upsurge in China.

To do this, it was also necessary to snap the ties between the bosses and big business and finance. Bank nationalisation was the answer. Not only would it enable the government to give a social purpose to banking, to change its direction so as to funnel credit to the small farmer and petty manufacturer and to backward regions. It would also give the government political control of the banking system and thus curb the malpractices of big business and the covert support of industrialists to anti-national and other subversive forces.

Broadcasting to the nation on the night of July 19, Mrs Gandhi announced that the 14 leading Indian banks had been nationalised by presidential decree. She assured private trade and industry that their legitimate needs for credit would be met. She justified nationalisation on two grounds: it would not starve the private sector of funds; and savings would now be mobilised for productive investment according to the government's planned priorities. Two days later she told Parliament: "The government believes that public ownership of the major banks, for which there has been widespread public support, will help in the most effective mobilisation and deployment of national resources so that our objectives can be realised with a greater degree of assurance."

There was not a doubt that the measure was very popular. It would have been foolish for the Syndicate to have challenged Mrs Gandhi before the nation on it. They preferred to bide their time and work hard to see that Sanjiva Reddy was elected President. Then they would show their mettle. They would either break her to their will or throw her out. Reporting this, I commented that Mrs Gandhi had "pulled out the joker she had up her sleeve and tossed it in the face of Mr Nijalingappa and his friends. It brought about the collapse of the united front they had been building to winkle her out of the prime ministership—at least temporarily."

I said this was not a clash of personalities as a sizable section of the Delhi press thought. "The antagonists in this battle represented two clearly divergent political trends in the Congress Party."

Before the banks were nationalised, Mrs Gandhi had to settle accounts with Desai. Since he was resolutely against this action, he could not hold the finance portfolio any longer. Mrs Gandhi decided to relieve him of it. She did not, however, lever him out of the cabinet as she would have been justified in doing but offered him another berth, at the same time permitting him to continue as Deputy Prime Minister. This was very generous treatment for a man who had openly disavowed a measure with far-reaching economic consequences, including a more equitable distribution of gainful opportunities, and a cardinal point in Mrs Gandhi's programme. Desai was quite clearly out of tune with the times. He could not understand the need for changes of the kind Mrs Gandhi wanted. He did not realise that by taking away some of the cream the big industrialists and landlords fattened on Mrs Gandhi was ensuring that they would not lose all. In the new social order she envisaged, these groups would find a place, provided they learnt to curb their itch for more riches than they merited and contributed their share to the general wellbeing of the nation.

Desai resigned on July 16. His resignation was not accepted immediately. Mrs Gandhi exerted herself to persuade him to change his mind. These efforts failed, and Desai was allowed to go three days later. The correspondence between the Prime Minister and her deputy preceding his departure was released on July 21. It revealed that Mrs Gandhi had told the Congress Chief Minister of Uttar Pradesh, C.B. Gupta, that some party leaders were "conspiring" against her. Mrs Gandhi denied this charge was directed at Desai, but Desai insisted that Gupta had confirmed it was.

The nation greeted the decree enthusiastically. The small man felt he would now come into his own. I wrote: "Never have there been such stirring times in the capital of Bharat as in these swinging days since bank nationalisation. Daily mass rallies outside No 1, Safdarjang Road (the house of the Prime Minister) to thank the Prime Minister for this act and to exhort her to perform more of a like nature. Mr Krishna Menon, a father figure of the near-left, leading processions of sans culottes through the streets of New Delhi...."

Now the battle for the presidency grew more furious. The Jana Sangh and Swatantra pledged their preference votes in the election to Reddy. This followed a deal Nijalingappa struck with the leaders of these conservative parties. The arrangement showed that the Syndicate was prepared to go to any lengths to get their man into Rashtrapati Bhavan, and this boded ill for Mrs Gandhi. Nijalingappa directed her by letter to issue a whip to Congress MPs to vote for Reddy. Reassuringly, he added that no bid would be made to toss her out of office before 1972, when the fifth general election was due, if she obeyed. In the light of consequent developments this piece of condescension is amusing. It reveals how out of touch he was with reality. Here was a man on the verge of political annihilation offering to let Mrs Gandhi continue in office at his pleasure if she was a good little girl and obeyed Uncle Gappa.

Mrs Gandhi replied on August 12, eight days before the election was to take place in Parliament and all the state legislatures, saying she could not constitutionally instruct the members of her party to vote as Nijalingappa wanted. She had been advised legally not to do so. Ananthasayanam Ayyangar, a former Speaker of the Lok Sabha, had said "the party cannot give directions to members even in regard to the election of a leader, and much less has it a right to give directions to members regarding election of a speaker or president, who are above parties." In any event, Mrs Gandhi added, the new circumstances resulting from Nijalingappa's deal with the right-wing parties ruled out support for Reddy. The note warfare raged until a few hours before the election. On August 15, Mrs Gandhi stressed the need for a free vote, as a refusal to permit this would "lead to a serious division in the party." Such a vote would on the other hand "rejuvenate the party, restore confidence and strengthen unity."

The Prime Minister's letter replied to one from Nijalingappa the day before, in which he threatened to discipline any Congressman who voted against his nominee. This was his riposte to her rejection of his directive about a whip. Mrs Gandhi's reply said: "I do think I was ignored in the Congress selection of the presidential candidate at Bangalore." She warned him that any disciplinary action after the election would be disastrous for the party. She explained: "I feel that the issues involved go beyond the presidential poll. The result of the election, one way or the other, will not resolve

the differences over the manner in which our basic policies of democracy, secularism, socialism, and nonalignment are implemented."

I wrote in *Now* that by demanding a free vote, which in effect
meant a vote for Giri, Mrs Gandhi had "committed herself irrevocably to the breakup of the Congress Party." I said this was not an
arbitrary decision, taken in a moment of pique. It was the logical
consequence of all she had said and done from the time her "stray
thoughts" exploded in the Working Committee in Bangalore in
July.

"Looking ahead to the general election in 1972, Mrs Gandhi
seems to have come to the conclusion that the Congress was doomed
to disaster at the polls if it did not do some vigorous housecleaning
and try to present a new picture of itself to the electorate two and a
half years from now," I observed. "Such an image, she and her ad-
visers seem to have argued, could only be created by weeding out the
fossilised elements in the party leadership and shifting the emphasis
in its economic programme to the small entrepreneur in the town
and the middle and small peasant in the village."

Around 10.30 on the night of August 20, the result of the election
was announced. Giri had won by a narrow margin. He became
the first President to be elected without the Congress label although
he was a Congressman of many years' standing. Reddy had not fared
as well as expected in some states where the Syndicate was believed
to be influential. Chavan's Congress supporters in Maharashtra
voted solidly for Reddy. If the spiteful, frustrated, and frightened
old men who had teamed up against Mrs Gandhi had craned their
inner ears, they would have heard the tolling of bells. The bells
were tolling for them, for their blasted political careers, for the end
of the particular brand of blarney they had peddled very successfully for more than two decades.

The wild jubilation in the streets of the city should have told them
that the jig was up. Had they been as wise as they had been thought
to be for so long, they would have packed their traps and retired
from the scene of their defeat quietly, leaving Mrs Gandhi to get
on with the task of reconstructing the Congress Party and giving
a new edge to government development programmes in keeping
with the economic policy she had framed in her note to the AICC.
But they continued to stay and make a desperate effort to turn the
tide that was running against them with growing velocity.

They did not see that the general election had unleashed political forces which were propelling people who thought and acted as they had done to where they belonged—the dustbin of history. Mrs Gandhi had read the writing on the wall correctly after the 1967 elections. She was moving with the historical processes set in motion by the people's urge that the political revolution which took place with the transfer of power in 1947 from Britons to Indians should continue so that the urgent need for social and economic change was fulfilled.

The Syndicate and its followers were set on a course of self-destruction, and Mrs Gandhi tried at this point to save them from the consequences of their blind opposition to history. She advised Nijalingappa that if he tried to punish the "rebels" who had voted for Giri he would bring disaster to the party. This was a moment of crucial decision for Mrs Gandhi and Nijalingappa and for the conflicting interests they represented.

Nijalingappa brushed her advice aside. He issued notices to her, Jagjivan Ram and Ahmed demanding that they explain why they should not be disciplined for favouring a free vote in the presidential election. Like King Canute, who many centuries before tried to discipline the waves, poor Gappa, who could not see politically beyond his nose, was trying to roll back the tide of history. He was to meet with as little success as Canute.

The Working Committee met in New Delhi on August 25. Chavan again played peace dove. This time he was also playing for his survival in the cabinet. Having backed the wrong horse in the presidential race, he was in the ticklish position of having to win back the confidence of the head of government. Mrs Gandhi could have had little reason to be pleased in spite of the prodigal's act of penitence. He had nearly lost her candidate the presidency by giving the solid block of Maharasthtra votes to Sanjiva Reddy. But this was not the time for settling scores, as the next round of hostilities was due any moment and anybody who made friendly gestures was welcome.

The nation had expected an epic confrontation at the meeting, but it ended with a whimper. Chavan presented it with two draft compromise resolutions. The second resolution, which was accepted, attempted to define the relations between the legislative and executive wings of the party. It said that while the Congress president "has the important task of running the organisation, which has the responsibility to lay down broad policies and rally the people in support of accepted policies," the leader of the parliamentary wing as Prime Minister and head of government "has wider responsibilities to the country as a whole in the national as well as international spheres." The draft, described as the unity resolution, ended on this wishful note: "Let us ... not say anything or do anything which is likely to widen the breach...."

The resolution recognised that the two wings were complementary and the Prime Minister was accountable to the people, one of the principles Mrs Gandhi had fought for. The executive wing was relegated to a subsidiary role, and the functions of its president were defined as looking mainly into organisational matters. The effective check on the Prime Minister was the parliamentary wing of the party, which had elected her its leader, and Parliament. Thus Chavan helped Mrs Gandhi assert the ministerial wing's independence of the executive.

Historic is a greatly overworked word in the Congress lexicon. There was a time when every session of the AICC was automatically described as historic in newspaper reports, just as swearing-in ceremonies of presidents and other notables are today almost unfailingly spoken of as "simple but impressive." But there is every justification for using the term in speaking of this Working Committee meeting which resolved in all solemnity that the factional schism in the party could be healed in a spirit of let's kiss and be friends. For, in spite of the verbal dexterity Chavan had displayed in his draft, the party remained irrevocably divided because the differences between the factions could not be bridged by pious wishes.

Acceptance of the independence and superiority of the parliamentary section of the party spelt the end of the unfettered reign of the overlords who had ruled the party at the state level for as long as they had played a guiding role in Congress destinies. Their authoritarian discipline, which stifled party democracy at all levels, was maintained through a mixture of bribes and threats. It was now on the way out. Now it was Mrs Gandhi's responsibility to get on with the job of thoroughly cleansing the Congress stable if she wanted to consolidate her control of the party machine. The bosses had been vanquished but not destroyed, although it was obvious to keen observers that the war of supremacy had been won and lost with the results of the presidential election five days earlier, probably even before that when Mrs Gandhi flouted Nijalingappa's diktat and called for a free vote.

The challenge of bossism would be met only by genuinely democratising the party in policy and administration and thus making it attractive to young men and women with political leanings who were now drawn to parties to right and left of the Congress. The party could be revived only by bringing into its ranks frustrated young people in whom fresh hopes had been kindled by Mrs Gandhi's revolt against the Old Guard. But this would happen on a large scale only when the death-hold of the tired old men on the party apparatus was removed. The party had to be made democratic from the grass-roots to its topmost pinnacle if it was to become a vital national force again. It had to become a party of under-thirties, not of over-sixties. This was the Herculean task of rejuvenation Mrs Gandhi undertook when she decided to defy the bosses.

Mrs Gandhi could not afford to let the battle with the bosses stop at the halfway stage. She was under pressure both from the rightwing and leftwing parties, and to meet this she had to cast the party in an altogether new image. Paternalism would have to go, the gravy train would have to be derailed, and a different type of party manager, a sophisticated technocrat, would have to be found to cope with the new political tasks facing it. The Syndicate had withdrawn from the battlefield after the loss of the presidency, but this was just a tactical retreat to treat its wounds and prepare for the next, and hopefully final, round. But delay would have been fatal to Mrs Gandhi. The bosses had to go speedily if the party was to be given a thorough cleanup, and there was no better time for these two operations then when her political fortunes were ascending rapidly.

The unity resolution was dead even before it was voted on in the Working Committee. The irrepressible Nijalingappa started a new hare, this time what he called the "personality cult" in the party. He described this cult as "a mischievous and dangerous trend in democracy." It needed no great insight to realise that he was sniping at Mrs Gandhi, whose popularity had soared greatly since bank nationalisation and the election of Giri. Mrs Gandhi's response to the charge was that "there is no change on the part of those who have vehemently opposed bank nationalisation. The reconciliation to the present situation was only tactical. They are waiting for their opportunity and will try to upset matters when they can."

Denied success at party headquarters in New Delhi, the bosses carried the war to the state capitals, where their strength lay. Kamaraj set the pace in Tamil Nadu. He forced Subramaniam, who was president of the state Congress, to resign on a cooked-up charge of discourtesy to Kamaraj. The Syndicate's game was deep. Its members planned to capture control of the Working Committee by reducing Mrs Gandhi's following in it to a minority. When she was outnumbered, they intended pointing their guns directly at her. Subramaniam was a member of the Working Committee in consequence of his membership of the AICC, which in turn he enjoyed because he led the party's Tamil Nadu branch. The Syndicate moved in for the kill when Subramaniam resigned. Nijalingappa, acting on behalf of the group, declared Subramaniam could no longer be a member of the Working Committee as he had lost his official position in the Tamil Nadu Congress.

If Subramaniam was removed from the committee, Mrs Gandhi would be vulnerable. The two factions would be evenly balanced, but Nijalingappa's casting vote as committee chairman would tilt the scales in the Syndicate's favour. Mrs Gandhi struck back by firing four of her junior ministers who were known to support the Syndicate. In individual letters asking them to resign, she explained that she was carrying out "certain changes which are necessary for a more cohesive and purposive direction of the work of the Council of Ministers." Mrs Gandhi was closing her ranks as a prelude for battle. Her action was a warning to some ministers of cabinet status who were secretly loyal to the Syndicate.

Simultaneously, Mrs Gandhi and her followers launched a signature drive urging an early session of the AICC to elect a new president before Nijalingappa's term ended. The target of this campaign met Kamaraj and Sanjiva Reddy in Bangalore and tabooed it as violating party discipline. On October 28, Nijalingappa sent Mrs Gandhi a six-page indictment listing all her alleged acts of defiance of his authority. Three days later Mrs Gandhi's supporters decided to boycott a meeting of the Working Committee Nijalingappa had summoned in New Delhi. The same morning, they held a parallel committee meeting and fixed November 22 for a session of the AICC in the city. Nijalingappa sacked Fakhruddin Ali Ahmed and

Subramaniam from his Working Committee on October 31.

He asked Mrs Gandhi to explain her "reported association" with the move to call an "illegal and unconstitutional" meeting of the AICC. She retorted that he had flouted the party constitution in expelling two members of the Working Committee. The very next day he accused Mrs Gandhi of "having committed an unpardonable act of gross indiscipline, a flagrant violation of the constitution of the Congress" in passing "a resolution on characterising some of my actions as unconstitutional and backing the move for a requisition to remove me from the [presidency] of the Congress and summoning a special session of the AICC in Delhi on November 22 and 23, 1969."

From now Mrs Gandhi's faction was known as the Requisition Congress and Nijalingappa's as the Organisation Congress until the first of them was able to establish its claim to be the legitimate Congress Party when, to distinguish it from the rump of organisation men, it was popularly known as the Ruling Congress. To make sure that its listeners would not be confused, All India Radio referred to the two bodies when the division was final as "the Congress presided over by Shri Jagjivan Ram" and "the Congress presided over by Shri Nijalingappa."

Events followed one another with whirlwind rapidity. On November 4, Mrs Gandhi asked Railway Minister Ram Subhag Singh to quit the cabinet for endorsing the views of Nijalingappa's committee. The two faction leaders met at lunch on November 7 to see whether they could settle their differences. To outside observers, however, it seemed clear that the rift had gone beyond the point where it could be patched up. Mrs Gandhi insisted on Nijalingappa's taking back the expelled members of the Working Committee while he demanded that she bring back into her Council of Ministers all those she had dropped since the Bangalore session of the AICC. The talks failed, mercifully for the future health of the Congress Party, people with a progressive outlook felt.

Mrs Gandhi spoke to the press on November 8. She saw no danger to national stability as a result of the crisis in the party. This was no clash of personalities but a combination of "many things" involving several basic issues. She ruled out seeking a vote of confidence from the Congress Parliamentary Party and repudiated the "insinuation" that she was "going Communist or relying on their support."

Noting that this "malicious" propaganda had been going on for some time, she said: "I am in no way getting aligned to these forces." Her main difference with the Communists was on means, not ends. She believed in persuasion, they in coercion. She rejected dissolution of Parliament as the only solution for the political crisis.

Before the Nijalingappa committee excommunicated Mrs Gandhi, Uttar Pradesh Chief Minister C.B. Gupta made a last-minute bid to bring about a compromise. He had tried earlier on November 11 in concert with other Congress chief ministers, but the effort had misfired.

On November 12, Nijalingappa's segment of the Working Committee expelled Mrs Gandhi from the party. It directed the Parliamentary Party to elect a new leader. The split was complete. By this act Nijalingappa and Company condemned themselves to political suicide. By cutting themselves off from Mrs Gandhi they were rejecting the most dynamic figure in Indian politics and withdrawing from its mainstream, the surest way of achieving political extinction. Supporters of the Prime Minister denounced Nijalingappa, saying: "We want to state categorically that the action taken by Nijalingappa is illegal and has no validity. The Prime Minister still continues to be a member of the Congress organisation and continues to be leader of the Congress Parliamentary Party." There was no mistaking on whose side most Congress MPs were.

Mrs Gandhi sent a six-page letter to the members of the AICC the same day. It said: "I do not want a split in our great national organisation, which has to fulfil its promises by building a new society." But she wanted unity on principles and methods of work. To spout socialism and secularism on public platforms but to be associated in the minds of people with those who opposed these objectives was no service to the Congress. She said arrogant use of authority by the bosses had made some party members resign or retire from active work. It also discouraged fresh streams of young workers from flowing into the party. The tendency to acquire factional control of the organisation had recently become more intense. This was linked with a desire to control the direction of government policy and economic life in line with the narrow purposes and interests of small elite groups.

Mrs Gandhi said that "outside the narrow confines of our party great and turbulent changes are taking place in the minds and hearts

of our people. There are new trends of thought. There are new aspirations. And there are new tensions apart from other older tensions.
Political consciousness has matured and deepened among the masses,
and in this process many ideas, some old and some new, are being
canvassed, and a kind of crystallisation has been steadily taking
place.

"Faced with this change in the national political environment,
our party has been in danger of losing its orientation—it has been
trying to cope with the situation by a ritualistic repetition of the
formal positions of the past without making fresh assessment of the
needs of the present and the future in accordance with its own living
revolutionary tradition.

"There is loss of confidence in ourselves and in the destiny both
of our country and our party. There is a tendency to be influenced
by the forces of reaction, revivalism, and vested interests.

"In this situation, it is necessary for the Congress to recognise
frankly that it no longer commands in full the loyalty and emotions
of the nation as it did in the past. It must also recognise that it cannot
discharge the role of leadership unless it redefines its position sharply
in relation to the competing points of view in the country—and it
can serve as an effective instrument of the national purpose only
if it revitalises its membership and its methods of functioning."

The break was completed on November 22 and 23 when the
Requisition Congress held its session in New Delhi. Subramaniam
presided. Out of 801 members of the undivided AICC, about 495
attended, proof, if any was necessary, that Mrs Gandhi commanded
the loyalty of the majority of Congressmen. The committee removed
Nijalingappa from the presidency, elected Subramaniam in his place
temporarily—Jagjivan Ram succeeded him in a few weeks—and
picked ten members for inclusion in the reconstituted Working Committee. All of them belonged to the old committee.

To sentimentalists among the old school of pre-independence
politicians the split in the Congress Party was synonymous with the
end of the world. Donning sackcloth and ashes and rending the air
with their wails, they blamed Mrs Gandhi for wrecking the party
which was the banner-bearer of Indian nationalism. These folk were
to be pitied because they had no historical perspective. They failed
to see that Mrs Gandhi was fulfilling a historic task. She was trying
to retool the Congress ideologically and organisationally to cope

with the democratic tasks confronting it and the nation. She was responding positively and constructively to the politics of protest first manifested in the 1967 elections.

The party as a whole was incapable of changing its economic and social outlook without a purge of its leaders in the states. They were too closely meshed with big business and the rich farmers to be able to generate enthusiasm in either themselves or their rank and file for democratising the Indian economy. They talked socialism but made no effort to take the nation towards it. The first requirement of a forward-looking socio-economic programme for India was fair distribution of land by limiting individual holdings legally and implementing the law effectively. The second was developing small and cottage industries in towns and villages by curbing the expansion of the capital-intensive sector, which was siphoning off most of the scarce resources of the community for its own needs.

The tieup between the state bosses and these elitist economic and social groups had been the main source of Congress political strength in the past. They provided the money to grease the Congress machine, especially in elections. So long as the small farmer and agricultural labourer could be dragooned into voting as the big farmer wanted, the Congress faced no problems in the countryside. But the burgeoning technological revolution in agriculture had changed the power structure in the village. The submerged layers of the rural population wanted to share in the fruits of this revolution. They saw in it a way of escaping from the bondage to which they have been subjected by the privileged in the village and their political allies in the Congress.

The troubles of the party began when these havenots began to do their own political thinking. The Congress could not, as the 1967 elections showed, hope to retain its political predominance without a sharp leftward slant in its sympathies and programmes of rural development. But it was too much to expect men who had prospered for more than 20 years on the support of the rich farmer to shift their social base in the village even if they realised the vital need for this. This switch could be effected only by a thorough shakeup of the party leadership, and at the same time democratising the party at the grassroots by turning more to the small farmer and landless labourer.

A change of this drastic nature could not be carried out from below because the state leaders had driven out almost all the independent-minded and politically courageous activists who could have taken the party in this direction. The party was packed with yesmen who could be depended upon to say and do as the bosses wished. These bogus members, by sheer numbers, smothered the small voice of protest on the rare occasions when it was heard. A change of state leaders could thus be brought about only from the top, through the party president and his Working Committee. The lower one travel-led down the party pyramid, the greater one discovered was the stranglehold of the bosses. Tammany Hall had nothing to teach these men in the art of machine politics and manipulation of people.

In refusing to accept Mrs Gandhi's new look in party policy and clinging, limpetlike, to the presidency, Nijalingappa was defending the vested rights of the state leaders who belonged to the Syndicate. Mrs Gandhi's proposals would, if implemented, undermine their autocratic grip on the machine. The crisis in the party could be resol-ved either by Mrs Gandhi surrendering to Nijalingappa or forcing a split, or by Nijalingappa's compromising with her. Her surrender would have been disastrous for the country as it would have strength-ened the Marxists and the Naxalites on the left. Nijalingappa's would have brightened the prospects of the Jana Sangh and Swatantra on the right, for the continuance of the conservative bosses in the party would have sabotaged Mrs Gandhi's efforts to give a leftward turn to its policies.

The split in the Congress and Mrs Gandhi's success in carrying much the larger part of the party with her was not the end of the war. It was only the end of the first stage. Mrs Gandhi's big tasks lay ahead. Long years of bossism had enervated the party. It had lost touch with the havenots in village and town who formed nine-tenths of the population. It was not enough to draw up an impres-sive-looking programme of social and economic reform. The party had to be restructured to be able to convince people who had lost faith in Congress promises that it meant business this time.

It was necessary to change the governmental bureaucracy to make it more receptive to the needs of the people instead of functioning as the state organ of elite interests. Most of the bosses had opted out of Mrs Gandhi's party, but a good number of them still remained. They too would one day have to be pushed out, for they had stuck

by Mrs Gandhi not because of their fervent belief in the rightness
of her cause but to ensure their own continuance in power. Men
of this kind were to be found in her cabinet as well as in the state
governments. The purge would have to go on until all these focal
points of infection were dispersed.

The struggle for democratising Congress policy and organisation
marked a turning-point in the party's history. It was equally a turning-point in the life of the nation, for the ripples of change did not
stop within the walls of the party but would soon engulf all the other
parties in India. The entire political process was to be radicalised
in a manner nobody dreamt of when Mrs Gandhi sent her stray
thoughts to the Working Committee in Bangalore four months before the split became a physical fact.

The story of this very significant development in Indian politics
after independence would not be complete without a look at how
the people on the other side of the fence from Mrs Gandhi viewed
her actions in this period. Let us turn to *The Split in the Indian National Congress,* written by that "voracious reader" Atulya Ghosh.
The introduction is by Nijalingappa, and it is undoubtedly his own
penmanship to judge by its barrenness of content and verbal infeli-
cities. Nijalingappa says that in her first year as Prime Minister
Mrs Gandhi "generally gave no cause for complaint [!!!] and it
looked as though her attitude would be one of democratic approach
to national problems and that collective leadership would prevail.
But after the same people did their best to have her re-elected to
prime ministership in 1967, her attitude has been one of autocracy.
She has been more concerned about herself, her authority and her
ambition to become a dictator of this country. . . ."

Instead of giving the credit for bank nationalisation to the Congress
Party, "she tried to make the people believe that she was the only one
responsible for it. . . . Having done so, she wanted to become a hero
[!!!] and with this end in view had demonstrations arranged and
statements made by her as though she was the only one person who
could implement socialistic policies."

Further on in his introduction he says: "The way the Prime
Minister behaved at the time of the election of the President of the
Union was totally unbecoming of a person holding her position in
the party and the government. It is a sordid tale."

What has Ghosh to say about these events? He asserts that "ideology, programme, and policy have nothing to do with the split. The fact of the matter was that the Prime Minister had wanted to get rid of certain individuals and PCCs [Provincial Congress Committees] in order to strengthen her personal position in the country even if it weakened the organisation. Since her installation as Prime Minister she had been trying to be in closer contact with the Communist Party of India on the all-India political level.... She was convinced of the idea that if she were to retain her prime ministership she would have to organise what could be called a sort of united front at the Centre with the help of the CPI and other regional parties."

According to Ghosh, "it has now become evident that there was, in fact, a conspiracy to bring about a cleavage in the Congress Party, and every step taken by the PM was actually aimed at achieving this object." Commenting on Mrs Gandhi's call for a "conscience" vote in the presidential election, Ghosh says: "This stand of the PM is not only novel in a political party, but also involves certain basic principles of ethics, quite unconnected with political manipulations. ... Shri Giri's name was first sponsored by the Muslim League and the Akali Dal, and yet, in spite of that, the PM had no hesitancy in supporting him."

Nijalingappa and Ghosh may be forgiven for lacking a sense of literary style. But they cannot be exonerated for being devoid of a sense of history. Individuals are the agents of the unconscious historic process. Mrs Gandhi is such an agent, and she has attained this position because of her awareness of the changes that have been taking in the minds and attitudes of the Indian people. She succeeded in worsting the fumbling men of the Syndicate not because of manipulations and manoeuvrings but because she had history on her side. But they have one consolation. Fossilised reaction thrown out of power in other parts of the world speaks in the same tone as they do. The backroom boys who formed the Syndicate had been bosses so long that they fell into the error of believing that bossism would continue for ever and ever.

CHAPTER EIGHT

ELECTION TRIUMPH

FROM THE BANGALORE session of the AICC to the final rupture in November was a period of great physical and mental strain for Mrs Gandhi. In addition to directing the running battle with the Syndicate, she had taken over finance when Desai quit in July. There was also the problem of giving the Congress Party a new look in policy and structure to present it to the nation as a democratic, progressive force capable of fulfilling the gigantic tasks of development. The strain showed when she presided over the first AICC meeting in New Delhi after the parting of the ways. Her voice was edgy when she delivered the opening address. At one point, while describing how the Nijlaingappa group had tried to expel her from the party, she broke down and wept into the microphone.

What struck me about the session as I sat in the packed press gallery in the temporary conference hall set up in the grounds of Constitution House was the businesslike manner in which the proceedings were conducted. This was strikingly different from the previous Congress gatherings I had attended. Those looked more like an annual district cattle show than a serious political meet of India's ruling party. This same *mela* (fair) atmosphere was evident at the Nijalingappa faction's rival session at Gandhinagar, the new capital of Gujarat State, in December. Amid heat and clouds of dust raised by hundreds of motor vehicles on a treeless plain, the delegates sprawled on mattresses laid on the ground in a tent and played with their toes while speaker after speaker crucified Mrs Gandhi with words.

Mrs Gandhi had two important aims at the New Delhi session. One was to establish continuity with the old undivided Congress in whose fortunes her family had played a considerable part. The other was to prove to doubting observers that the new Congress she was intent on building was genuinely committed to socio-economic change, about which the boss-ridden organisation had talked

much but done little. To prove the first she had veterans like Govind
Das and T.T. Krishnamachari take a prominent part in the proceedings. Govind Das had an unbroken parliamentary record going back
to the 1920s and was known for his fervour in expelling English
from India and banning cow slaughter totally. He created a problem
when he refused to read in English the motion he had been asked
to propose for the removal of Nijalingappa from the party presidency. For a few seconds the large audience heard angry mutterings
between Mrs Gandhi and him over the microphone.

Krishnamachari was a businessman of Madras who had proved
India's most competent Finance Minister under Nehru and Shastri.
He unfurled the party flag before the session began and spoke on the
resolution for ousting Nijalingappa. His appearance on the platform
and Subramaniam's temporary appointment as president were designed to offset Kamaraj's claim that the entire Congress organisation
in Tamil Nadu was behind him.

Parliament opened on November 17, five days before the session.
For the first time in 22 years of independence, the Congress Government was in a minority at the Centre. About 55 Congress members
of the Lok Sabha had gone into opposition, but Mrs Gandhi had
nothing to fear. Earlier calculations had shown that she would have
an assured working majority with the support of regional parties
like the DMK in Tamil Nadu and the Akali Dal in Punjab and the
Bharatiya Kranti Dal (Indian Revolutionary Party, the spokesmen
of the rich farmers of North India) and some members who were
not attached to any party. The two Socialist groups could also be
depended upon to support her, and thus she could beat off attacks
from the right even without the votes of the pro-Moscow Communists and the Marxists. This was important because the Nijalingappa
faction and its rightwing allies were trying to make out that Mrs
Gandhi was a captive of the Communists and would sell India to
the Russians.

Her first test came on the opening day of Parliament's winter
session when she faced a motion of censure for sending an official
delegation to participate in the Islamic Conference at Rabat the
previous September. The debate started as a motion of no-confi-
dence and, with the government subjected to severe fire from several
sides, there was a chance that it might have been passed. This might
have impelled Mrs Gandhi to ask for dissolution of Parliament and

an early election. But not even those who were in a great hurry to topple her were prepared for elections before the prescribed date, early 1972. So the motion was watered down to one of adjournment, which she won easily. The weakness of Mrs Gandhi's rightist opponents had been bared, and she could now go ahead with the new policies she wanted to introduce knowing she had a shifting but certain majority in the Lok Sabha.

Some political wiseacres advised Mrs Gandhi to form a coalition government with some of the small opposition parties. The claims of the two Socialist parties were pressed by their sympathisers, while there were others who advocated bringing the Moscow-leaning CPI into the government. What these partisans did not realise was that a fundamental change was taking place in Indian politics. Decisions were no longer taken on the narrow parliamentary plane but on the much wider national plane. Mrs Gandhi was going over the the heads of the political parties, including her own, and appealing to the people. She had no need to broadbase her government by adding the representatives of other parties when she was creating a much more powerful and durable foundation for it among the dispossessed and the havenots and the underprivileged.

The main task facing the Congress Party that was reborn at the New Delhi session was to build an organisation reaching down to the grassroots. The party apparatus was still in the hands of the bosses even in those states where the government had declared itself for Mrs Gandhi. While her party controlled the Centre, the bosses were still very powerful in the state capitals. The Organisation Congress had governments of its own in two states, Gujarat and Mysore, and control of a sizable section of the Congress machine in five others—Bihar, Kerala, Tamil Nadu, Uttar Pradesh, and West Bengal.

What was more, there were many supporters of the Syndicate who had stayed on in the new Congress of Mrs Gandhi because they did not want to reveal their sympathy for the other side until they felt it was strong enough to challenge her a second time. Till then they would function as a fifth column, scuttling every attempt her committed followers made to implement the party programme.

The crux of any serious policy of social advance was land reform. Bank nationalisation was a dramatic step designed to remove the control of big business over the main channels of credit in the country. By itself it could not achieve much although it gave the government leverage in industry. Mrs Gandhi therefore turned her attention to land reform as a first priority. She called the Congress chief ministers to New Delhi and told them they must get a move on and implement the reform acts that had been inscribed in the statute book but remained mostly inoperative. They were told that if they wished to enjoy New Delhi's favour they must make a serious effort to bring about a juster distribution of land resources so that the small farmer and agricultural labourer could participate in the "green revolution" which was making the rich farmer richer and widening class differences in the Indian village.

Writing about the meeting, I said: "Land reform has to be coupled with the availability of easy credit to the petty farmer. The takeover of the banks has to be followed with more vigorous measures to raise their deposits and funnel a large part of them to the village.... Land reform combined with a flow of capital from the city to the village will provide a solid base for consolidating the political leadership of the new Congress Party. The question is whether the chief ministers who belong to it can carry out the task the Centre has assigned them. Will they continue, on the other hand, to drag their feet because of local pressures while the non-Congress governments push ahead with reforms?"

Land reforms and the provision of credit and other inputs to the small peasant had to be accompanied by a drive to end social discrimination on grounds of caste or religion. Land hunger and social disabilities went together, and one could not be ended without ending the other.

The meeting was not a success. The chief ministers made half-hearted promises which they promptly forgot on getting back to their home bases. If they were not members of the farm lobbies organised by the Indian equivalent of kulaks in the state capitals, they were pretty close to them, and it was inconceivable that they would take land reforms of the kind Mrs Gandhi proposed seriously. Two years later, such reforms are still a vague aspiration rather than a reality. It was obvious at the end of the meeting that any meaningful and integrated policy of reform to meet the urges of the small farmer and the landless would require a different set of leaders.

Could the Congress Party in its new avatar produce such leaders? The answer would appear to be no. To put more radical elements in charge of party affairs in the states seemed at that time to require a complete reconstruction of the socio-economic base of the party and the elimination of the existing power blocks in it. In the process Mrs Gandhi would have to part company with most of the men whose help she had sought to get control of the Congress Party at its apex. This action had to await the approach of the general election in March 1972. Even that surgery did not go deep enough to remove the canker in the party.

The 73rd plenary session of the Congress was held in Bombay late in December under the presidency of Jagjivan Ram, then Food and Agriculture Minister. He was the most influential leader of the 60 million or so untouchables in the country. He was therefore an asset to Mrs Gandhi in this respect, but he was a liability in others. The opposition had found him a weapon to embarrass her. Questions in Parliament, said to have been inspired by former Finance Minister Desai, elicited the information that Jagjivan Ram had not filed income-tax returns for ten years. Asked at a meeting at the Press Club of India, New Delhi, about this matter, Mrs Gandhi ascribed it to "forgetfulness." Jagjivan Ram settled his accounts soon after, without paying any of the penalties an ordinary citizen would have had to pay for such a lapse of memory.

The Bombay Congress confirmed the evidence of the earlier session in New Delhi that the bulk of the party was behind Mrs Gandhi. About 500 members of the old AICC attended. The delegates endorsed fully the 10-point programme they had approved in 1966 and told her to go right ahead in fulfilling it. They emphasised the need to implement speedily five points—a limit on holdings of urban property; restoring to Parliament the authority to amend the section of the Constitution on fundamental rights which the Supreme Court of India had vetoed; funnelling key imports through state-owned commercial undertakings; curbs on monopolies and restrictive business practices; and priority to agriculture in framing national plans for development and fiscal policy.

In an interview on the role of the public sector, Mrs Gandhi outlined her industrial development policy. She said a mixed economy, part public and part private sector, was viable and could be the main path leading to a socialistic society. At the moment the public sector had a prominent position in the national economy in name but not in fact. It would be given that position in fact

immediately. Since the available capital resources of the nation
were limited, public-sector investment would be most suitable in
areas where social returns were highest. She did not propose to
limit the private sector if it functioned "as it should function, realising its own limitations, realising the public compulsions."

She said: "In the circumstances here in India it would be difficult to change entirely and suddenly what we have been committed
to. We have been committed to the concept of a mixed economy.
Within that, there is considerable room for movement." She and
her party believed in remaining centrists—but left of centre. She
drew a sharp line demarcating the objectives of the two sectors.
The private sector worked for profit in terms of money. The
objective of the public sector was profit in social terms.

This did not mean, however, that a money profit was without
honour in the public sector instead of escalating losses. But such
profits were not the main purpose of creating the public sector.
Its results were to be measured in terms of social gain, but at the
same time it had to be operated in a rational, scientific manner
to avoid recurring losses and to pay back to the state the investment
made in it from the national pool of capital. Further, public-sector
undertakings must not only provide the capital needed for their
own expansion but also create a surplus for investment in fresh
ventures.

Mrs Gandhi presented her first budget to the Lok Sabha on February 28. She declared in her introductory speech that the object
of the government's fiscal policies was growth with stability, with
due regard for the welfare of the weaker sections of the community—
the small farmer, the landless agricultural worker, the petty artisan,
untouchables, and tribes living in economically backward areas.
Providing adequate opportunities for gainful work was a necessary
component of the development strategy of a poor country. She
said: "It is generally accepted that social, economic, and political
stability is not possible without the growth of productive forces
and the augmentation of national wealth. Also, that such growth
and increase in wealth cannot be sustained without due regard
to the welfare of the weaker sections of the community.

"Therefore, it is necessary to devise policies which reconcile the
imperatives of growth with concern for the well-being of the needy
and the poor. Measures have to be devised which, while providing

welfare, also add momentum to productive forces. Any severance of the vital link between the needs of growth and of distributive justice will produce stagnation or instability. Both must be avoided.

"The provision of adequate employment opportunities is not just a welfare measure. It is a necessary part of the strategy of development in a poor country which can ill afford to keep any resources unutilised or underutilised. Greater attention to dry farming areas is not merely to avoid inequalities in rural areas. It is also an essential part of any programme to achieve sustained increase in agricultural production.

"Encouragement to small enterprises and to new entrepreneurs is vital to build up managerial and entrepreneurial talent, which is all too scarce today. Without some restraint on urban values and individual ownership of urban property, we cannot adequately develop housing and other amenities necessary to wrest the maximum benefit from the vast productive investments already made in our overcrowded towns and cities. The weaker sections of society are also the greatest source of potential strength. We cannot provide for all the urgent needs of society with our limited resources. But a balance has to be struck between outlays which may be immediately productive and those which are essential to create and sustain a social and political framework which is conducive to growth in the long run."

Here in brief was Indira Gandhi's economic philosophy, permeated with a strong desire for social justice. This was to be the guiding motif of the new Congress. This was the answer to the jitterbugs and detractors who were crying out that she was leading the nation to totalitarian communism. To anybody who could understand what she said in her budget speech, it should have been clear that her aim was to create a society in which the glaring economic and social inequalities endemic in India would be removed by a gradual process of reform. Mrs Gandhi was much closer to Lord Beveridge and the Fabian Socialists of Britain than to Marx and Lenin.

Inspired reports began appearing in the foreign press that democracy was withering away in India. They said economic growth had halted, and the wrangling in the ramshackle coalition governments in various states, coupled with paralysis at the Centre, was dragging the country towards anarchy. Speculation about the likely entry of the armed forces into what had until then been the close preserve of the politicians increased. There seemed to be a strong body of opinion which believed Mrs Gandhi could not last long as Prime Minister as her government was shaky, and a military dictatorship was the only way to prevent chaos and spreading violence of the Naxalite type.

The prospect of India abandoning democratic ways and coming under the army was causing much bother in Western capitals which found no difficulty in accepting a military dictator in Pakistan. Mrs Gandhi was interviewed on this topic by a correspondent of *US World and News Report*. She said India was too big a country for the army to seize power. The Indian people were too politically conscious to give up their democratic prerogative of choosing the kind of government they wanted.

Not only had democracy taken firm and deep roots in India but Indians had "examples of military rule close by which should be a warning." She did not think that parliamentary democracy was seriously threatened by the flareup of violence in many states. All Indian political parties were undergoing "some kind of disruptive division," she said, adding that this was "a healthy sign."

Mrs Gandhi told the correspondent: "People have joined parties without too much thought. The new developments will bring us all to greater realism, greater appreciation of the need for national unity, cooperation between states and the people of India." She reassured her interviewer on another point which was troubling many Americans greatly. This was the fear that India was going communist and would nationalise its economy completely. She told him: "Our plans do not call for socialising the entire economy or even the greater part of it. We do want the commanding heights of the economy to be in state hands—basic industries, defence industries and, to a large extent, import trade. This is essential for India.

"We seek means of easing political and social tensions . . . these means are to some extent economic and involve providing the Central Government with economic powers through socialisation. We do not intend to stifle the private sector—far from it. We are very much aware of the value of enlightened private initiative." The United States had helped India much, and "we are grateful for the help." She might have added that gratitude did not mean abdicating the right to take her own decisions on domestic and international affairs and to disagree with Washington, loudly and strongly, if necessary, when the occasion demanded.

Mrs Gandhi demonstrated her pragmatic and flexible approach to economic policy in a parliamentary debate on the Fourth Five-year Plan in August 1970. The plan should have come into operation in April 1967, but had been put off because of the unsettled economic conditions resulting from widespread drought in 1965 and 1966. Its start was postponed till April 1969, but more than one year after that date it had not received Parliament's assent.

In the prevailing economic conditions, Mrs Gandhi said in the Rajya Sabha, big business houses would be permitted to expand their operations in the interest of increasing industrial production and stepping up the rate of overall economic growth. Her government was committed to ensuring equitable distribution of income and wealth, but this could not be done overnight without seriously jolting the economy. (Under the existing system of production and distribution, greater inequalities seemed inescapable before a juster social order could be brought into existence. Similarly, to become economically selfreliant, one of the chief aims of the Fourth Plan, India would have first to borrow more abroad to meet the foreign exchange requirements of the plan.)

At this time the Socialists and the Communists had launched a land-grab movement aimed at taking away the surplus land of big farmers and giving it to the landless. This action was a protest against the unwillingness of the state governments to respond to Mrs Gandhi's urgings that they implement agrarian reforms without delay. One of the targets of Socialist attack was a piece of land, four acres in area, on the outskirts of Delhi belonging to the Prime Minister.

In her speech on the plan in the Rajya Sabha she said the grab movement was based partly on hatred and envy and partly on acquisitiveness. These motives could not lead to social justice. She had no time for people who claimed that the movement was modelled on the teaching and practice of Mahatma Gandhi. He would never have condoned forcible takeover of land when there was a possibility of peaceful reforms. Persuasion and peaceful means were the correct methods to be employed in a democracy, not the "big stick."

August and September 1970 were crucial months. They saw a bid by the government to abolish the privy purses and privileges of the former rulers of "native states" in preindependence India. As a reward for agreeing to merge their territories ranging from Kashmir and Hyderabad, which were larger than many countries in Europe, to petty principalities of a few square miles, the princes were assured of special treatment under covenants and treaties of accession which the Nehru Government signed with them.

They were given purses ranging from several million rupees to a few hundreds yearly, and a number of rights which made them a very privileged elite group in a country which was pledged to equality and fair shares for all. On the death of the original rulers, these rights passed on to their heirs. Thus this parasitic outgrowth of colonialism—most of these princes and princelings were British creations—appeared as though it would continue to burden the Indian nation for several generations.

India became a sovereign, democratic republic within the Commonwealth of Nations on January 26, 1950. Under the new republican Constitution approved by the Constituent Assembly on November 26, 1949, all Indian citizens were promised: social, economic, and political justice; liberty of thought, expression, belief, faith, and worship; equality of status and of opportunity. The rulers of the nation were also pledged to promote fraternity, assuring the dignity of the individual and the unity of the nation. But the princes continued to be more equal than other citizens of the new republic. Their privy purses, exempted from income tax, were guaranteed by the Constitution, and so were their privileges and dignities, including gun salutes and importing goods without paying duty.

Mrs Gandhi decided that these anachronisms had to be removed. They were incongruous in a democratic setup in which all men and women were supposed to be on a level before the law. A bill to amend the Constitution for the 24th time (between 1950 and the end of 1971 there were 27 amendments, of which ten were in the last six years) was introduced in the Lok Sabha. Before it was voted on, Mrs Gandhi told the house: "If we do not take this step, we shall be swept aside." While abolishing purses and privileges might not solve the problem of poverty, unemployment or any other problem facing India's millions, it would be a step in the direction the country "wants to go, and will go in spite of anybody. The Constitution-makers could not foresee all eventualities. We must make the Constitution serve the aspirations and the needs of the people."

The bill went through the Lok Sabha with the two-thirds majority required to alter the Constitution. The Socialist and Communist factions voted with the government, as did regional parties like the DMK. Members belonging to the Organisation Congress opposed it, thus ratifying the death wish of their leaders. Hailed throughout the country except by the upholders of the old order, the bill ran into difficulties in the upper house. It was lost by a fraction of a vote less than that needed for its passage. This was in mid-December.

After the government's failure in the Rajya Sabha, President Giri issued an order withdrawing recognition of the special status the former rulers had been given under the Constitution. Their privy purses were also stopped. Some aggrieved princelings went to the Supreme Court complaining against the order. The court upheld them, saying the order was bad in law. This was the immediate reason for Mrs Gandhi's decision to seek a popular mandate.

The cabinet held an emergency meeting on the evening of December 27. After consulting her colleagues, Mrs Gandhi drove to Rashtrapati Bhavan and asked President Giri to dissolve Parliament—more than a year before its term ended—and hold fresh elections. This was the first time since Parliament was born out of the old Legislative Assembly in 1950 that a snap election was being held. The presidential communique issued the same evening said the Prime Minister had advised dissolution of the Lok Sabha to enable the government to seek a fresh mandate "to effectively implement its socialist and secular programmes and policies." The President called upon Mrs Gandhi to continue in office as head of a caretaker government.

Broadcasting to the nation later the same night, Mrs Gandhi hoped the fourth Lok Sabha would meet well before the financial year ended on March 31, 1971, indicating the possibility that elections would be held about two months after the third was dissolved. In a calm, measured voice she said: "There comes a time in the life of a nation when the government of the day has to take an unusual step to cut through difficulties in order to solve the pressing problems with which the country is beset.

"The present is such a time. Therefore, on the advice of Council of Ministers, the President has dissolved the Lok Sabha before its full term. In a parliamentary democracy this is not unusual, but in India it has happened for the first time."

Why was she taking this unusual step? "It is because we are not merely concerned with remaining in power but with using that power to ensure a better life to the vast majority of our people and to satisfy their aspirations for a just social order. In the present situation, we feel we cannot go ahead with our proclaimed programme and keep our pledges to our people."

She conceded that after the split in the Congress in November 1969 the government had lost its status as a party with an absolute majority in the Lok Sabha. But she maintained that it commanded majority support in the house and thus retained its confidence. She was sure most of the people were behind her government and accused "vested interests" of exploiting the country's economic problems. In these circumstances, the government had decided to accept their challenge. She said: "Power in a democracy resides with the people. That is why we have decided to go to our people and to seek a fresh mandate from them. . . . The old year is ending. I wish you a year of renewed hope and common endeavour to realise the great goals which we have set for ourselves."

The announcement of fresh elections ahead of time was the signal for the Jeremiahs in India and abroad to raise their voices in lamentation, some of them with secret glee. Mrs Gandhi had already destroyed the Congress Party by splitting it. Now she was trying to destroy Indian democracy, and she would end up by destroying the nation, they said. That was what came of entrusting the management of the country to a woman, even if she happened to be Nehru's daughter.

If these attacks upset Mrs Gandhi, she did not reveal her perturbation in public. Her fighting spirit was up, and the more critics sniped at her the stronger was her determination to win the elections. Her confidence stemmed from her unshakable belief in the good sense of the people, the little people in the villages and towns who were neglected and spurned by selfseeking politicians who had no use for them except at election time. They would vote her back to power because they recognised only her as their leader, and they had implicit faith in her promises to give them a better deal.

She launched her party's election campaign at a press conference in New Delhi on December 29. At it she bombarded the special

interests and business groups which were withholding fresh investment in industry because they wanted the government to change
its economic policies. When—not if—her party was returned to
power, she promised to introduce more constitutional amendments
to promote the interests of the many against those of the few. Her
party did not want "to take away the right to hold and enjoy property," but she suggested that it might alter the Constitution so
that property-holding would not be treated as a fundamental right.

She said that her party was not against any group or section of
society. But in a country like India, with great disparities of wealth
and wellbeing, it would be impossible to maintain social stability
unless the gulf between the haves and havenots was narrowed. This
was not a task that could be accomplished overnight. "If we can
show we are moving towards greater equality, our people will be
patient." She denied deteriorating economic conditions had forced
her to an early poll and claimed that the economy was in "far better
shape" than before.

The World Bank endorsed her view. A report prepared by a team
of experts which visited India to study its development said that
the country ended the 1960s "with a favourable and extended
period of economic improvement," with national income rising
by 5 per cent in real terms in 1969-70. The economy had picked up
from 1967 after two years of drought, industrial recession, and
inflation. "Promising gains were at last made in introducing new
agricultural technology and in raising the volume of grain produced.
The foundation of a sound population control programme was
laid and industrial output and exports moved up.

"The upswing in the dominant rural sector had a favourable
impact throughout the economy," the report said. Industrial advance
was somewhat uneven, with additional output of 6 to 7 per cent in
each of the last two years, and with an increase in the export of
manufactures in response to official incentives and goading. "The
other relevant development indicators that go beyond the gross
measures of economic growth show that a good deal of progress
has been made in India during the past two decades. India has
created a large and complex industrial structure; laid the foundations for accelerated agricultural growth; developed her transport
network and progressed in the fields of education and public health."

As in 1967, Mrs Gandhi shouldered almost the whole burden

of the election campaign of the Congress Party. But this time her responsibility was even heavier. Not only was she the only leader of the party with a national standing but also the only one the new wave of voters—the most submerged layers of rural society who had often been terrorised into keeping away from the polling booth at previous elections, and young people of the first generation born after independence—would listen to. They wanted only her to spell out to them the new deal she had prepared for the nation.

One of the most significant points about this election was the attraction the Congress had for youth. Those who were too young to vote busied themselves canvassing for party candidates and organising cheer squads at mass rallies where Mrs Gandhi spoke. They made up for the deficiencies of the party organisation at the state and district level.

Four states were holding elections to their legislatures at the same time. These were Tamil Nadu, Orissa, West Bengal, and Nagaland. The Congress refused to form electoral alliances with any party on a national basis, but was ready to join hands with likeminded parties in states where its prospects were not considered bright enough to ensure victory on its own. It made alliances with the Communist Party of India in Tamil Nadu, Bihar, Uttar Pradesh, and West Bengal, the DMK in Tamil Nadu, and the Muslim League and the Bangla Congress in West Bengal.

Four opposition parties—the Nijalingappa Congress, the Jana Sangh, Swatantra, and the Samyukta (United) Socialist Party—formed a similar alliance with the sole object of overthrowing Mrs Gandhi. But they could not reach a satisfactory understanding on apportioning constituencies among themselves, with the result that they fielded 543 candidates. The Congress, on the other hand, put up only 442 of its own men, leaving 76 to its allies. Of the Congress candidates, 257 had not sat in Parliament before. More than half the candidates were under 40. The only other party with pretensions to bigness, on a national scale, the Communist Party of India (Marxist), was on its own except in West Bengal, where it had the support of two or three splinter parties.

The Congress election manifesto was a "12-point programme for progress." It asked the nation for a clear mandate to "continue the advance to socialism through the democratic process and devise an administrative system capable of speedy implementation."

It committed the party to "defend secularism and safeguard the interests of the minorities and the weaker sections of the community, particularly the scheduled castes, scheduled tribes, and the backward sections so that they may attain 'equality of status and opportunity and fraternity, assuring the dignity of the individual'."

The party promised the farmer that it would "accelerate efforts to provide basic requirements to our people to develop a dynamic programme of agricultural development by the application of science and technology and thereby usher in a new phase of rural prosperity which will improve the condition of small farmers, in dry areas, the landless, artisans and others. . . ." The role of the public sector was to be enlarged and its performance improved, the private sector was to be encouraged to play its proper role in the economy, while concentration of economic power and wealth was to be curbed. To fulfil these and other pledges the manifesto contained, the Constitution would be amended "as may be necessary."

Mrs Gandhi spent 41 of the 52 days between January 13 and March 5 on the campaign trail. She was in New Delhi for just three days in February. She covered 30,000 miles in this period by airplane and helicopter, 3,000 by car, jeep, and train. She addressed 252 scheduled meetings, including 13 in her constituency, Rae Bareli. The number of unscheduled meetings she addressed at wayside halts was 157. Other highlights of this fantastic performance were:

Attendance at scheduled meetings	13 million
Attendance at wayside meetings	7 million
Average meetings daily	10 scheduled and 5 wayside
Average highest and lowest attendance	200,000 and 50,000
Largest number of meetings in one day	14
Files from New Delhi attended to daily	30
Telephone calls attended to personally	30
Individual interviews	20
Meetings with groups and deputations	5
Working hours	18
Sleep and rest	4 to 5 hours
Meetings cancelled because of indisposition or fatigue	0

A memorable incident in this whirlwind campaign which took her to 15 states and three Union territories was the forcelanding on the afternoon of March 1 of the Air Force plane she was travelling in at an airstrip at Jaykaypur, between Bhubaneswar and Jeypore in Orissa. Mrs Gandhi was talking with Mrs Nandini Satpathy, who was Deputy Minister of Information and Broadcasting, about the cancellation of a meeting at Jaykaypur because the landing strip was not fit for use. Mrs Satpathy suggested that the aircraft circle the airstrip so that the thousands who had gathered to welcome the Prime Minister would not be disappointed. The plane was going round when the pilot, Wing Commander V. Krishnamurthy, noticed oil running out of one engine, followed by smoke.

Swiftly, the strip was cleared of people and the plane landed at 3 o'clock. As soon as it touched ground, people rushed to it shouting "Indira Gandhi ki jai." They were unaware how narrowly disaster was averted. If the plane had not circled the landing place, it would have been in serious difficulties. Mrs Gandhi used the opportunity created by the enforced halt to address a meeting at Rayagada in Koraput district.

Meanwhile, newspaper pundits, "scientific" pollsters and astrologers in New Delhi were working overtime studying the electioneering of the various parties and forecasting the outcome of the poll. Teams of reporters traversed the country, interviewing anybody who would talk to them, and their political studies in depth took down to the village grassroots. No previous elections in India had received such extensive and at the same time minute coverage as this one. For not merely the fate of Mrs Gandhi and her party but also that of the democratic system of government depended on the result. Back in New Delhi, recovering in their airconditioned cubicles from their unaccustomed sojourn in the countryside, these gentlemen, with a few exceptions, concluded that the Congress should consider itself lucky if it got as many seats as it had in the dissolved Lok Sabha.

Inevitably, they saw a gloomy vista of political instability ahead, with Mrs Gandhi having to enter into a coalition with the Communists to stay in office. Reports from Tamil Nadu foretold a victory for the Organisation Congress, thanks to the indefatigable efforts of Kamaraj, who was trying hard to make a political comeback in his home state. From Calcutta came the news that the Marxists

had had their innings and would be fortunate to escape annihilation, though it was doubtful whether the Congress would be strong
enough to form a government on its own.

The results ran contrary to all these guesstimates, mainly based
on gossip. Mrs Gandhi's incredible exertions were very amply re-
warded. In the voting for the Lok Sabha between March 1 and 10,
more than 150 million voters turned up at the polls out of a total
272.7 million. In a landslide victory, it carried off 350 seats, about
120 more than it had after the split in November 1969. The three
main rightwing parties, the Nijalingappa Congress, the Jana Sangh,
and Swatantra, shrank considerably. The only party besides Mrs
Gandhi's which bettered its position in the Lok Sabha was the
CPI(M), which raised its strength to 24.

The DMK was returned to power in Tamil Nadu with a larger
majority in the state Legislative Assembly, while the Marxists just
edged the Congress out of first place in the West Bengal legislature.
But even with the support of their allies they were unable to show
an absolute majority and the Congress formed a coalition government which was, however, shortlived. West Bengal then returned
to President's rule until the next round of elections in March 1972.

What brought about Mrs Gandhi's sensational, and mostly
unexpected, victory when, according to the knowalls on the sidelines, she should have been fortunate to continue as Prime Minister.
It was positively not the Nehru charisma, which those who could
not find any better reason for her triumph grasped at in their puz-
zlement. The simple fact was that, while in 1967 the politically
literate voter—and political literacy did not necessarily go hand
in hand with education—had turned against the Congress because
it had failed to redeem its past pledges and given the opposition
parties a chance to run the affairs of state, he turned back to the
Congress in 1971.

He did so because the opposition parties had made an absolute
mess, showing a degree of opportunism and downright chicanery
without parallel in India's experience of parliamentary democracy
since 1947. The split in the Congress and the filtering out of the
conservative elements in it gave the voter confidence that Mrs
Gandhi would be able to carry out the radical reforms she had
constantly been advocating from the Bangalore AICC in July 1969.

The adverse vote for the Congress in 1967 was an unmistakable sign that the voter had matured and that he no longer, by and large, voted according to caste or religion or parochial pulls. His swing back to the Congress in 1971 was evidence of his further maturity. The democratic experiment the Congress undertook under Nehru when it introduced adult franchise under the new Constitution in 1950 was a success. The academic researchers who thought India was taking a big, and unjustified, gamble in entrusting its destinies to unlettered peasant masses who, in their opinion, couldn't tell chalk from cheese and would be swayed by emotional appeals and not by sound commonsense were proved as wrong as the newspaper columnists and editorial writers.

Mrs Gandhi had brought stability back to Indian politics. She had charted a new course, and it was now up to her to steer the nation through the economic and other hazards on its journey to a juster social order. At the end of these elections, most of the parties which claimed to be national in outlook and influence appeared irrelevant in relation to the socio-economic tasks that had to be undertaken. The only two national parties that were relevant were the Congress and CPI(M). At the regional level, there was only one credible survivor, the DMK. The Jana Sangh, which in 1967 appeared to pose a dynamic alternative to the Congress in the Hindi-speaking belt in northern and central India, seemed to have passed its zenith. It had lost much of its demagogic fire and was on the defensive. It was now trying to adjust itself to the new political forces sweeping the country and to cloak its obscurantist, reactionary face with the mask of modernism.

At the end of the 1971 elections Mrs Gandhi could chalk up two big achievements to her credit. She had won the first round in her bid to purge the Congress of the bosses who were propped up by the kulak and big business lobbies and had stifled inner-party democracy. She had followed this up by demonstrating the irrelevance of the existing party system to the development needs of the country. She had reversed the process of political polarisation which some observers thought was taking place, and the process of political atomisation which others saw in action, and had drawn the main currents of national politics back into a safe, middle-of-the-road channel.

The results of the 1971 elections opened up exciting possibilities. Confidence in the nation's future was reborn. The darkness which had descended with the Chinese invasion in 1962 and Nehru's death in 1964 had lifted. Mrs Gandhi's vision of a brave new India seemed as though it would take tangible shape in the not too distant future.

CHAPTER NINE

AGONY AND ECSTASY

BUT NEW FORCES intervened. Events beyond Mrs Gandhi's control exploded and occupied her attention and that of the Indian people for the rest of 1971. She was unanimously elected leader of the Congress Parliamentary Party on March 17. President Giri asked her the same day to form a new government. A 36-member Council of Ministers was sworn in on March 18. Seven cabinet ministers were dropped, while another did not seek re-election. One cabinet minister, five ministers of state, and 12 deputy ministers were added on May 2, raising the strength of the Council of Ministers to 55. Among the senior ministers Chavan, Fakhruddin Ali Ahmed, Jagjivan Ram, and Swaran Singh stayed on. Chavan was now in charge of finance, Ahmed replaced Jagjivan Ram in agriculture, and Swaran Singh handed over defence to Jagjivan Ram and moved over to foreign affairs. Mrs Gandhi kept home and information and broadcasting for herself.

Even when the elections were taking place, signs of danger were visible in East Pakistan, across the border from West Bengal. The Awami League of Sheikh Mujibur Rahman had won an overwhelming victory in the national assembly elections held there in December 1970, capturing 167 of the 169 seats allocated to the eastern province. As the leader of the majority party in the 131-member assembly, Mujib should have been asked to form a government for all Pakistan. But on March 1, President Yahya Khan postponed the inaugural session of the assembly fixed for March 3 in Dacca without consulting Mujib.

The military dictatorship in Islamabad had deliberately engineered a confrontation between the eastern and western wings of the state, thus giving it an excuse to stall the meeting of the assembly to frame a popular, democratic constitution that would restore civilian rule after 12 years of iron dictatorship. Yahya Khan's catspaw in this operation was Zulfiqar Ali Bhutto, who was to succeed him as President of Pakistan in December 1971 after Yahya had been booted out by his own generals, who were looking for a scapegoat for the crushing defeat their country had suffered in war with India.

Before this climax was reached and East Pakistan became the independent republic of Bangladesh, the 75 million Bengalis who lived there were to undergo horrors of a kind unheard of in the history of civilised man at the hands of the militarists of West Pakistan. As the members of the national assembly were gathering in Dacca for the opening, Bhutto went through the well-rehearsed motions of boycotting the session, thus giving Yahya Khan the excuse he wanted to call off the meeting. All preparations were made for a military crackdown on the Bengali nationalists if the Awami League reacted strongly, as it was expected to, against postponement of inaugurating the assembly.

Yahya Khan's announcement sparked an outburst of mass anger in Dacca, backed by similar demonstrations in other towns in the province, far beyond that expected by the military junta and its agents in the east. Crowds gathered at Paltan Maidan, the military parade ground in Dacca, and outside the hotel where the Working Committee of the Awami League was holding an emergency session. Mujib called for an immediate general strike and followed this up on March 3 with a call for a provincewide strike and an indefinite satyagraha of an intensity andt horoughness never seen in undivided India even at the height of the independence movement.

This was the beginning of a well-organised and mostly peaceful struggle involving millions of Bengalis against a military regime which was determined to quell it, no matter how much blood was shed in the process. Operation Butcher was entrusted to Lieutenant-General Tikka Khan, the new governor and military administrator of the province who had already earned a reputation for bloodthirstiness in putting down a revolt some years earlier in Baluchistan. While Pakistani troops and war material poured into the eastern province by air and sea, Yahya Khan played for time by conducting mock negotiations with Mujib in Dacca. When all was ready for the bloodletting on a mass scale, Yahya Khan flew back to Islamabad on the night of March 25, leaving the field clear for his cohorts to teach the obstreperous Bengali nationalists a lesson.

Popular reactions in India to the campaign of terror the Pakistani army, backed by armed gangs they had organised in the province, were very strong. Throughout the country as well as in Parliament demands were made that the Indian Government intervene to stop the butchery that was going on India's own borders of people who had until a few years ago been part of one nation. Mrs Gandhi was asked to act militarily if necessary to help the Bengalis achieve selfrule.

Not very long after the killings began, with systematic ruthlessness, of those suspected of belonging to the Awami League or of harbouring sympathies for the League, the first trickle of refugees began entering India. Soon the trickle turned to a flood. Thousands of terrified peasants and townsfolk crossed the border daily wherever they could find an escape outlet and sought refuge in India. At the peak the influx rose to about 50,000 a day.

It became obvious that there was method behind the onrush of refugees. The Pakistani militarists were aiming at disrupting the liberation movement in the east by making out that it was Indian-inspired and that the Hindus in the province were playing a subversive role to break up an Islamic state. Therefore, in the the name of Islam, the *kafirs* (unbelievers) must be exterminated or driven into Hindu India. The landed property and business concerns and other assets of the Hindus would go to loyal Muslims.

Thus the first waves of refugees were mainly Hindus, for whom staying in East Pakistan meant death by horrible means. When this game failed to split the nationalists and the guerilla operations began to trouble the occupying army and it seemed that the pacification of the rebellious province would take long, the guns and knives of the Pakistanis were turned against all Bengalis, no matter what their professed religion. The operation became genocide. Being a Bengali was sufficient reason to invite death. Apart from the three million to four million who were murdered in Bangladesh, around ten million were driven across the border into India.

India's involvement in the liberation struggle thus became a national policy issue instead of being only emotional. The Pakistanis were trying to solve the political problems they faced by pushing as many Bengalis as they could into India. When, as they hoped, the movement was quelled, they would not let the refugees return because they were "traitors" to Pakistan—and to Islam too—in seeking shelter in a non-Muslim country. For India, already over-burdened with millions of rural unemployed who were increasing daily, the permanent absorption of 10 million destitutes would have been economically crippling. It would set back planned development, and at the same time provide tinder in the highly explosive conditions caused by overpopulation and unemployment in the eastern region of the country.

This was indeed the aim of the Pakistani military junta. Thus India was sucked reluctantly into the war of liberation in Bangladesh. Its outcome became a matter of vital interest to this country and its government, for it seemed clear that the point of a negotiated settlement within the framework of Pakistan had been passed and only the creation of an independent, sovereign Bangladesh could ensure the safe return of the refugees.

Such a result served other, larger purposes too. The very existence of Indian democracy depended on a victory for the liberation movement over the border. With the restoration of military rule there and the economic strains imposed by the refugees over a long period, the seeds of unrest would find fertile soil. This would be the opportunity for religious and other sectarian forces within India to undo the democratic gains of Mrs Gandhi's great victory at the polls in March 1971. The Pakistani militarists were the best friends of right reaction in India, which was waiting for a chance to raise its battered head.

The resurgence of sectarianism in such circumstances could very well have led to the breakup of India, a contingency which the militarists in Islamabad and their foreign friends would have welcomed. The official climate in the capitals of many countries which claimed to be friendly to India was distinctly cold to appeals from New Delhi for international action to stop the bloodbath in Bangladesh. Their governments felt that India was meddling in what was Pakistan's internal affair, and they were ready to swallow the Pakistani charge that India was at the bottom of the Bengali demand for independence.

While this was undoubtedly false, Bengali independence was now of the utmost importance for India, for the reasons I have already mentioned as well as for the fact that the separation of Bangladesh from its colonial oppressors in the west would weaken the economic structure of that truncated state. This in turn would make it impossible to maintain the huge military machine that had been built up, primarily with American and Chinese aid, against India unless the foreign patrons of the generals in Islamabad converted the residual Pakistan into a garrison state almost solely dependent on them economically and militarily. With this constant threat removed, India could devote its undivided attention to the gigantic tasks of socio-economic development which were becoming more important daily.

At the start of the refugee wave, there was little awareness abroad of the immensity of the human tragedy that was being enacted in the eastern region of the subcontinent. When a few courageous Western newspapermen and cameramen revealed the depths of the misery and suffering of the refugees, the conscience of the world was stirred, but few governments took this seriously enough to help. The burden was carried almost alone by India, short of resources for its own people, in the first few months.

Once the relief operations got moving under the supervision of the Indian Ministry of Rehabilitation, the refugees were guaranteed adequate shelter, food, clothing, and medical attention. Most of them were probably better off than they had ever been in their village homes in Bangladesh, and they were certainly better off than their Indian neighbours in the villages surrounding the camps in which they were lodged.

I visited several camps at the height of the influx. I saw men, women, and children wounded by Pakistani shellfire on villages which were thought to be helping the Mukti Bahini, the guerilla army of the freedom movement, in Indian hospitals which were so overcrowded with refugee patients that sick Indians had to be turned away. I heard many of the refugees narrate their stories. With tears in their eyes they spoke of the kindness and care they had received in India. They all wanted to go back when Bangladesh became a reality, but they would never forget how they had been cared for in India. I also saw the singleminded devotion with which Indian district officials and doctors and nurses worked among the refugees, often well beyond their normal hours and ungrudgingly. The refugee relief operation was one of the greatest acts of humanity ever carried out to ease the plight of millions of people who shrank in fear at the mention of the terrible things they had seen done to others or had undergone themselves in their homeland.

India performed a job that would have strained the resources of the world's richest nations, inflicting in the process heavier tax burdens on its own people to pay the bill. The Indian people rallied behind Mrs Gandhi when she called on them to tighten their belts a few notches more to help those whose economic condition was not much worse than that of many of them. Meanwhile, other nations pledged to upholding democracy dragged their feet in succouring the helpless victims of the most ferocious military dictatorship in history.

When they offered aid—haltingly—later, they tried to hog the credit for rescuing the refugees from death while India's great effort was scarcely acknowledged. I met representatives of foreign governments and international relief agencies who had no good word for India, and made charges, unsubstantiated, that foreign supplies for the refugees were being diverted to aid Indians.

Yahya Khan exploited the latent anti-Indianism which was now surfacing in foreign capitals. He said India was preparing war against Pakistan, with the purpose of dismembering it. Many so-called friends of India believed this charge. The argument that Yahya Khan was imperilling democracy in India, the only big country in the developing world where the democratic parliamentary system had survived, fell on deaf ears.

Mrs Gandhi told Parliament on May 26: "We have heard much talk of democracy. The allies claimed that the Second World War was fought to save democracy. But when democracy is so flagrantly and so brutally being destroyed, we do not hear much comment, nor do we see the sort of spontaneous strong responses which the situation warrants. Could there be a greater or a clearer expression of democracy than the one we witnessed in the elections in Pakistan? . . .

"We are told by some countries that while they may disapprove of what is being done by the military rulers they cannot be a party to the disintegration of Pakistan. Is it suggested that we wish the disintegration of Pakistan? Have we not, as many members have pointed out, at every step tried not only for propriety in our relationship but also for friendship? If there is a struggle between the two parts of Pakistan, it is certainly not of our making but of the rulers of Pakistan. Is it anybody's contention that the methods being used today can achieve any integration or stability worth the name now or in the future?

"The question of secession is also raised.... This is distortion of facts. It is conveniently forgotten that the majority of Pakistan's people live in the eastern region. In a democratic system, the majority does have certain rights. They cannot be accused of secession if they assert those rights. However, if today there is such strong feeling amongst our people, it is not merely because the democratic rights and liberties of 75 million people are being crushed but because of the damaging effect which this cruel tragedy is having on our entire country economically, politically, and socially."

Mrs Gandhi ended: "It is a problem created by calculated genocide that is resulting not only in the murder of tens of thousands of men, women, and children but also forcing many more to seek refuge and shelter in India. It is a problem that threatens the peace and security of India and, indeed, of Southeast Asia. The world must intervene to see that peace and security is re-established and maintained."

Such statements of plain, unvarnished fact, although repeated often by Indian spokesmen in many world forums, did not impress people who were determined to believe what they thought suited their political interests. Big India was the aggressor, and poor little Pakistan its victim. Because India could not defeat the brave Pakistanis on the battlefield it was resorting to the devious way of subversion to undermine it. This refrain was to be heard with sickening sameness from many lips at diplomatic parties in New Delhi in those months of agony for the revolting Bengalis, and not only from diplomats of countries which were known to be hostile to India but also from the representatives of others whose cause India had championed in world forums over the years. It is an irony of history that the Chief Executive of the world's most powerful democracy should have espoused the cause of one of the most savage military tyrannies that struck with its mailed fist at a popular movement for freedom.

Some months later, after Pakistan warred against India, Mrs Gandhi wrote a statesmanlike letter to President Nixon to explain what his coldness to the legitimate struggle of the people of Bangladesh and unabashed support of Yahya Khan meant in terms of suffering to millions of people in the subcontinent. She said: "There are moments in history when brooding tragedy and its dark shadows can be lightened by recalling great moments of the past. One such great moment which has inspired millions of people to die for liberty was the Declaration of Independence by the United States of America.

"That declaration stated that whenever any form of government becomes destructive of man's inalienable rights to life, liberty, and pursuit of happiness, it was the right of the people to alter or abolish it. . . .

"This tragic war, which is continuing, could have been averted if, during the nine months prior to Pakistan's attack on us on December 3, the great leaders of the world had paid some attention to the fact of revolt, tried to see the reality of the situation and searched for a genuine basis for reconciliation. . . .

"War also could have been avoided if the power, influence and authority of all the states, and above all of the United States, had got Sheikh Mujibur Rahman (whom Yahya Khan held prisoner in West Pakistan) released. Instead, we were told that a civilian administration was being installed (in the east). Everyone knows that this civilian administration was a farce; today the farce has turned into a tragedy. . . .

"The fact of the matter is that the rulers of West Pakistan got away with the impression that they could do what they liked because no one, not even the United States, would choose to take a public position that while Pakistan's integrity was certainly sacrosanct, human rights, liberty were no less so and that there was a necessary interconnection between the inviolability of states and the contentment of their people."

Mrs Gandhi assured Nixon that India did not covet any territory of West Pakistan. India wanted lasting peace with its neighbour. She asked: "But will Pakistan give up its ceaseless and yet pointless agitation of the last 24 years over Kashmir? Are they willing to give up their hate campaign and posture of perpetual hostility towards India?"

This appeal to reason was lost on Nixon. Why did he, as well as the leaders of nations much nearer to India both geographically and in world outlook, refuse to see "the reality of the situation" as Mrs Gandhi asked them to? The reason was not that they did not see the truth. It was against their interest to accept it and act accordingly. The truth was that the breakup of Pakistan would bring about a radical change in the power balance on the Indian subcontinent, and ultimately in South and Southeast Asia. With Pakistan shrunk drastically and economically impotent, the balance which the United States and China had worked hard to achieve, and many other countries had come to accept as a fact of life, would be upset.

Without Pakistan to worry about militarily, India could devote all its energies to economic growth, and this would in the course of a few years raise it to the status of a big Asian power. Hence the strong dislike of Pakistan's disintegration, which had not been engineered by India, as Nixon professed to believe, but by the stupidity of the West Pakistan militarists. Pakistan had destroyed itself, and in the process changed the power balance in the subcontinent in India's favour. The civil war in Bangladesh and the war with India were the work of the military rulers in Islamabad and brought about their downfall. The natural answer to this problem by those who wanted to contain India was to rebuild Pakistan militarily, as China and the US are doing as fast as they can.

For the rest of 1971 Bangladesh and the confrontation with Pakistan, which seemed painfully inevitable as the days passed, occupied most of the attention of the Indian Government, Parliament, and public. Mrs Gandhi warned the Rajya Sabha on June 15 that "we will have to go through hell" to meet the challenge of developments in that unhappy territory whose people were ground under the jackboot of militarism.

The problems created for India by the upsurge on the other side of the border would "hurt us in many ways." But she had no doubt the nation would pull through the crisis if it was handled with courage, determination, and vigilance. India would have to pay a heavy price in financial as well as physical terms for befriending the heroic people of Bangladesh. But the price was worth paying because this was a "very important" cause.

Her government stood for a political settlement between the leaders of Bangladesh and the rulers of Pakistan. But it would never endorse a settlement "which meant the death" of the new Bengali-speaking nation that was coming into being. But the chances of a settlement were receding daily. A peaceful solution might have been possible in the early stages of the civil war if the big powers, as well as other nations with influence in Islamabad, had tried effectively to restrain the military junta.

India was not "begging" for help from abroad to cope with the flood of refugees. But it wanted other nations to share the burden because the refugees were not India's problem alone but of the international community as a whole. "We are going to do our very best for them," she said, even if this meant that "we have to go hungry." She felt the house would understand, as well as support, the need for sacrifice. "This is something we cannot avoid." The government had no intention of letting the refugees settle in India, but it would not push them back into Bangladesh "to be butchered."

As the resistance movement in Bangladesh became more effective and the stream of refugees continued unabated and Pakistan grew increasingly belligerent towards India, it became evident to observers in New Delhi that war would be thrust on India whether it wanted or not. Indeed, Pakistan had already started making war on India by driving large masses of refugees across the border, knowing that this would strain the Indian economy severely and have political repercussions which would add to the government's difficulties. With the Nixon Administration and China decidedly hostile to India, it was necessary to prepare for the worst. New Delhi had to make sure that in the event of a not unlikely attack by Pakistan, when the junta found that the tide was running against it in Bangladesh, it had a strong and willing friend to turn to in need.

This friend had to be a power big enough to cancel the advantage Pakistan enjoyed in winning the support of Peking and Washington. Moreover, India was virtually isolated on the issue of Bangladesh in the developing world, while the Western nations did not venture beyond expressions of sympathy for the refugees, backed with some—but not overgenerous—supplies for their relief.

The only nation which fitted the bill was the Soviet Union, which had stood by India over Kashmir in the United Nations Security Council whenever Pakistan raised the subject, helped build India's heavy industrial base and modernise its defence forces, and had promoted a rapid escalation of balanced trade between the two countries on the basis of the rupee. Moscow's interest in the Hindustan Peninsula had grown steadily from the time of the Tashkent Agreement, when it had initiated serious efforts to draw Pakistan away from close dependence on China and the US to a less aligned stance.

This had been interpreted in some circles in India not very friendly to Moscow as part of a sinister game to sell this country down the river. Stories, often emanating from American or Indian or other channels, magnified the arms supplies the Soviet Union was giving Pakistan. There was no doubt that from 1966 onwards there were people very keen on creating a rift between Moscow and New Delhi.

New Delhi's search for a powerful and reliable ally who could provide it with a sheet-anchor in the difficult and dangerous times that were now evidently ahead found a ready response from Moscow. The need was mutual. Moscow also needed a trusted friend among the developing nations in the face of Nixon's efforts to strike a deal with Peking at the expense of the Soviet Union.

The result was the Treaty of Peace, Friendship, and Cooperation, signed by Soviet Foreign Minister Andrei Gromyko and his Indian counterpart Swaran Singh in New Delhi on August 9, 1971. This marked a turning-point in India's foreign policy. While the 20-year pact could not be correctly termed a military alliance, it came pretty close to one since it implied mutual aid if either signatory was threatened militarily by a third nation. Article 9 of the treaty said: "In the event of either party being subjected to an attack or a threat thereof, the high contracting parties shall immediately enter into mutual consultations in order to remove such threat and to take appropriate effective measures to ensure peace and the security of their countries."

This article had immediate relevance to the ballooning threat of war from Pakistan. In such an event, US intervention on the side of Pakistan, either directly or more likely indirectly, could not be ruled out. Peking was also making ugly noises and accusing India of poking its nose into Pakistan's affairs, although it did not say a word against Sheikh Mujib or the freedom struggle in Bangladesh. What it might or might not do in the event of a third war between India and Pakistan was a matter of conjecture, but New Delhi could take no chances.

The treaty was the answer to India's problem. With the Soviet Union underwriting its security, the chances of American or Chinese intervention, or intervention by both powers, if war broke out on the subcontinent receded, but did not disappear. Should they intervene, they would have to be prepared to confront the Soviet Union since the treaty gave India the right to seek Moscow's help in precisely such a development. India could now go ahead with preparations to meet the impending Pakistani threat without too great concern about attacks from other quarters.

This was the first treaty of its kind India had made with any big power, and to that extent there was a significant shift in its foreign policy. This did not mean abandoning nonalignment but recognising the realities of Pakistan's threat to national security, aided and abetted by its close friends, and taking the necessary steps to meet it effectively. It was not a treaty directed against any other nation, but in the circumstances in which it was signed it fitted India's immediate needs. If India appeared to be aligned, this was due to the unfriendly attitude adopted by other nations working in league with Pakistan.

On India's part, it wished to be on good terms with China, Pakistan, and the United States and was not therefore aligning itself permanently with the Soviet Union. Those who were aligned against India would find India aligned against them, but this was not a matter of India's choosing. And it certainly did not want this state of affairs to continue. If alignment meant a rigid posture to be maintained over a given period, India was not aligned.

It regarded the alignment with the Soviet Union as a temporary phenomenon arising out of the hostility of two big powers and one of their client states. India would be aligned with the Soviet Union against them so long as this hostility continued, which might be for a long or short period. But India was not a willing party to this state of hostility. On the contrary, it wished its speedy end so that it could normalise its relations with all three countries.

Speaking from the ramparts of Red Fort in Delhi on the 24th anniversary of independence six days after the treaty was signed, Mrs Gandhi said the treaty did not mean the end of nonalignment as some critics thought. India would continue to follow this policy, as it was most beneficial to countries of the Third World. Evidence of this determination to stay nonaligned if permitted was available when she met newspapermen in Calcutta on September 1.

Mrs Gandhi said her government was taking "concrete steps" to establish normal relations with China, broken off nine years earlier. She refused to tell what these steps were, but added that she had written to Premier Chou-En-lai, and "our charge d'affaires in Peking is in constant touch." She appealed to newspapers "not to project anything in such a way as makes bilateral relations more difficult, whether it is China, USA, or some other country. Headlines create a lot of misunderstanding." These were not the words of somebody who was turning her back on nonalignment.

For a lucid exposition of the doctrine of nonalignment and the treaty of friendship one must turn to Jai Dev Sethi, reader in economics at Delhi University and former director of studies at the Indian Council of World Affairs, New Delhi. He draws a distinction between nonalignment as a policy and as a strategy, or what Nehru called "approach to foreign policy." A strategic approach implies the optimal use of national resources, expertise, diplomatic, and other techniques to achieve desired objectives in foreign policy, he wrote in an article published in *India Quarterly*, the Council's bulletin, in 1971.

This strategy emphasises independence of policy from the beginning, because this is the only choice for countries which have emerged from a long period of colonial rule to freedom after a prolonged struggle. Such countries are unlikely to surrender once again their independence in framing their policies and executing them. Since most nonaligned countries are militarily and economically weak, they have to depend on the international system represented by the UN or on the balance of power for their security. Like the strategy of alignment, this means buying time by maintaining the utmost independence of policy possible. This in turn involves keeping out of cold-war politics and employing this breathing-time to strengthen a nation's economic, and later military, sinews.

India is the only threshold power among the nonaligned, says Sethi, and nonalignment has special significance in relation to it. The most important attribute of nonaligned strategy is its utility in transforming a potential power into an actual one and removing external constraints on achieving this goal. If this assertion is correct, India's policy of nonalignment since Nehru first enunciated it in the late 1940s has paid golden dividends, for who will deny that India is on the verge of becoming a real power, indeed the only indigenous power, in the Indian Ocean region.

Sethi sets two aims in India's relations with other nations: opposing those nations which wish to undermine its objective of becoming an effective power; and cooperating with those which have no such desire. He notes: "It is quite possible, and India is not unaware of it, that small nonaligned countries in the region may oppose her power goal more than powers situated outside the region. Thus a natural conflict arises between one nonaligned country and another. The strategy of power thus does not exclude India having closer political or even military relations with one of the big powers. So far as the other middle powers are concerned, there is a natural affinity between them and a nonaligned, potential power like India. Paradoxically, this strategy aims at India ultimately getting out of the nonaligned group, for after India becomes a fullfledged power its continued membership of the nonaligned group becomes anathema."

The strategy of nonalignment is essentially an attempt to use all components of this posture in foreign policy to build up a nation's economic and military might so that it does not have to seek the protection of bigger nations. The treaty with the Soviet Union came when India's security was threatened and several external restraints were imposed on its efforts to become an independent power. Sethi says India can use the treaty as an umbrella while building up its own power with Soviet help. Such help will be forthcoming because Moscow is threatened with isolation as a result of the Peking-Washington understanding, and because Soviet power has overextended itself globally and need a strong ally in India.

This academic point of view is complemented by the pragmatic approach of Mrs Gandhi. Writing as a practical-minded statesman, she said in September 1971: "We do not want to be tied to any group or any country but are trying to stand squarely on our own feet. In foreign policy, our ideal and practical interests are the same since no government, however idealistic it may be, can afford to leave or neglect the practical interests of the country.

"We have believed, and we do believe now, that freedom, peace, and economic prosperity are all indivisible, and these are the fundamentals on which our policy, both inside and outside the country, is based. . . .

"The most dangerous change that has come over the world in recent times is a veiled neocolonialism, and the great difficulties arising from it are now confronting the developing nations. And we can face them not merely by idealism or sentimentalism but by very clear thinking and hardheaded analysis of the world situation." A nation could strengthen itself through alliances, but that would be a sort of borrowed strength which may deceive it into a feeling of complacency and lead it into certain dangerous consequences. "I think our security lies in strengthening the people and in being confident of ourselves," she wrote. "Conviction, courage and national pride are therefore the intangible elements in our foreign policy."

In an address to the AICC on October 9 at Simla, Mrs Gandhi referred to the treaty with the Soviet Union and said India was free to exercise such options as it wanted in the national interest without any restraint. This was evidently intended to counter newspaper comments that the treaty hobbled India's freedom of action in relation to Bangladesh. Although the government might consult other nations, and occasionally seek their advice, on vital issues, she said it would never give up its right to decide and act independently, as this would mean surrendering national sovereignty. The treaty defined certain mutual interests, but placed no restraints on India. Ultimately, India had to take foreign policy decisions on its own, keeping in mind its economic, social, and political interests.

Towards the end of October, Mrs Gandhi set out on a tour of Western Europe and the United States to inform the policy-makers of the countries in her itinerary that zero hour was approaching in the subcontinent and they should do something about it. Specifically, she told them that the Indian Government could not sit back and watch refugees pouring into the eastern states, thus creating unsettled conditions in this sensitive region as well as being a drag on the national economy. With Yahya Khan taking an increasingly aggressive attitude to India, the time was not far off when India might be compelled to take strong measures to protect its own security and integrity. The consequences of such action might be another armed confrontation with Pakistan.

Yahya Khan's plans were becoming clearer as the fighting between his troops and the freedom forces in Bangladesh became fiercer. He wanted a speedy solution in his own blustering, bullheaded military way, which meant crushing the liberation movement and returning Bangladesh to its colonial servitude. For this, contact between the freedom fighters and the neighbouring states of India had to be snapped. How did Yahya Khan propose to do this? By building up tension through a series of incidents on the border and giving his foreign friends a chance to tell the UN that India was acting aggressively and it was necessary to seal off the border by getting the UN to police it.

Once this was done, he thought he would be free to deal with the Bengali resistance as he pleased. China was now a member of the UN, and also had a permanent seat in the Security Council with the power of veto. It could be depended upon to back the Nixon Administration's manouevrings to pull its client Yahya Khan out of the hole into which he had plunged himself.

Mrs Gandhi was received and heard sympathetically in Bonn, London, Paris, and Vienna. She got the cold shoulder in Washington. Later, when fighting broke out between India and Pakistan after Yahya Khan's air force attacked air bases over a wide area in north-western India, Britain and France proved very helpful in the Security Council and General Assembly by abstaining from supporting their senior partner in the North Atlantic Treaty Organisation in its frantic efforts to save Yahya Khan from the doom that was coming to him.

As November drew to a close the dark shadows of war closed in over New Delhi. It was only a matter of days before Yahya Khan would strike in desperation, political observers felt. Four months earlier, Gen Kaul had said in his book, *Confrontation with Pakistan*, that to divert attention from the unsettled economic and political conditions in both wings of Pakistan Yahya might provoke war with India. But this would be a big gamble. If he lost, as was likely, it would be Pakistan's death, "Time is on India's side," Kaul said, "as it is a bigger and a more stable country with larger resources. So Pakistan must act now or never. But if it bites India alone, now or ever, [the] chances are that it will come to grief."

In his rare moments of sobriety, Yahya Khan must have known this. He was a shrewd operator, although he outsmarted himself over the Awami League's demand for autonomy and the restoration of democratic rights in East Pakistan. His military instinct must have told him that in a war on two fronts against India, without the direct intervention of his big brothers China and the US, he stood no chance of success. But such intervention seemed ruled out by the India-Soviet treaty.

What then led him to undertake an operation which, on the face of it, appeared a mad gamble entailing certain disaster? He could not have done so unless he had received assurances from his patrons that they would bail him out by invoking the authority of the UN against India. They probably banked on the Soviet Union not using its veto on India's behalf in the Security Council because it did not want a war on the subcontinent and the dismemberment of Pakistan, which seemed an inescapable consequence of the liberation of Bangladesh.

On the evening of December 3, Yahya Khan's air force made a pitifully feeble attempt to emulate the Israeli attack on Egyptian bases in June 1967: I had packed my bag and was leaving my house for Delhi airport. I was going to Calcutta, and from there to Bangladesh. Suddenly the air-raid sirens shrieked and the street lights went off. The civil defence authorities had announced a practice raid the next day, and my wife said they had probably advanced the date to take people by surprise. But I felt this was the real thing. A few minutes later my friend Sundar Dhingra phoned to say that sneak raids had taken place on several forward bases. The night before I had trunk-called a friend in Calcutta to say I would seek his hospitality while I was in transit to the border. He was surprised. "Why are you coming?" he asked. "We are expecting war on the fifth."

In the early hours of December 4, the Prime Minister broadcast to the nation. She said Pakistan had declared fullscale war on India. But this wanton and unprovoked aggression would be repelled decisively. A state of emergency had been declared and India was prepared for all eventualities. What was at stake was not merely India's territorial integrity but the basic ideals which had given strength to this country.

The next day was Saturday and Parliament was summoned specially to hear her statement on the war. She was leaving Calcutta for Delhi when news of the attack came. As soon as she got back, she consulted her cabinet and the leaders of the opposition parties. A truce was declared to political bickering and all parties pledged their support to the war effort. Mrs Gandhi said: "Our feeling is one of regret that Pakistan did not desist from the ultimate folly and sorrow that at a time when the greatest need of this subcontinent is development the peoples of India and Pakistan have been pushed into war. We could have lived as good neighbours, but the people of West Pakistan have never had a say in their destiny. In this grave hour our own dominant emotion is one of confidence and faith."

The Indian Government had repeatedly drawn the attention of the world to the annihilation of a whole people in Bangladesh by the military regime, which had committed "heinous crimes, unmatched for their vindictive ferocity," and whose actions also menaced India's security. Governments to which India had appealed for action to control the Pakistani militarists seemed "morally and politically paralysed." India's tradition was to stand "not with tyrants but with the oppressed. And so their anger has been turned upon us." She ended: "We have stood for peace, but peace itself has to be defended. We are fighting to safeguard our territorial integrity and national honour. Above all, we are fighting for the cause of human freedom."

Thirteen days after the war began, Yahya Khan's commander in Dacca, Lt-Gen A.A.K. Niazi, surrendered tamely with all his troops, to the deep chagrin of Yahya's many admirers among the foreign newsmen who had assembled in New Delhi to cover the war and confidently expected the Pakistanis to come out on top. The surrender was preceded by some exciting moments. A task force of the US 7th Fleet was reported to have passed through the Straits of Malacca and to be heading for the Bay of Bengal. Some Western newspapermen who talked as if they had inside information were certain a dramatic rescue of the Pakistani general and his men was in the offing. They were disappointed when Niazi chose to give in without a fight before the fleet could reach coastal waters and send helicopters to Dacca to rescue the beleaguered garrison, according to one version of the proposed operation I heard.

The scene in the Lok Sabha on the afternoon of December 16, when the Prime Minister announced the end of hostilities in Bangladesh, was unforgettable. At the end of her brief statement members jumped up and cheered as they had never done before. They were drunk with joy. Even the Speaker forgot momentarily his nonpartisan role and joined in the rejoicing.

Mrs Gandhi said the Indian forces had strict orders to treat Pakistani prisoners of war in accordance with the Geneva Convention and deal with all sections of the inhabitants of Bangladesh humanely. A foreign diplomat who was in Dacca at the time of the surrender and for some days after told me the behaviour of the Indian troops was a model to the soldiers of any other nation. He marvelled at their discipline and modest bearing. He had seen the advance of the victorious Allied forces into Germany at the end of the Second World War and could make a comparison.

Mrs Gandhi said the Indian objectives were limited to assisting "the gallant people of Bangladesh and their Mukti Bahini to liberate their country from the reign of terror and to resist aggression on our own land." Indian troops would not stay in Bangladesh "any longer than is necessary." All nations who valued the human spirit would recognise the liberation of Bangladesh as "a significant milestone in man's quest for liberty."

Yahya Khan, who had pledged in a broadcast the same day that Pakistan would fight to the end, accepted Mrs Gandhi's offer of a ceasefire on December 17. His gamble had failed. Pakistan had suffered an overwhelming defeat. It had lost its eastern province and nearly four and a half divisions of men and vast quantities of arms. A few thousand square miles of territory in the west wing was under Indian occupation. Pakistan's major port, Karachi, had been bombarded heavily from air and sea. Its navy had been crippled. Its air force had been driven out of the skies. The invincibility of Pakistani arms had been disproved. The foreign friends of Pakistan who believed that one Pakistani soldier equalled five Indians would have to think up another myth to keep up their sagging morale.

December 17, 1971 did not mark just the end of another war. Like August 15, 1947, it was a turning-point in the political life of the Indian subcontinent. It marked one more step in the process of banishing colonialism from the region. In 1947, under external and internal pressures, India split in two. These pressures had one aim: to keep India economically and politically weak by creating a bogeyman which would constantly threaten its existence. That bogeyman was Pakistan.

Emergence of an independent Bangladesh neutralised the poisonous influence of Pakistan. That was the great historic task that was fulfilled by the nine-month agony of the people of what was once East Pakistan and the war that had been thrust on India much against its will. That agony, felt as much by the people of India as by those of Bangladesh, had turned into ecstasy. Bangladesh was free, India had won freedom from the nightmare of constant attack from a neighbour which would remain relentlessly hostile so long as it was ruled by a coalition of feudalists, militarists, and bureaucrats who denied democracy to their own people.

By withstanding the challenge of the military junta in Islamabad and its foreign buddies and underwriting with Indian blood the freedom the people of Bangladesh had bought so dearly, Mrs Gandhi performed a historic mission which would have far-reaching consequences not only in the subcontinent but also in the whole of South and Southeast Asia. Freeing Bangladesh was not merely the fulfilment of the cherished wish of its 75 million people. It served notice on the forces that sought to reimpose colonialism, in pursuit of their global power aims, on Indo-China and other places in the Indian Ocean region that they must quit.

The message was not meant for the US alone. It was intended too for Peking, Washington's new partner which not so long ago spoke of revolutionary struggles against imperialism throughout the Third World. Alas for the power aims of Peking and Washington in the Indian Ocean, they would no longer be able to use a militarised Pakistan as a stick to beat India with. But if this doubly motheaten—this was the expression Jinnah used to describe Pakistan as the British bequeathed it to him in 1947—caricature of a nation holds together in the west, which is problematic, New Delhi must see that no big power is permitted to put fresh military muscles in place of those it has lost. Arms in Pakistani hands will automatically be turned against India.

A meaningful peace in the subcontinent must be built on the firm assurance that Pakistan will be defanged and that no big power will rearm it. If any foreign nation wishes to be friends with India, it must as a token of its sincerity subscribe to the proposition that everything that happens in the Indian Peninsula, within India's borders or in its neighbours' territories, is a matter of direct concern to New Delhi. Thus rearming Pakistan cannot, and must not, be undertaken over New Delhi's disapproval, for arms have always been used in the past against India. Peace and stability can be assured in the subcontinent only if Pakistan is demilitarised, and if the Pakistani ruling classes will not do it those who provided them with lethal weapons to use against India should do so. If they shirk their responsibility, India must not hesitate to undertake this job because it vitally concerns its security.

Mrs Gandhi has made history by casting India in a new role in Asia. In sponsoring the cause of Bangladesh when others spurned it, hypnotised by the empty boasts of the warriors of West Pakistan, she injected a dynamism into India's foreign policy which it never had in the preceding 24 years. India had fought three wars before, one against China and two against Pakistan. But these were a negative response to external threats, reflex actions without clearly defined political aims. Nobody has yet disproved Clausewitz's dictum that war is politics by other means. War, in the present world

power setup, is the most potent instrument of national policy and
will continue to be so until the world community can find a better,
more civilised way of solving international problems. A toothless,
backboneless United Nations which reflects the pulls and pushes
of various pressure groups cannot provide the answers.

War was forced on India in December 1971 for the third time
with Pakistan precisely because this organisation was unable to fulfil the main purpose for which it had been created and to guarantee
the safe return to their homeland of nearly 10 million refugees thrust
on this country by acts of barbarity the UN was unable to prevent.
When this supine body finally bestirred itself, it was at the instiga-
tion of those powers which were interested in saving Yahya Khan
from the retribution that was his just due. The third, and one hopes
final, round with Pakistan was, on India's side, a carefully thought
out action with well-defined political objectives set out well in
advance of the expected Pakistani attack.

Success would not have been assured without the support of the
Soviet Union. The cornerstone of India's foreign policy is the treaty
of friendship and the consequences that flow from it. Much more
than the military supplies Moscow has provided, its political backing
has given New Delhi confidence to pursue national aims in the international field with determination and zeal. There are, of course,
Indians and India's foreign "friends" who shake their wise heads
in despair because, they say, Mrs Gandhi is turning, or has already
turned, this country into a satellite of Moscow. They should still
their quaking hearts, and if they would then spend some time in
quiet meditation they would surely realise that India is too big to
become the satellite of any power.

India is too big not just physically but industrially, militarily and
politically as well. This bigness sticks in the craw of the geopolitical
strategists in Peking and Washington. If only India could be trim-
med to manageable proportions, all would be well with the Third
World. The assumption on which the India-Soviet treaty is founded
is a partnership of equals to work for their mutual advantage. The
agreement is workable only on that basis, not on that of patron and
client. There is no reason to believe that the Soviet leaders look at
the treaty in a different light.

The significance of the 14-day war was fully realised in Washington. Nixon and his adviser Henry Kissinger knew that it was not

just another spat between neighbours but the vehicle of a fundamental shift in the balance of power in the Indian Ocean region. That is why Nixon tried, in the final stage of the bitterly cruel drama that began in Bangladesh on the night of March 25, to swing back the pendulum of history by giving a sophisticated nuclear dimension to the crude gunboat diplomacy of 19th century imperialism and sending a naval task force into the Bay of Bengal.

What would have been the outcome of this show of might against India, and the Soviet Union, if Niazi had held out another 48 hours? Nixon must be taught, as the magnificent people of Vietnam are demonstrating, that atomic blackmail is a paper tiger, a favourite expression of his new chum in international arm-twisting, Mao Tse-tung. India, the true voice of the Third World that is struggling to find its rightful place in the sun, must stand up determinedly against the revamped old-style imperialism of Washington and the neo-imperialism of Peking. This will usher in a new era in the life of the downtrodden nations of the earth.

CHAPTER TEN

UNCHALLENGED LEADER

ALL ATTENTION IN the last nine months of 1971 was focused on the war of liberation in Bangladesh and the growing refugee problem and their climax, the short, swift and decisive military operations against Pakistan in December. Significant developments were also taking place at home. Mrs Gandhi was continuing the democratic process begun after independence of putting together the bits and pieces into which India had been broken up under British rule. After the consolidation of territories begun in 1947 came the formation of states in the 1950s on the basis of language. But within these new language entities there were, further, differences of regional culture and of stages of economic growth, and movements for autonomy developed on these lines.

Accordingly, four new states were created in 1971, bringing the total of fullfledged units of the Indian Union to 21. The new states were Himachal Pradesh, in the Himalayan foothills north of Delhi, and Manipur, Meghalaya, and Tripura, all in the northeast. Two new autonomous regions under the Central Government were also created in the same region. These were Arunachal Pradesh and Mizoram. The northeastern region is the most backward, economically and culturally, in India, and its political reorganisation is the first step towards grappling with the problems of development in an area that is very vulnerable to troublemaking outsiders. A regional council will coordinate the economic and social plans of the different units.

Three constitutional amendments Parliament passed in this period were very important because they cleared the way for implementing the socio-economic reforms the government is pledged to carry out under the popular mandate Mrs Gandhi received in the elections in March 1971. The 24th amendment gave back to Parliament and the Indian people the sovereign right to change the Constitution which the Supreme Court had sought to limit. The court had ruled in what came to be known as the Golaknath Case that Parliament lacked the power to amend the fundamental rights listed in the Constitution. The amendment reversed the court's verdict, thus reaffirming the essence of parliamentary democracy, where the people are supreme and Parliament derives its authority from the people and is accountable only to the people.

The 25th amendment was intended to remove another roadblock the Supreme Court had raised in the way of the rapid achievement of the government's programmes for social justice and democratisation. It arose from a judgment in a case regarding the nationalisation of banks the government had carried out in 1969. The case hinged on whether compensation for nationalised properties should be based on their market value or on a just computation of what the government thought the owner was due. By substituting "amount" for "compensation" in the relevant article the amendment implied that payment made when acquiring private property would be what the legislature considered reasonable. Such payment could not be challenged in a court of law. The purpose of the amendment is to avoid the time-consuming legal wrangles resulting from the takeover of large agricultural holdings and monopolistic industrial concerns. It is directed at less than 0.1 per cent of the Indian people. Property to be nationalised under it is only what is meant for exploiting the labour of others and not possessions like a house or a car designed for personal use. The social purpose of this change becomes evident when one remembers that 90 per cent of Indians own no property while 9.9 per cent own very little.

The 26th amendment enabled the government to end the privy purses and privileges of the princes and withdraw recognition of their princely status. The burden of maintaining these aristocratic parasites in luxury might not have cost the national exchequer more than Rs 50 million a year, but the effect of this legislation was not to be measured in rupees and paise but in its psychological impact of the mass of people. The existence of the maharajas and nawabs as perpetual pensioners of the government did not jive with the nation's aims of social equality and fair shares for all. They were a standing affront to the democratic concepts the government was propagating, and the end of their special status was convincing evidence to millions of people who had a marginal standard of living that the government meant to fulfil its pledges to the hungry and the workless, the shirtless ones who took Mrs Gandhi at her word and voted her to power.

The year was also important for certain moves Mrs Gandhi initiated within the Congress Party in preparation for the general election in 1972. The 1971 elections saw a cleanup at the Centre and many youthful new faces appeared on the Congress benches in the Lok Sabha. But clusters of power, based on privilege and special interests, still existed in many state capitals. No headway was possible in the government's programme of economic reform and social democratisation until these clusters were dispersed. To do this, the chief ministers who were their nucleus had to be removed.

Mrs Gandhi set about doing this very firmly and effectively. The men whom she had marked for political liquidation were summoned to New Delhi and quietly, but ruthlessly, advised to resign. Their protests, if any, were cut short and they were summarily sent back to their state capitals to perform their separate acts of renunciation. In this way Mohanlal Sukhadia, who had been Chief Minister of Rajasthan continuously from 1954, had to step down. In his place came Barkatullah Khan, and Rajasthan became the second Indian state to have a Muslim chief minister. Kashmir already had Mir Qasim.

Brahmananda Reddy of Andhra Pradesh went the same way, giving place to P.V. Narasimha Rao. M.M. Chaudhury of Assam suffered the same fate. So did S.C. Shukla in Madhya Pradesh. The ease with which these men, the founts of patronage and influence in their states, fell showed what a commanding position Mrs Gandhi occupied in national politics. For members of her own Council of Ministers this must have been an awe-inspiring spectacle, for Mrs Gandhi was said to be planning a thorough shakeup of her team after the dust of the elections had settled.

This was the only way in which the pressure groups in the states could be broken up. Mrs Gandhi's choice of replacements for the deposed satraps was revealing. She picked men who belonged to minority groups which were outside the power game in the states of whose administration they now took charge. Since they did not have much political leverage in them, and they owed their appointment to her, it was logical to expect that their first loyalty would be to her. She could depend on them to implement the policies she had decided to give top priority in the big process of social engineering, involving 550 million people, she was about to set in motion.

Barkatullah Khan was a Muslim heading the government in a state in which the Muslims counted little politically. Narasimha Rao was a Brahmin in a state where the tussle for supremacy was between Reddy and Khamma. In Assam the nominee of the majority faction in the state Congress organisation was ousted to make place for a member of a minority faction which leaned towards Mrs Gandhi. Sethi, the new Chief Minister of Madhya Pradesh, did not belong to either of the two dominant castes in Madhya Pradesh, the Brahmins and Rajputs.

This set the shape of things to come when Congress candidates were chosen for seats in the state legislatures and when new ministeries had to be formed after the elections. In drawing up lists of candidates, the heads of six more chief ministers rolled. Only three Congress chief ministers, in addition to the four whom Mrs Gandhi had chosen in the months preceding the elections, survived. One of them, V.P. Naik, weathered the storm in Maharashtra because he belonged to a socially backward group, and the strongest contender for his post was a member of the dominant Maratha community. The other two survivors of the hurricane from New Delhi which caused such havoc among the lordlings of the Congress Party were Bansi Lal of Haryana and Y.S. Parmar of Himachal Pradesh. Their removal at this juncture might have resulted in the collapse of the entire Congress power structure in their states.

But this was not Mrs Gandhi's purpose. It was to replace the existing independent, localised focuses of power by one centre located in New Delhi whose nucleus would be herself. In doing this, Mrs Gandhi was not seeking absolute power. She was only adjusting her strategy to the realities in the Congress organisation. Its inner-party democracy had been so eroded by many years of bossism that it had to be reshaped from the summit down to its foundation to fulfil the democratic national tasks ahead. This transformation needed drastic surgery by a skilled hand which did not depend for its sanction on any of the numerous lobbies in the party.

Strict conditions were laid down for selecting Congress candidates. Age, ideological bent, non-adherence to dominant factions, characters unbesmirched by charges of corruption or skulduggery were among them. The selection was mainly in the hands of groups which had been named by Congress president Sanjivayya and the Working Committee to run the state party organisations after the permanent bodies which performed these functions had been sacked for too much involvement in factional politics. To insulate the process of selection still further from factional mischief, this operation was performed in New Delhi under the watchful eyes of handpicked observers of the AICC.

Mrs Gandhi took a personal hand in deciding whether state government ministers should be given party tickets. Some 50 ministers were denied them for various reasons such as corruption, their unprogressive outlook and suspected connections or sympathy with the Organisation Congress. But whether it was a question of choosing chief ministers or ministers or ordinary legislators the underlying aim was the same: to instil in them the consciousness that their loyalty was first and last to the party apex in New Delhi and not to provincial blocks created to defy the high command.

Mrs Gandi's intervention in the process of selecting candidates was necessary to ensure that the power combines and pressure groups which had gravely damaged the prestige of the Congress Party by their constant infighting were dissolved. Their destruction was necessary to democratise and modernise the party and fit it for the role of national leadership in changing social conditions. This was not the action one would expect from a person who was solely interested in building up her own image as an infallible, unquestionable leader who depended on her charisma to win the hearts and minds of people.

Mrs Gandhi is today on a political pinnacle where she holds absolute power and could, if she wanted, do without the party, she has achieved this by purely democratic, parliamentary processes. If she is in a position to dictate today, she is there by the people's unfettered will, expressed through free elections. She is a political phenomenon, in a class by herself. Her sanction is the people. Their votes put her in power despite the attempts of various elite groups to see that she was shut out of its portals.

In the circumstances, she cannot rule without Parliament or periodic elections. If she tried to, she would cut herself off from her source of strength. If she dispensed with these instruments of democracy, she would lay herself open to pressures from the vested interests in town and village whose hold on the levers of power she must weaken if she wishes to rule effectively. Mrs Gandhi's independence of power blocks hinges on the popular support she enjoys. She speaks direct to the people today, over the heads of her own party men, who need her much more than she needs them. She has her own charisma today, no part of it inherited from her father. She has created it herself in the last three years.

Mrs Gandhi used the opportunity provided by Sheikh Mujibur Rahman's stopover in New Delhi for a few hours on his way from London to Dacca in January 1972 to prove her credibility to the voters, just as the 1971 elections had been used to project her image as a progressive wedded to improving the lot of the havenots and opposed to entrenched privilege. She reminded them at a mass rally she addressed with Mujib of four crucial promises she had fulfilled: she had liberated Bangladesh; India had won the war against Pakistan; Mujib had been released; and the refugees were returning to their homes.

The Congress Party's election manifesto spelt out the programme in great detail. It also invited attention to other pledges the party had redeemed after the 1971 elections. These included the three amendments of the Constitution already mentioned, nationalisation of general insurance, self-sufficiency in grain, and special programmes to provide more gainful employment, especially for the weaker sections of society. The manifesto then listed the urgent tasks to be fulfilled. Self-reliance was placed at the top of the list, and this was necessary in view of the stoppage of US economic aid after the start of the war the previous December.

Self-reliance was one of the main themes of Mrs Gandhi's election speeches, and with it were linked emphatic declarations that India would not touch aid which was tied to conditions no self-respecting nation could accept. The manifesto put this resolve in these words: "While we shall not deny ourselves such friendly assistance as will enable us to strengthen critical sectors of the economy, we shall redraw our economic programmes and mobilise our material and intellectual resources as to be able to do without foreign aid." The other tasks to be fulfilled to become self-reliant were: (1) to remove the inefficiencies in the economy which had created idle capacity in key industrial sectors; (2) to alter the pattern of production to make more essential consumer goods which would generate more jobs and strengthen the nation's defence; (3) to mobilise more resources, which would involve cutting the consumption of those classes of society which had benefited most from the social investments already made; and (4) labour-management harmony and introduction of modern managerial methods, with emphasis on labour participation in management at every level of the productive process.

Progress towards self-reliance must be accompanied by greater efforts to reduce social and economic inequalities. As a first step, certain quantities of essential goods would be supplied to vulnerable sections of the community at fixed, reasonable prices. "Land reforms hold the key to greater efficiency in agricultural production and the evolution of a more egalitarian social order in rural areas," the manifesto said. It spoke of a limit on farm holdings on the basis of a family of five, ranging from 10 to 18 acres of perennially irrigated land. With the passage of the 25th amendment to the Constitution, it said the way was clear for setting a limit on urban property, again based on the family unit.

On foreign relations, the manifesto said: "We are determined that India's strength and size shall never become a cause of apprehension to any of our neighbours. We are pledged not to interfere in the internal affairs of our neighbours in any way but to live with all countries in a spirit of coexistence, equality and mutual respect. We reject the great power chauvinism....

"To the new state of Bangladesh, born out of sacrifice and dedication to freedom, we offer friendship and cooperation. We say to the people of Pakistan that India wishes to live in peace and unity with them. Peace and security can be achieved only through cooperation and not through confrontation. All the nations of our region have one supreme challenge, the eradication of poverty. Let us work together to conquer this common enemy."

If proof was needed of the sincerity of these words, India's actions after the liberation of Bangladesh speak for themselves. The manner in which it set about helping in the gigantic task of economic and social reconstruction in that war-racked state is a model for relations between developing nations. The talk set in motion by unfriendly foreigners that the Indian Army would stay on in Bangladesh whether the leaders of the new state wanted it or not, and that the new republic would be turned into a colony to profit the businessmen of Calcutta, has been proved a malicious piece of fiction.

No private Indian capital has been permitted to enter Bangladesh, and trade between the two countries, except for border sales of fish, vegetables and fruits, is channelled through state-owned agencies. Far from forcing Bangladesh to depend on India for its requirements of consumer and other goods, New Delhi has released foreign exchange from its greatly strained reserves so that Bangladesh may import what it needs from other countries. Instead of trying to keep Bangladesh an agricultural colony, as Pakistan did, India is seeking ways of providing lipuid capital and technical know-how and skills to build new industries in the state sector. The economic partnership between India and Bangladesh could lay the foundation for a wider community embracing neighbours like Nepal, Burma and Ceylon, and Pakistan too when that troubled country finds leaders who are prepared to exorcise the psychotic fear of India that has been deliberately fostered over the years and collaborate in the immense and urgent task of fighting the common enemy of all their peoples—poverty.

The Treaty of Friendship, Cooperation, and Peace Mrs Gandhi and Mujib signed in Dacca on March 19 should serve as a guide to the Indian Ocean countries in ordering their relations with each other. The 25-year treaty binds Bangladesh and India "to strengthen and widen their mutually advantageous and allround cooperation in the economic, scientific and technical fields. The two countries shall develop mutual cooperation in the fields of trade, transport and communications ... on the basis of the principles of equality, mutual benefit and the most-favoured nation principle."

The two nations have agreed to undertake joint studies and action for flood control, river basin development and irrigation. They have decided to establish a permanent joint river commission, a very necessary step to protect the entire northeastern region of the subcontinent from annual floods, develop the vast potential of the Brahmaputra-Ganga river system for generating electricity, and organise a rational system of transport along the region's magnificent natural waterways.

National newspapers carried full-page advertisements on March 10 of a letter Mrs Gandhi had addressed to the Indian voter. It said that India won the war against Pakistan because of its people's "unity and adherence to high ideals, and because they voted for a strong government at the Centre which was able to take right and timely action." Now, she continued, "we must turn again to the bigger war—the war against poverty—and win it with the same unity and determination."

If the war on poverty was to succeed, the states should have governments "committed to democracy, secularism and socialism and which act in partnership with the Centre. The Congress alone can provide such governments. Parties which advocate communalism, regionalism or violence, parties which support vested interests cannot serve the national interest."

"The world is watching you," Mrs Gandhi said. "Make India self-reliant and strong so that no power can pressurise a great country inhabited by a great people. Raise the country to new heights of effort and achievement."

At stake in the elections was the fate of seven national political parties as well as the future pattern of Indian politics. The future of the Congress was as much involved as that of the opposition parties. The big question the coming polls would answer was whether the voting trend in 1971 was ephemeral or represented a genuine shift in popular opinion in favour of the Congress. All the objective factors favoured a Congress victory, for this was the only party that could guarantee national stability. No other party which claimed to be national had any chance of getting a majority in some states and emerging as the main opposition in others, or at least of becoming the main opposition party in every state where elections were to be held.

The Congress made an electoral pact with the CPI. Critics of Mrs Gandhi said this was the payoff for the Indian Communists for the support the Soviet Union had given her on Bangladesh. But this was not correct. There were three states—Bihar, Punjab, and West Bengal—where the Congress strategists had reasonable grounds for doubting whether their party would get an absolute majority. They thus hit on the tactic of an electoral pact with the Communists, with no promise that they would find a place in the state governments if the Congress came out on top.

No risk was involved in this tactical move because the CPI had long ceased being a serious political force and there was no possibility of its being a contender for power in the foreseeable future. It could only function as an appendage of the Congress and play the role of a loyal opposition. In spite of the purge in the Congress ranks after the great split in November 1969, Mrs Gandhi's party continued to be associated in the minds of large numbers of voters in these states with social and economic privilege. The electoral alliance with the CPI was expected to remove this impression.

The Congress won the March elections overwhelmingly. Its most spectacular success was in West Bengal, where it won 216 seats, double the number it secured in 1971, while the Marxists lost around 100 seats to end up with a bare 14. The Marxist share of the total vote fell from 34.8 per cent to 27.6, but the number of votes they gathered in 1972 was significantly higher than in 1971 because the turnout of voters was much heavier in 1972. The CPI, with 35 seats, became the second largest party in the state legislature, a figure which was very flattering to its actual political weight in West Bengal.

The only party besides the Congress to win more seats in these elections which, together with those in 1971, have changed the face and content of Indian politics, was the CPI. But these gains were registered only in those states where it had an electoral pact with the Congress. Elsewhere it fared as badly as the other opposition parties. In the first group of states, the Communists won 90 of the 129 seats it contested; in the other group where it was on its own, its tally was a meagre 18 out of 206.

The Congress bag was 1,926 seats out of 2,529, and for the first time it secured more than half the votes cast in many states. The three main rightwing parties were prostrate. The Organisation Congress won 88 out of 868 contests Swatantra was virtually wiped out, with 16 successes out of 346 contests. The Jana Sangh secured 105 seats out of 1,229. The Socialist score was 57 out of 644.

The elections in 1971 enabled Mrs Gandhi to build a parliamentary party to her own specifications and to cut the opposition parties to a manageable size. Those one year later enabled her to extend this process to the states. Every Congress minister, and chief minister, in the states owes his position to Mrs Gandhi, and he knows from recent examples that he is liable to be out any time he gets out of step with the Centre.

Mrs Gandhi has received two clear mandates from the people of India within 12 months. This does not end her troubles. They have just begun, both on the home and foreign fronts. To few countries is Nixon's visit to Peking in February 1972 more fateful than to India. The red signal went up for India when the Nixon-Chou communique was published in Peking. The American and Chinese leaders agreed on their estimate of what they should jointly and individually do in the Indian subcontinent after India had worsted their protege Yahya Khan. That was to circumscribe in every way possible India's influence and power in the region.

Otherwise, was there any need for both sides to issue nothing less than a directive, primarily aimed at New Delhi, for Indian and Pakistani troops to withdraw to their respective borders? They must have been aware that Pakistan has waged war on India, although they pretended to believe that India was the aggressor, that Pakistan may do so again, and that it has not recognised the finality of independent Bangladesh. Thus there can be no Indian troop withdrawal until what remains of Pakistan agrees to a peace settlement which over the next few years at least will rule out the possibility of another war with India or even the adoption of hostile attitudes which might lead to war.

Pakistan must be demilitarised as a precondition for peace. But nothing in the communique issued in Peking on February 27 indicates that this was realised by the American and Chinese leaders, and there was still less indication that they desired such action to defuse the potentially explosive military state of the subcontinent.

Indeed, everything points in the opposite direction. The communique implies an escalation of tension between India and Pakistan, for what else is meant by the Chinese declaration that Peking "firmly supports the Pakistan Government and people in their struggle to preserve their independence and sovereignty, and the people of Jammu and Kashmir in their struggle for the right of self-determination." In this single sentence there is enough inflammatory material to spell mischief on India's Himalayan border for years to come. This means that Peking wants to undo the accession of Kashmir to India, and the possibility of a fresh flareup in Ladakh in the pursuit of this objective cannot be ruled out.

Victory in the 14-day war does not promise to usher in a period of peace in which the energies of the nation can be directed to tasks of development which have been seriously neglected in the search for military security since the Chinese attack in 1962. It means greater vigilance on the borders, entailing a heavier burden on the country's resources. Some people may derive comfort from the American silence on Kashmir. They may argue that Nixon has not endorsed the Chinese attitude on Kashmir. But the US Administration has decided to renew the supply of arms to Pakistan, with the clear purpose of restoring, if this is possible, the balance of power in the subcontinent which has tilted heavily in India's favour since the events of December.

American policy on the Indian subcontinent since the Dulles era has had this aim. The militarisation of Pakistan begun by him has been designed to prevent India from developing into an Indian Ocean power. This was to be effected by building Pakistan's military sinews to the point where that country could act continuously as a watchdog on India without actual war. But the inner political compulsions of Pakistan compelled its military rulers to attack India, and the latest of these acts has resulted in disastrous defeat. If Washington wishes to restore the power balance it has sought to maintain for nearly two decades, rearming Pakistan becomes an absolute necessity.

Such a policy meshes with the avowed Chinese intention of supporting "the Pakistan Government and people in their struggle to preserve their independence and sovereignty." It would have been indiscreet for Nixon to endorse this in the communique when his role in the recent developments in the subcontinent has caused so much bitter criticism in the US and elsewhere. Steering parallel courses, Washington and Peking have one purpose: the political and military downgrading of India. This country must be kept weak and in a state of constant insecurity so that it cannot play a pivotal role in the system of counterbalance the Soviet Union is attempting to create in Asia to meet the possibilities of a China-US combination of forces against it in this region.

One thing is clear from the Nixon-Chou communique. The American and Chinese leaders have had a close look at each other and decided that they can do business together. They have identified their areas of agreement and of disagreement, and on balance they have discovered that the pluses outweigh the minuses.

A new era of super-power politics has come. India cannot isolate itself from this development. Whether it likes or not, it is a part of this system and must accordingly trim its foreign policy to face this grim reality. To ignore the danger signal hoisted in Peking would be fatal.

China is India's rival for leadership of the havenots. While it may be ready to do business with Bangladesh after some kind of stability has been effected in Pakistan, it appears to have made up its mind to be relentlessly hostile to India. This hostility is likely to intensify as India gets stronger and plays a more positive role in the Third World. But this should not deter New Delhi. It should spur the government to greater efforts to curb China's bids to prop up reaction as a counter weight to this country. India's economic growth and political stability depend on its ability to create similar conditions in the rest of the Indian Ocean region. China's aim is the opposite. It may seek in the coming months to stir up mischief against India in Pakistan, Ceylon, and Nepal, even in Bangladesh if it has the opportunity.

If India is to play an increasingly important role in the Indian Ocean, for which all the circumstances are good today, it cannot obviously depend on another power to protect its sealanes or land boundaries. This is its own responsibility. Further, it cannot ever allow a repetition of incidents like the appearance of a part of the US Seventh Fleet in the Bay of Bengal in a critical situation. India must have the strength to meet any threat from land or sea with determination. This could probably be done effectively through collective measures in collaboration with its neighbours.

Building a navy big enough and strong enough to defend the ocean approaches to India is very costly, and one that would take several years to achieve. A quicker and cheaper alternative exists. This is nuclear power. The missile may be India's answer to any power that threatens its sovereignty from the sea. Building a nuclear missile force may be one of the inevitable consequences of the new role India has perforce assumed in helping liberate Bangladesh. This is only the beginning of a new wave of political restructuring in South and Southeast Asia to further the task of liquidating colonialism which began after World War II.

At home, the big test is whether the government can work up sufficient thrust to get its *garibi hatao* programme to take off. Big thinking on this subject has been done. A strategy for going about it has been prepared. Now is the time for acting big. The crux of the problem is land reform, real reform that will give land to the millions of landless families who hunger for it. So far, the agricultural revolution has benefited only the big farmer to any considerable extent, and that too only in certain irrigated areas of the country. If the revolution is to really transform Indian agriculture, it must spread to the small farmer, particularly in the dry farm areas which cover about 60 per cent of the cultivated land.

Taking away land from the big farmer and giving it to men without land is not an act of charity. It is sound economics, and even sounder politics. Giving land to the landless will create more employment in the countryside and raise the standard of living of countless families which will be able to cultivate a holding of their own. With improved methods of cultivation and multiple-cropping patterns, it has been established that small holdings of even two acres are viable in India.

The most outstanding feature of Mrs Gandhi's political career has been courage. "My grandfather once told me," she recalled in an interview with the *New York Times*, "that there are two kinds of people: those who do the work and those who take the credit. He told me to try to be in the first group; there was much less competition there." Mrs Gandhi has always been a doer, and she has done what she felt should be done courageously. Her biggest political test is now coming—meaningful land reforms speedily implemented to provide a sound base for the other economic and social tasks she wants to carry out. This will need greater courage than she has ever been called upon to show before.

Once this hump is crossed, even greater things lie ahead. Today, Mrs Gandhi is the unchallenged leader of India. At the head of an economically strong, politically stable, modern and democratic nation, the day may not be far off when she will lead Asia away from colonialism and big-power rivalries and enervating wars to seek its destiny in cooperation and understanding and peace.

APPENDIXES

SELECTIONS FROM THE SPEECHES AND WRITINGS OF MRS GANDHI, 1966-72

A Servant of the Nation

I have always considered myself a *desh sevika* (servant of the nation) even as my father regarded himself as the first servant of the nation. I also consider myself a servant of the party and of the great people of this country. (Speech to Congress Parliamentary Party after election as Leader of the party, January 19, 1966.)

A Pledge

My own approach to the vast problems which confront us is one of humility. However, the tradition left by Gandhiji and my father, and my own unbounded faith in the people of India give me strength and confidence. Time and again, India has given evidence of an indomitable spirit. In recent years, as in the past, she has shown unmistakable courage and capacity for meeting new challenges. There is a firm base of Indianness which will withstand any trial.

The coming months bristle with difficulties. We have innumerable problems requiring urgent action. The rains have failed us, causing drought in many parts. As a result, agricultural production, which is still precariously dependent on weather and rainfall, has suffered a sharp decline. Economic aid from abroad and earnings from exports have not come to us in the measure expected. The lack of foreign exchange has hurt industrial production. Let us not be dismayed or discouraged by these unforeseen difficulties. Let us face them boldly. Let us learn from our mistakes and resolve not to let them recur. I hope to talk to you from time to time to explain the measures we take and to seek your support for them.

Above all else we must ensure food to our people in this year of scarcity. This is the first duty of government. We shall give urgent attention to the management and equitable distribution of foodgrains, both imported and procured at home. We expect full cooperation from state governments and all sections of the people in implementing our plans for rationing, procurement and distribution. Areas like Kerala which are experiencing acute shortage will receive particular attention. We shall try especially to meet the nutritional needs of mothers and children in the scarcity-affected areas to prevent permanent damage to their health. We cannot afford to take risks where basic food is concerned. We propose, therefore, to import large enough quantities of foodgrains to bridge this gap. We are grateful to the United States for her sympathetic understanding and prompt help.

Only greater production will solve our food problem. We have now a well-thought-out plan to reach water and chemical fertilisers and new high-yielding varieties of seed as well as technical advice and credit to farmers. Nowhere is self-reliance more urgent than in agriculture, and it means higher production not only for meeting the domestic needs of a large and increasing population but also for growing more for exports. We have to devise more dynamic ways of drawing upon the time and energy of our rural people and engaging them in the tasks of construction. We must breathe new life into the rural works programme and see that the income of the rural labourer is increased.

Our strategy of economic advance assigns a prominent role in the public sector to the rapid expansion of basic industries, power and transport. In our circumstances, this is not only desirable but necessary. It also imposes an obligation to initiate, construct and manage public sector enterprises efficiently and to produce sufficient profits for further investments. Within the framework of our plans, there is no conflict between the public and private sectors. In our mixed economy, private enterprise has flourished and has received help and support from government. We shall continue to encourage and assist it.

Recent events have compelled us to explore the fullest possibilities of technological self-reliance. How to replace, from domestic sources, the materials we import, the engineering services we purchase, and the knowhow we acquire from abroad? Our progress is linked with our ability to invent, improvise, adapt and conserve. We have a reservoir of talented scientists, engineers and technicians. We must make better use of them. Given the opportunity, our scientists and engineers have demonstrated their capacity to achieve outstanding results. Take the shining example of Dr Homi Bhabha and the achievements of the Atomic Energy Establishment. The path shown by Dr Bhabha will remain an inspiration. ...

In economic development, as in other fields of national activity, there is a disconcerting gap between intention and action. To bridge this gap, we should boldly adopt whatever far-reaching changes in administration may be found necessary. We must introduce new organisational patterns and modern tools and techniques of management and administration. We shall instil into governmental machinery greater efficiency and a sense of urgency and make it more responsive to the needs of the people.

In keeping with our heritage, we have followed a policy of peace and friendship with all nations, yet reserved to ourselves the right to independent opinion. The principles which have guided our foreign policy are in keeping with the best traditions of our country, and are wholly consistent with our national interest, honour and dignity. They continue to remain valid. During my travels abroad, I have had the privilege of meeting leaders in government and outside and have always found friendship and an appreciation of ourstand. The fundamental principles laid down by my father, to which he and Shastriji (Lal Bahadur Shastri) dedicated their lives, will continue to guide us. It will be my sincere endeavour to work for the strengthening of peace and international cooperation, so that people in all lands live in equality, free from domination and fear. We seek to maintain the friendliest relations with our neighbours and to resolve any disputes peacefully. The Tashkent Declaration is an expression of these sentiments. We shall fully implement it in letter and spirit.

Peace is our aim, but I am keenly aware of the responsibility of government to preserve the freedom and territorial integrity of the country. We must, therefore, be alert and keep constant vigil, strengthening our defences as necessary. The valour, the determination, the courage and sacrifice of our fighting forces have set a magnificent example. My thoughts go out today to the disabled and the families of those who gave their lives.

Peace we want because there is another war to fight—the war against poverty, disease and ignorance. We have promises to keep with our people—of work, food, clothing and shelter, health and education. The weaker and underprivileged sections of our people—all those who require special measures of social security— have always been and will remain uppermost in my mind.

Youth must have greater opportunity. The young people of India must recognise that they will get from their country tomorrow what they give her today. The nation expects them to aspire and to excel. The worlds of science and art, of thought and action beckon to them. There are new frontiers to cross, new horizons to reach and new goals to achieve.

No matter what our religion, language or state, we are one nation and one people. Let us all—farmers, and workers, teachers and students, scientists and technologists, industrialists, businessmen, politicians and public servants—put forth our best effort. Let us be strong, tolerant and disciplined, for tolerance and discipline are the very foundations of democracy. The dynamic and progressive society, the just social order which we wish to create, can be achieved only with unity of purpose and through hard work and cooperation.

Today I pledge myself anew to the ideals of the builders of our nation—to democracy and secularism, to planned economic and social advance, to peace and friendship among nations. (Broadcast over All India Radio, January 26, 1966.)

A Great Renewal

I speak to you tonight to seek your support, cooperation and blessings in the discharge of the tremendous responsibility placed on me once more in heading the Government of India.

I rededicate myself to this task with humility. I know that in the people of this country, I have 500 million colleagues and constituents, critics and friends.

Never have we faced such a testing time. There are demands and expectations on every side. I respect these. We must fulfil the basic aspirations of our people for a better and fuller life, free from want and fear. But I expect from you—as you have a right to expect of me and my colleagues—the highest quality of service, wherever you may be, in whatever you do, at all times and in all circumstances. . . .

I should like to congratulate you on the conduct of the elections and on the results. You—the free citizens of India—have not merely made your choice of elected representatives but, even more triumphantly, demonstrated our common faith in the democratic system.

The majority enjoyed by the ruling party has been reduced in the Centre and in many States. In some others, one or other party or parties, previously in opposition, have come to power either singly or in coalition. This is a significant development. Democracy implies choice. Choice involves alternatives. It is a healthy sign that alternatives are emerging and competing. . . .

I do not think there is any ground for uncertainty or dismay at the fact of reduced majorities or political changes in government. India is a stable and going concern. It has been my hope that popular ministries would be installed in all the states. I am glad that this has in fact happened with commendable smoothness and speed. The one exception has regrettably been Rajasthan, which has had to be brought under President's rule. In the circumstances, there appeared to be no reliable alternative. However, the assembly has not been dissolved and I hope that it will soon be possible to restore normal responsible government in that state.

For the rest, the ministries which have been formed in the states are, regardless of party affiliations, full partners with the Centre in the exciting enterprise of building a new united, prosperous India based on the principles of democracy, secularism, social justice, and equality of opportunity. I have written to my colleagues, the Chief Ministers, and have assured them, on behalf of the Central Government, that they will receive every support and cooperation in all constructive endeavours. Equally, I look forward to their full cooperation. Whatever our differences, I know that at heart we all have a common interest—the well-being of our patient, thoughtful, courageous people. . . .

In the economic sphere, our goal is swadeshi and *arthik swarajya* (economic independence), and we mean to demonstrate that self-reliance is as much a process as an objective. . . .

Although we are immediately confronted with a critical shortage of foodgrains, I do not believe we can afford to ignore the long-term and equally basic problem of malnutrition, which affects the health, physique and stamina of the mass of our people. Here again, I think it is necessary and possible to draw up a forward-looking charter under Article 47 of the Constitution to improve the nutritional standards of the people. . . .

If the general elections have pointed a moral, it is that the country wants performance, progress, change. Power and responsibility are passing to a new generation. The wisdom and experience of age must blend with the idealism and vitality of youth. Jai Hind. (Broadcast over All India Radio, March 15, 1967.)

Industry and Social Objectives

Mr President, I am glad that you have talked about government and business sharing common objectives. At the same time you have referred to possible differences in the approach to these objectives. Perhaps you would like to see obedience to the laws of market economy in the hope that it would help to produce wealth and that wealth so produced would ultimately reach down to the people. This proposition could have been considered at some other periods of human history, but not today. The world now is qualitatively different from what it was any time before. India is very much a part of the world. In fact, some of the movements which exist elsewhere are found in greater intensity in our country. There is a stirring of consciousness that riches and poverty are not God's creation but man's. There is a crisis in civilisation, a restlessness of spirit, and a revolt against unimplemented declarations and hypocrisy. There is a demand for participation and involvement. Are we who work in the political field, or you who work in the field of commerce and industry, capable of responding to this mood of the people?

The mood is more understandable in a country like ours where the poor outnumber the rich in overwhelming proportion. But the same mood prevails even in countries which boast of affluence and opulence. No system is perfect, but we have to realise that no economic solution can ignore the social or political context. To allow a haphazard growth of productive forces and to wait for the satisfaction of human needs in God's good time is not an answer to the problems which confront us. The first essential in our country today is to provide the elementary needs of our people.

Our objective is to infuse social purpose at strategic points in decision-making while avoiding cumbersome and unnecessary intervention. I am fully aware that sometimes our methods have been cumbersome. But in the last few years the structure of controls has been considerably simplified. A number of industries have been exempted from the licensing provisions of the Industries Act. Much greater freedom has been given to industry in the matter of adjusting production to changing requirements. Capital issues control has also been greatly simplified. Distribution and price controls have been progressively streamlined and, in fact, removed from a number of commodities. Licensing of imports for priority industries is on the basis of requirement.

In a society where affluence and power are tiny specks in the vast sea of poverty, it is not unnatural that monopoly should attract strong hostility. Industrial development is regarded by many in our country as an instrument which has benefited only a few. The problem of the concentration of economic power will have to be dealt with inter alia by the adoption of suitable policies by our financial institutions. It is reasonable to expect that large industrial groups should raise a substantially larger part of the finance required for projects than is feasible in the case of smaller groups.

Although the rate of growth is important, progress cannot be adjudged by it alone, but more by the composition of the national product and by the nature of the forces which are generated by development. Governmental decisions and policies are apt to be judged by individuals according to their own preoccupations. Within the same party or organisation there are different approaches and evaluation. You have often spoken about the size of the plan being too large; at the same time you have urged greater public investment in infrastructure as well as in productive industrial activity. . . .

The import of technology is useful and may even be essential in several sectors, but we have to rely increasingly on our own resources. Industry has sometimes complained that indigenously developed knowhow cannot be applied because it has not been carried to the production stage. Our national research institutions are taking steps to remedy this defect. At the same time, industry should not always opt for the easy path of importing established knowhow but should make a genuine effort to utilise what is indigenously available. In fact, much development work could take place in our factories, quite apart from the research work which is being done in the national research institutions. Industry should devote a greater quantum of resources to improvement of our own technology.

If we must import technology, we should do so as cheaply as possible. There has been an unnecessary controversy with regard to the centralised purchase of knowhow. The Minister of Industrial Development has fully clarified the position and I hope that there are no misgivings on this score now. The point is simple enough—when a number of units are to be set up in an industry simultaneously or within a limited period, the possibilities of saving foreign exchange by unified purchase of knowhow should be explored. When it is to the national advantage to purchase knowhow on a unified basis, this possibility should not be overlooked. (Address at the annual session of the Federation of Indian Chambers of Commerce and Industry, New Delhi, March 15, 1969.)

A Fresh Mandate

There comes a time in the life of a nation when the government of the day has to take an unusual step to cut through difficulties in order to solve the pressing problems with which the country is beset.

The present is such a time. Therefore on the advice of the Council of Ministers, the President has dissolved the Lok Sabha before its full term. In a parliamentary democracy this is not unusual, but in India it has happened for the first time.

Why did we do this when it is conceded on all sides that our government could have continued in power for another 14 months?

It is because we are concerned not merely with remaining in power but with using that power to ensure a better life to the vast majority of our people and to satisfy their aspirations for a just social order. In the present situation, we feel we cannot go ahead with our proclaimed programme and keep our pledges to our people.

In the years since independence, the nation has many achievements to its credit: vast and complex industrial enterprises, agrarian reforms, including the abolition of zamindari system; mass education, including substantial expansion of university and technical education; major social reforms and advances in many other spheres particularly in science and technology.

But despite this progress, many problems still await solution. Millions live in backwardness and poverty in town and the countryside. Justice—social, economic and political—which is the basis of our Constitution, is yet a goal to be fought for and attained. Our people are rightly impatient in their ardent desire for a speedier and more resolute advance towards this goal.

Our recent political initiatives reflect this urge. The decision to nationalise the banks, the setting up of the Monopolies Commission and the attempt to abolish privy purses were welcomed by large masses of people throughout the country.

These attempts to accelerate the pace of social and economic reform have naturally roused the opposition of vested interests. Reactionary forces have not hesitated to obstruct in every possible way the proper implementation of these urgent and vitally necessary measures.

The present political situation has set in motion a process of rethinking on major political issues within every political party.

With the division in the Congress, we lost our party majority although throughout we have retained the confidence of Parliament. The amendments to the Constitution designed to pave the way to abolish privy purses and princely privileges were lost by a fraction of a vote in the Rajya Sabha. The presidential order derecognising the princes has been struck down by the Supreme Court as unconstitutional.

Economic difficulties and the growing impatience of the people are being exploited by political elements. Violent activities are being organised by extremists. Reactionary groups are arousing communal passions and trying to divide our people. This has often led to a breakdown of law and order and dislocation of normal life, causing suffering to our people. The challenges posed by the present critical situation can be met only by the proper effective implementation of our secular socialist policies and programmes through democratic processes.

Time will not wait for us. The millions who demand food, shelter and jobs are pressing for action.

Power in a democracy resides with the people. That is why we have decided to go to our people and to seek a fresh mandate from them. We hope the elections will be completed in time for the new Lok Sabha to assemble in March 1971, well before the end of the current financial year.

The old year is ending. I wish you a year of renewed hope and common endeavour to realise the great goals which we have set for ourselves. (Broadcast over All India Radio, December 27, 1970.)

Bangladesh

We have heard much talk of democracy. The Allies claimed that the Second World War was fought to save democracy. But when democracy is so flagrantly and so brutally being destroyed, we do not hear much comment, nor do we see the sort of spontaneous strong responses which the situation warrants. Could there be a greater or a clearer expression of democracy than the one we witnessed in the elections in Pakistan? Let me remind the house that although the elections were held under the rules formulated by the military regime, immediately afterwards military repression was used mercilessly to halt the process leading to the formation of a democratically elected Government in Pakistan.

We are told by some countries that while they may disapprove of what is being done by the military rulers they cannot be a party to the disintegration of Pakistan. Is it suggested that we wish the disintegration of Pakistan? Have we not, as many members have pointed out, at every step tried not only for propriety in our relationship but also for friendship? If there is a struggle between the two parts of Pakistan, it is certainly not of our making but of the rulers of Pakistan. Is it anybody's contention that the methods being used today can achieve any integration or stability worth the name now or in the future?

The question of secession is also raised, if I may say so. This is distortion of facts. It is conveniently forgotten that the majority of Pakistan's people live in the eastern region. In a democratic system, the majority does have certain rights. They cannot be accused of secession if they assert those rights. However, if today there is such strong feeling amongst our people, it is not merely because the democratic rights and liberties of 75 million people are being crushed but because of the damaging effect which this cruel tragedy is having on our entire country economically, politically and socially.

This is the reality of the situation. It is not propaganda or the figment of anyone's imagination. Our experience of the influx of refugees and the preposterous propaganda by Pakistan has reinforced the fact that what is happening in Bangladesh does have manysided repercussions on our internal affairs. That is why I have said that this cannot be considered merely as an internal problem of Pakistan. It is an Indian problem. More, it is a worldwide problem. The international community must appreciate the very critical character of the situation that has now developed. Any failure to do so may well lead to disastrous consequences. For what is happening in Bangladesh is not just a political and economic problem. It is a problem of the very survival of the people of that whole area, the people of Bangladesh.

It is a problem created by calculated genocide that is resulting not only in the murder of tens of thousands of men, women and children but also forcing many more to seek refuge and shelter in India. It is a problem that threatens the peace and security of India and, indeed, of Southeast Asia. The world must intervene to see that peace and security is reestablished and maintained. (Speech in Parliament, May 26, 1971.)

War with Pakistan

This morning the Government of West Pakistan has declared a war upon us.

Last evening the West Pakistan Air Force violated our air space wantonly and attacked a large number of our airfields. Simultaneously their ground forces shelled our positions along the western border. Their propaganda media have made totally baseless allegations that India had launched an assault.

The news reached me just as I was leaving Calcutta. Immediately on my return I took counsel with my colleagues and with the leaders of the opposition parties. We were all of one mind and united in our resolve that the nation's freedom should be defended, and unanimous that the aggressor should be beaten back.

I am sure that the same sense of solidarity will mark our work in the difficult days ahead.

A state of emergency has been proclaimed. We are approaching the house to adopt the Defence of India Bill.

Our feeling is one of regret that Pakistan did not desist from the ultimate folly and sorrow that at a time when the greatest need of this subcontinent is development the peoples of India and Pakistan have been pushed into war. We could have lived as good neighbours, but the people of West Pakistan have never had a say in their destiny. In this grave hour our own dominant emotion is one of confidence and faith.

For over nine months, the military regime of West Pakistan has barbarously trampled upon freedom and basic human rights in Bangladesh. The army of occupation has committed heinous crimes, unmatched for their vindictive ferocity. Many millions have been uprooted: 10 million have been pushed into our country.

We repeatedly drew the attention of the world to this annihilation of a whole people, to this menace to our security. Everywhere the people showed sympathy and understanding for the economic and other burdens and the danger to India.

But governments seemed morally and politically paralysed. Belated efforts to persuade the Islamabad regime to take some step which would lead to a lasting solution fell on deaf ears.

The wrath of the West Pakistan Army has been aroused because the people of Bangladesh have stood and struggled for values which the army is unable to comprehend, and which it has suppressed in every province of Pakistan.

As the Mukti Bahini's effectiveness increased, the West Pakistani Army became more desperate. Our tradition is to stand not with tyrants but with the oppressed. And so their anger has been turned upon us.

West Pakistan has escalated and enlarged the aggression against India.

War needs as much patience and self-restraint as does peace. The military regime of West Pakistan will go all out to sow suspicion and rumour in the hope of fomenting communal tension and internal trouble. Let us not be taken in by their designs. We must maintain unity and a sense of high purpose. We should be prepared for a long struggle. High production, agricultural and industrial, is the foundation upon which defence rests. The courage and fighting capability of the jawans have to be backed by the dedication of the farmer, the worker, the technician and the trader.

The business community has a special responsibility to resist the temptation to hoard or to charge higher profit.

Artists and writers, teachers and students, the nation looks to you to defend our ideals, to keep high our morale.

To the women of our country, I make a special appeal to save every possible grain and rupee to avoid waste. The sacrifice of each of us will build the nation's strength and enduring power.

We have stood for peace, but peace itself has to be defended.

We are fighting to safeguard our territorial integrity and national honour. Above all, we are fighting for the cause of human freedom. (Statement in Parliament, December 4, 1971.)

Surrender

Mr Speaker, Sir, the West Pakistani forces have unconditionally surrendered. Dacca is now the free capital of a free country.

The instrument of surrender was signed at Dacca at 16-31 hours (IST) today by Lt-Gen A.A.K. Niazi on behalf of the Pakistan Eastern Command and Lt-Gen Jagjit Singh Aurora, GOC-in-C in command of the Indian and Bangladesh forces in the eastern theatre, accepted the surrender.

This house and the entire nation rejoice in this historic event. We hail the people of Bangladesh in their hour of triumph. We hail the brave young men and boys of the Mukti Bahini for their valour and dedication. We are proud of our own army, navy, air force and Border Security Force who have so magnificently demonstrated their quality and capacity. Their discipline and devotion to duty are well-known.

India will remember with gratitude the sacrifice of those who have laid down their lives and our thoughts are with their families.

Our armed forces are under strict orders to treat Pakistani prisoners of war in accordance with the Geneva Convention and to deal with all sections of the population of Bangladesh in a humane manner.

The commanders of the Mukti Bahini have issued similar orders to their forces. Although the Government of Bangladesh has not yet been given the opportunity to sign the Geneva Convention, they have also declared they will fully abide by the convention.

It will be the responsibility of the Government of Bangladesh, the Mukti Bahini and the Indian armed forces to prevent any reprisals.

Our objectives were limited to assist the gallant people of Bangladesh and their Mukti Bahini to liberate their country from the reign of terror and to resist aggression on our own land.

Indian armed forces will not remain in Bangladesh any longer than is necessary.

The millions who were driven out of their homes across our borders have already begun trekking back.

The rehabilitation of this wartorn land calls for dedicated teamwork by its government and the people.

We hope and trust that the father of this new nation, Sheikh Mujibur Rahman, will take his rightful place among his own people and lead Bangladesh to peace, progress and prosperity.

The time has come when they can together look forward to a meaningful future in their Sonar Bangla. They have our good wishes.

The triumph is not theirs alone. All nations who value the human spirit will recognise it as a significant milestone in man's quest for liberty. (Statement in Parliament on ceasefire in Bangladesh, December 16, 1971.)

A Letter to the Voter
Dear Voter,

Elections are with us again. Your vote will decide whether India will be strong and prosperous.

Communalism cannot strengthen the country. Nor will parties which champion vested interests or those who preach violence. Provincial parties cannot promote national unity.

From the very beginning of the Gandhi-Nehru era the Congress has stood for liberty, equality and tolerance; for democracy, secularism and socialism.

Last year, when the elections were held for the national Parliament, we little knew that we would soon be fighting a military war.

Our people won the war because of their unity and adherence to high ideals, and because they voted for a strong government at the Centre which was able to take right and timely action.

We have kept our promises to help free Bangladesh and to ensure the return of 10 million refugees to their homes in honour and safety.

Now we must turn again to the bigger war—the war against poverty and win it with the same unity and determination.

The people and administration must work together. Don't be a spectator. Join as an active participant.

Many of our programmes can only be implemented by state governments. If the Garibi Hatao (drive out poverty) programme is to succeed, we need governments in the states which are committed to democracy, secularism and socialism and which act in partnership with the Centre.

The Congress alone can provide such governments. Parties which advocate communalism, regionalism or violence, parties which support vested interests cannot serve the national interest.

The world is watching you. Make India self-reliant and strong so that no power can pressurise a great country inhabited by a great people. Raise the country to new heights of effort and achievement.

I sincerely hope that your vote will enable my party to form the government in your state with an overwhelming majority.

I appeal to you to vote for the Congress candidate by putting the mark on the cow and calf symbol.

Jai Hind. (Advertisement in newspapers, March 10, 1972.)

Greater Equality

I am grateful to you for the kind words that you have said.

Whatever victory we have gained is due to the people of India. Although they have been a much maligned people—and every time one opens foreign magazines and newspapers, one sees something about them which is very far from the truth—I feel the experience of all those of us who have worked among the people has been of their maturity of thought, of their solid commonsense. If we have won, it is only we have been able to walk in step with them to some extent, to the goodness of their heart, and confidence they have reposed in us.

I can only hope that we—I, as a person and we as the party—will prove worthy of their confidence. I have always believed that India has a great destiny, and again it is because I have known the people at the village level, at the slum level, at all the different levels. I do not mean to say that I don't have a very high opinion of the intellectuals and others, because they also have fine qualities.

But I feel that our major weakness has been in trying to follow paths which have been drawn out and mapped by outside countries. I think the time has come when we should measure growth, achievement, and advance, by our own standards. It does not mean that we want less growth than in other countries. But, we have seen that even in rich countries poverty exists. Therefore that is not necessarily the answer to our problems.

The Congress President was very correct when he said that this victory has imposed a great responsibility on us. The only way we will be able to discharge it is if we can chart new paths and if we are again able to convince the people to do their part of the work because no leadership and no party alone can solve the tremendous problems which the country faces. We can have programmes for giving employment, we can have programmes for building houses, we can have programmes for irrigation, but none of these is going to solve the problem of poverty or the problem of equality.

We have amended the constitution when that became necessary. But that again gives only national equality. It is not real equality. Real equality will only come when there is amongst the people equality of opportunity. I know that this cannot be absolute. But nevertheless, we do want a greater equality than has so far been achieved by any nation in the world.

Therefore, I think the time has come for us to think very seriously about these things and not to stop the programmes which we have in hand. We have to go ahead with them, but in every sphere whether it is education or health or giving justice to the people, we have to think along new lines.

In this matter we are completely on an uncharted path. We have to make the chart. We have to make the experiments. We will have to make our mistakes even; but I think that we owe to the people, even if it is a mistake, even if it has cost us something in popularity. I think we owe it the people that we give this guidance at this difficult stage.

It is not only India which is in difficult stage. All the world is trying to grope around for new methods, new paths, but many of them are not able to shake off old thinking. They think that merely if they transfer, or make new friendships or something like that, the problems will be solved.

What is needed is new thinking. I am sure that with the help of all of you, with the help of the people, the intelligentsia as well as all other sections of the people, we can make a beginning. I do not think that we can come to the end of this because this is a very long journey. But if we make a beginning and if the people see that we have made a beginning, I think that itself will be a great achievement.

Even without this victory, the responsibility on us was very heavy. The responsibility of the last victory—the victory of the war itself—has given a new and different type of burden. Today we have the advantage of knowing that the people of India are with us and I am sure we can evolve the kind of united working cooperation from all sections of people which is the only way to make democracy real.

As you know, I am not one of those who believe in leadership. My whole attempt is how to create a society in which people do not need leaders. I do not mean you do not need a leader, you do not need a Prime Minister. But in this country, we still have a very dependent attitude in every section. They are looking towards somebody to do something, somebody to show the way, whether it is in our party whether it is even in other parties, whether it is in different sections. Now we must attempt a far more self-reliant attitude of mind amongst our people, specially amongst the younger people.

As I said earlier, I think they have the quality, and we have let again the Western notions of the importance of literacy and so on guide our own work. Literacy is important to be in touch with the thinking of the world. But not being literate does not condemn a man to stupidity or lack of sense. So, we have to look at our people in this light that each one of them, whether they are literate or illiterate, have something to contribute and we have the responsibility of helping them to blossom whatever talent or capacity they have and putting it to the use of the country in wider sense of the word.

I don't mean by development merely more schools or more hospitals but development of society as a whole towards a better life that the people themselves feel that they have better life which is, for instance, not the case with the so-called affluent countries of today. I am not also saying that the only answer is spiritualism, because it is not. The people must have adequate food; they must have adequate shelter; they must have the opportunity of good employment.

But as I said myself—I must confess—I am only groping. I have many ideas on what changes should take place. But, I am not definite about them. I don't think I can be definite till I have discussed with all of you, or each of us has discussed it on a much wider level in our constituencies, in universities, and in many different such forums. It is out of that that we can evolve something which will involve the whole country, the whole people, to advance towards new goals and new higher levels of functioning and of living.

It is strange that people think that electioneering means a lot of hard work. But I can tell you, for me it does not, because it is the only time when I can do a great deal of reading. In helicopters, in planes, while one is sitting here, one is involved in meeting people somewhere. It is the only time during the last election that I read a great deal, and during these last 25-29 days I've done a enormous amount of reading and I find that in many, many countries they are groping towards the future but no one has found the answer. All that they know is that the society in their country today is merely creating dissatisfaction. We aim at more schools and more hospitals, but we have statistics from Latin America and from other parts to show that you can have more and more schools and yet you are not reaching all the people. They are spending more and more. Somehow out of that amount, although it is meant to bring education to the lowest level in the village, it is only a very small proportion of the people who benefit from that money. We have seen that in our own country.

Therefore, the answer is not not to have schools or not to have hospitals. You must have them. But we must evolve some way in which the benefit of this really reaches the people and not just the higher strata or even the middle strata. So I think that after the victory is the best time to think deeply and seriously about these methods. We tend to get excited and spend our time in congratulating each other and time goes very fast.

So, I hope this time, although I should like to congratulate all of you because I know that you have all worked in your constituencies, and many of you had been sent as observers or in other capacities to different states, and my reports are that very good work has been done and it is only because of your good work and of the good work of the Congress workers that this victory was possible. My contribution is merely to give a pat on the back. I think I am going to cheer up everybody and urge everybody to work hard.

I hope that we will now be inspired to a greater extent because of what we want we must do now, not in five years but in three years. I think we should set a target that in three years we have to achieve a certain target. I think if we work as we worked for this election, as you worked for the parliamentary election, as you worked during the war, if you work with that spirit of unity and dedication, there is no reason why we should not be able to reach all our targets.

Once again, I would like to say thank you very much indeed. Now, of course, we come to the real business, which is that we meet once again in Parliament, and you have a taste of what is to come from the President's address. You saw also that the President was able to hold his own in spite of the much younger people trying with all their strength (to prevent him from addressing). He still could hold his own. It was they who were tired and went out.

So, let us deal with Parliament in the same manner—that is not to get too excited, that is to be calm and patient. Let us understand the people who were defeated. Let us not rub salt into their wounds. So, since we have the victory we can afford to be generous in these matters, and we should just see that work proceeds and the standard of work high amongst us—that is unity and a high level of functioning. Thank you very much. (Speech to Congress Parliamentary Party, March 13, 1972.)

LETTER TO PRESIDENT NIXON
WRITTEN ON DECEMBER 15, 1971

Dear Mr President,

I am writing at a moment of deep anguish at the unhappy turn which the relations between our two countries have taken.

I am setting aside all pride, prejudice and passion and trying, as calmly as I can, to analyse once again the origins of the tragedy which is being enacted.

There are moments in history when brooding tragedy and its dark shadows can be lightened by recalling great moments of the past. One such great moment which has inspired millions of people to die for liberty was the Declaration of Independence by the United States of America.

That declaration stated that whenever any form of government becomes destructive of man's inalienable rights to life, liberty and pursuit of happiness, it was the right of the people to alter or abolish it.

All unprejudiced persons objectively surveying the grim events in Bangladesh since March 25 have recognised the revolt of 75 million people, a people who were forced to the conclusion that neither their life, nor their liberty, to say nothing of the possibility of the pursuit of happiness, was available to them.

The world press, radio and television have faithfully recorded the story. The most perceptive of American scholars who are knowledgeable about the affairs of this subcontinent revealed the anatomy of East Bengal's frustrations.

This tragic war, which is continuing, could have been averted if, during the nine months prior to Pakistan's attack on us on December 3, the great leaders of the world had paid some attention to the fact of revolt, tried to see the reality of the situation and searched for a genuine basis for reconciliation.

I wrote letters along these lines. I undertook a tour in quest of peace at a time when it was extremely difficult to leave the country in the hope of presenting to some of the leaders of the world the situation as I saw it. It was heartbreaking to find that while there was sympathy for the poor refugees the disease itself was ignored.

War also could have been avoided if the power, influence and authority of all the states, and above all of the United States, had got Sheikh Mujibur Rahman released. Instead, we were told that a civilian administration was being installed. Everyone knows that this civilian administration was a farce; today the farce has turned into a tragedy.

Lip-service was paid to the need for a political solution, but not a single worthwhile step was taken to bring this about. Instead, the rulers of West Pakistan went ahead holding farcical elections to seats which had been arbitrarily declared vacant.

There was not even a whisper that anyone from the outside world had tried to have contact with Mujibur Rahman. Our earnest plea that Sheikh Mujibur Rahman should be released, or that, even if he were to be kept under detention, contact with him might be established, was not considered practical on the ground that the US could not urge policies which might lead to the overthrow of President Yahya Khan.

While the United States recognised that Mujib was a core factor in the situation and that unquestionably in the long run Pakistan must acquiesce in the direction of greater autonomy for East Pakistan, arguments were advanced to demonstrate the fragility of the situation and of Yahya Khan's difficulty.

Mr President, may I ask you in all sincerity: was the release or even secret negotiations with a single human being, namely, Sheikh Mujibur Rahman, more disastrous than the waging of a war?

The fact of the matter is that the rulers of West Pakistan got away with the impression that they could do what they liked because no one, not even the United States, would choose to take a public position that while Pakistan's integrity was certainly sacrosanct, human rights, liberty were no less so and that there was a necessary interconnection between the inviolability of states and the contentment of their people.

Mr President, despite the continued defiance by the rulers of Pakistan of the most elementary facts of life, we would still have tried our hardest to restrain the mounting pressure, as we had for nine long months, and war could have been prevented had the rulers of Pakistan not launched a massive attack on us by bombing our airfields in Amritsar, Pathankot, Srinagar, Avantipur, Uttarlai, Jodhpur, Ambala and Agra in the broad daylight on December 3, 1971, at a time when I was away in Calcutta, my colleagues, the Defence Minister, was in Patna and was due to leave further for Bangalore in the South, and another senior colleague of mine, the Finance Minister, was in Bombay.

The fact that this initiative was taken at this particular time of our absence from the capital showed perfidious intentions. In the face of this, could we simply sit back trusting that the rulers of Pakistan or those who were advising them, had peaceful, constructive and reasonable intent?

We are asked what we want. We seek nothing for ourselves.

We do not want any territory of what was East Pakistan and now constitutes Bangladesh.

We do not want any territory of West Pakistan. We do want lasting peace with Pakistan. But will Pakistan give up its ceaseless and yet pointless agitation of the last 24 years over Kashmir? Are they willing to give up their hate campaign and posture of perpetual hostility towards India? How many times in the last 24 years have my father and I offered a pact of non-aggression to Pakistan? It is a matter of recorded history that each time such an offer was made Pakistan rejected it out of hand.

We are deeply hurt by the innundoes and insinuations that it was we who have precipitated the crisis and have in any way thwarted the emergence of solutions. I do not really know who is responsible for this calumny. During my visit to the United States, United Kingdom, France, Germany, Austria and Belgium, the point I emphasised publicly as well as privately was the immediate need for a political settlement.

We waited nine months for it. When Dr Kissinger came in August 1971, I had emphasised to him the importance of seeking an early political settlement. But we have not received, even to this day, the barest framework of a settlement which would take into account the facts as they are and not as we imagine them to be.

Be that as it may, it is my earnest and sincere hope that with all the knowledge and deep understanding of human affairs you, as President of the United States and reflecting the will, the aspirations and idealism of the great American people, will at least let me know where precisely we have gone wrong before your representatives or spokesmen deal with us with such harshness of language.

With regards and best wishes.

Yours sincerely,
Indira Gandhi

TREATY OF PEACE, FRIENDSHIP AND COOPERATION BETWEEN THE REPUBLIC OF INDIA AND THE SOVIET UNION, AUGUST 9, 1971

Desirous of expanding and consolidating the existing relations of sincere friendship between them,

Believing that the further development of friendship and cooperation meets the basic national interests of both the states as well as the interests of lasting peace in Asia and the world,

Determined to promote the consolidation of universal peace and security and to make steadfast efforts for the relaxation of international tensions and the final elimination of the remnants of colonialism,

Upholding their firm faith in the principles of peaceful coexistence and cooperation between states with different political and social systems,

Convinced that in the world today international problems can only be solved by cooperation and not by conflict,

Reaffirming their determination to abide by the purposes and principles of the United Nations Charter,

The Republic of India on the one side, and the Union of Soviet Socialist Republics on the other side,

Have decided to conclude the present treaty, for which purpose the following plenipotentiaries have been appointed:

On behalf of the Republic of India:

Sardar Swaran Singh,

Minister of External Affairs,

On behalf of the Union of Soviet Socialist Republics:

Mr A.A. Gromyko,

Minister of Foreign Affairs,

Who, having each presented their credentials, which are found to be in proper form and due order, have agreed as follows:

Article I

The high contracting parties solemnly declare that enduring peace and friendship shall prevail between the two countries and their peoples. Each party shall respect the independence, sovereignty and territorial integrity of the other party and refrain from interfering in the other's internal affairs. The high contracting parties shall continue to develop and consolidate the relations of sincere friendship, good neighbourliness and comprehensive cooperation existing between them on the basis of the aforesaid principles as well as those of equality and mutual benefit.

Article II

Guided by the desire to contribute in every possible way to ensure enduring peace and security of their people, the high contracting parties declare their determination to continue their efforts to preserve and to strengthen peace in Asia and throughout the world, to halt the arms race and to achieve general and complete disarmament, including both nuclear and conventional, under effective international control.

Article III

Guided by their loyalty to the lofty ideal of equality of all peoples and nations, irrespective of race or creed, the high contracting parties condemn colonialism and racialism in all forms and manifestations, and reaffirm their determination to strive for their final and complete elimination.

The high contracting parties shall cooperate with each other states to achieve these aims and to support the just aspirations of the peoples in their struggle against colonialism and racial domination.

Article IV

The Republic of India respects the peaceloving policy of the Union of Soviet Socialist Republics aimed at strengthening friendship and cooperation with all nations.

The Union of Soviet Socialist Republics respects India's policy of nonalignment and reaffirms that this policy constitutes an important factor in the maintenance of universal peace and international security and in the lessening of tensions in the world.

Article V

Deeply interested in ensuring universal peace and security, attaching great importance to their mutual cooperation in the international field for achieving those aims, the high contracting parties will maintain regular contacts with each other on major international problems affecting the interests of both the states by means of meetings and exchanges of views between their leading statesmen, visits by official delegations and special envoys of the two governments, and through diplomatic channels.

Article VI

Attaching great importance to economic, scientific and technological cooperation between them, the high contracting parties will continue to consolidate and expand mutually advantageous and comprehensive cooperation in these fields as well as expand trade, transport and communications between them on the basis of the principles of equality, mutual benefit and most-favoured-nation treatment, subject to the existing agreements and the special arrangements with contiguous countries as specified in the Indo-Soviet Trade Agreement of December 26, 1970.

Article VII

The high contracting parties shall promote further development of ties and contracts between them in the fields of science, art, literature, education, public health, press, radio, television, cinema, tourism and sports.

Article VIII

In accordance with the traditional friendship established between the two countries, each of the high contracting parties solemnly declares that it shall not enter into or participate in any military alliance directed against the other party.

Each high contracting party undertakes to abstain from any aggression against the other party and to prevent the use of its territory for the commission of any act which might inflict military damage on the other high contracting party.

Article IX

Each high contracting party undertakes to abstain from providing any assistance to any third party that engages in armed conflict with the other party. In the event of either party being subjected to an attack or a threat thereof, the high contracting parties shall immediately enter into mutual consulations in order to remove such threat and to take appropriate effective measures to ensure peace and the security of their countries.

Article X

Each high contracting party solemnly declares that it shall not enter into any obligation, secret or public, with one or more states, which is incompatible with this treaty. Each high contracting party further declares that no obligation exists, nor shall any obligation be entered into, between itself and any other state or states, which might cause military damage to the other party.

Article XI

This treaty is concluded for the duration of 20 years and will be automatically extended for each successive period of five years unless either high contracting party declares its desire to terminate it by giving notice to the other high contracting party twelve months prior to the expiration of the treaty. The treaty will be subject to ratification and will come into force on the date of the exchange of instruments of ratification which will take place in Moscow within one month of the signing of this treaty.

Article XII

Any difference of interpretation of any article or articles of this treaty which may arise between the high contracting parties will be settled bilaterally by peaceful means in a spirit of mutual respect and understanding.

The said plenipotentiaries have signed the present treaty in Hindi, Russian and English, all texts being equally authentic and have affixed thereto their seals.

Done in New Delhi on the ninth day of August in the year one thousand nine hundred and seventy one.

TREATY OF FRIENDSHIP, COOPERATION AND PEACE BETWEEN THE REPUBLIC OF INDIA AND THE PEOPLE'S REPUBLIC OF BANGLADESH, MARCH 19, 1972

Inspired by common ideals of peace, secularism, democracy, socialism and nationalism,

Having struggled together for the realisation of those ideals and cemented ties of friendship through blood and sacrifices which led to the triumphant emergence of a free, sovereign and independent Bangladesh,

Determined to maintain fraternal and goodneighbourly relations and transform their border into a border of eternal peace and friendship,

Adhering firmly to the basic tenets of nonalignment, peaceful coexistence, mutual cooperation, noninterference in internal affairs and respect for territorial integrity and sovereignty,

Determined to safeguard peace, stability and security and to promote progress of their respective countries through all possible avenues of mutual cooperation,

Determined further to expand and strengthen the existing relations of friendship between them, convinced that the further development of friendship and cooperation meets the national interests of both states as well as the interests of lasting peace in Asia and the world,

Resolved to contribute to strengthening world peace and security and to make efforts to bring about a relaxation of international tension and the final elimination of vestiges of colonialism, racialism and imperialism,

Convinced that in the present-day world international problems can be solved only through cooperation and not through conflict or confrontation,

Reaffirming their determination to follow the aims and principles of the United Nations Charter, the Republic of India, on the one hand, and the People's Republic of Bangladesh, on the other, have decided to conclude the present treaty.

Article 1

The high contracting parties, inspired by the ideals for which their respective peoples struggled and made sacrifices together, solemnly declare that there shall be lasting peace and friendship between their two countries and their peoples, each side shall respect the independence, sovereignty and territorial integrity of the other and refrain from interfering in the internal affairs of the other side.

The high contracting parties shall further develop and strengthen the relations of friendship, goodneighbourliness and allround cooperation existing between them, on the basis of the abovementioned principles as well as the principles of equality and mutual benefit.

Article 2

Being guided by their devotion to the principles of equality of all peoples and states, irrespective of race or creed, the high contracting parties condemn colonialism and racialism in all forms and manifestations and are determined to strive for their final and complete elimination.

The high contracting parties shall cooperate with other states in achieving these aims and support the just aspirations of peoples in their struggle against colonialism and racial discrimination and for their national liberation.

Article 3

The high contracting parties reaffirm their faith in the policy of nonalignment and peaceful coexistence as important factors for easing tension in the world, maintaining international peace and security and strengthening national sovereignty and independence.

Article 4

The high contracting parties shall maintain regular contacts with each other on major international problems affecting the interests of both states, through meetings and exchanges of views at all levels.

Article 5

The high contracting parties shall continue to strengthen and widen their mutually advantageous and allround cooperation in the economic, scientific and technical fields. The two countries shall develop mutual cooperation in the fields of trade, transport and communications between them on the basis of the principles of equality, mutual benefit and the most-favoured nation principle.

Article 6

The high contracting parties further agree to make joint studies and take joint action in the fields of flood control, river basin development and the development of hydroelectric power and irrigation.

Article 7

The high contracting parties shall promote relations in the fields of art, literature, education, culture, sports and health.

Article 8

In accordance with the ties of friendship existing between the two countries each of the high contracting parties solemnly declares that it shall not enter into or participate in any military alliance directed against the other party.

Each of the high contracting parties shall refrain from any aggression against the other party and shall not allow the use of its territory for committing any act that may cause military damage to or constitute a threat to the security of the other high contracting party.

Article 9

Each of the high contracting parties shall refrain from giving any assitance to any third party taking part in an armed conflict against the other party. In case either party is attacked or threatened with attack, the high contracting parties shall immediately enter into mutual consultations in order to take appropriate effective measures to eliminate the threat and thus ensure the peace and security of their countries.

Article 10

Each of the high contracting parties solemnly declares that it shall not undertake any commitment, secret or open, toward one or more states which may be incompatible with the present treaty.

Article 11

The present treaty is signed for a term of 25 years and shall be subject to renewal by mutual agreement of the high contracting parties.

The treaty shall come into force with immediate effect from the date of its signature.

Article 12

Any differences in interpreting any article or articles of the present treaty that may arise between the high contracting parties shall be settled on a bilateral basis by peaceful means in a spirit of mutual respect and understanding.

12-POINT PROGRAMME FOR PROGRESS (FROM CONGRESS PARTY ELECTION MANIFESTO, 1971)

The Congress appeal to the people to return its candidates to the Lok Sabha and thus give it a clear mandate to:

1   continue the advance to socialism through democratic process and devise the administrative system capable of speeding implementations;

2   put down the forces of violence and disorder so that all our citizens can live in peace and harmony;

3   defend secularism and safeguard the interests of the minorities and the weaker sections of the community, particularly the scheduled castes, scheduled tribes and the other backward sections so that they may attain "equality of status and opportunity and fraternity assuring the dignity of the individual";

4   end anachronistic privileges such as privy purses, etc. and reduce glaring disparities in income and opportunity;

5   accelerate efforts to provide basic requirements to our people by undertaking a dynamic programme of agricultural development by the application of science and technology and thereby usher in a new phase of rural prosperity, which will improve the condition of small farmers, in dry areas, the landless, artisans and others, who eke out their existence through diverse skills;

6   provide fresh avenues of employment and thus widen the participation of our citizens in nation building activities;

7   enlarge the role of the public sector and improve its performance;

8   give scope to the private sector to play its proper role in the economy, while curbing the concentration of economic power and wealth;

9   control prices and ensure to the people the supplies of essential commodities at reasonable rates;

10   launch upon a programme of child welfare to provide nutritious diet to pre-school children;

11   provide elementary education to all children and reshape secondary and higher education to suit the needs of the country; and

12   for these purposes, to effect such amendments of the constitution as may be necessary.

Extracts from Election Manifesto, 1972

Even in the midst of great upheaval and the burdens it imposed upon our country, the Congress did not neglect some of the most important of the promises which the Party had made in 1971.

By the 24th Amendment, the powers of Parliament to amend any part of the constitution has been restored. The Directive Principles enjoin that the ownership and control of the material resources of the community should be so distributed as best to subserve the common good and that the working of the economic system should not result in the concentration of wealth and means of production to the common detriment. By the 25th Amendment, these principles have been given their due position. The needs of the masses have been put above those of the privileged few.

The 26th Amendment redeems the pledge to abolish privy purses and princely privileges, thereby ending an outdated and anachronistic system.

We promised to take over general insurance; this has been done. We emphasised that the public sector would be extended in those areas where state ownership is vital and our taking over of the coking coal mines and of certain areas of foreign trade are steps in that direction.

We promised to concentrate on the speedy development of agriculture. The production of foodgrains reaching 108 million tons has enabled us to stop the import of cereals....

Self-reliance has been the objective of our plans of development since 1951. Today it assumes prime urgency. Fortunately, we are in a position to achieve self-reliance, provided we put in that extra effort which national interest demands.... While we shall not deny ourselves such friendly assistance as will enable us to strengthen critical sectors of the economy, we shall redraw our economic programmes and mobilise our material and intellectual resources as to be able to do without foreign aid.

To achieve economic independence, we have to undertake a number of measures with utmost urgency. First of all, we have to remove the inefficiencies in our economy which have resulted in the existence of idle capacities in important sectors of the economy, such as steel, fertilisers and others. Secondly, we must restructure our production pattern with the greatest emphasis on essential consumer goods and investment goods which are necessary for generating employment and for the defence of the country.

In order to achieve these objectives, we must mobilise more resources. This will mean curtailment of consumption by those strata of society who have benefited most from the social investment that has already been carried out. It is not enough to have more savings; it is necessary that some of these savings should accrue to the public sector. That will also help to create public property on a greater scale and hasten the transition to a socialist society.

There should be a more harmonious pattern of work between labour and management. The introduction of modern methods of management must be expedited with emphasis on participation of workers in management at every level in the production process.

Progress towards self-reliance must be accompanied by greater efforts to reduce social and economic inequalities. The levels of income of the weakest section of the population have to be raised so that the minimum necessities of life become available to them. As a first step, Congress will establish a system which will ensure minimum quantities of essential goods at fixed and reasonable prices to vulnerable sections of the community. . . .

Education is a major instrument for the achievement of our social objectives and to generate self-confidence among the people in accordance with national culture and ethos. Among the major tasks facing education is the inculcation of new social values, promotion of secularism and national integration and the spreading of a humane, rational and self-reliant outlook. It must contribute to the development of a self-generating economy, based on advanced science and technology. It must enable the fuller development of the students' personality and equip them to face the challenges of a fast-changing world. The system of education and examinations must consequently undergo radical reform. . . .

The Congress Party has resolved to provide compulsory school education up to the age of 11 for every child by 1975 and up to the age of 14 by 1980. The present quality of primary education has still not benefited our masses in a meaningful way. The party, therefore, aims at raising the standard of primary education by improving the curriculam, providing an adequate number of model primary schools with suitable reservation for the socially and economically backward sections of the community and by employing modern educational technology to improve teacher-training facilities. . . .

In fulfilment of the commitments made in the Congress election manifesto of 1971, the Union Government has already initiated several special programmes of high priority to provide additional employment and to promote greater opportunities for the weaker sections. These include programmes for rural works in drought prone areas, the crash scheme for rural employment, and special schemes for the benefit of small farmers, marginal farmers and agricultural labourers. A special provision was also made in the Central Budget of 1971-72 for schemes, many of which have been sanctioned, for absorbing the educated unemployed in general and engineers and technicians in particular. . . .

Land reforms hold the key to greater efficiency in agricultural production and the evolution of a more egalitarian social order in rural areas. The Centre has taken the lead in the formulation of a national policy on legislation on land ceilings. . . . Celing should be applicable for the family as a whole, the term family being defined so as to include husband, wife and minor children. Where the number of members in the family exceeds five, additional land may be allowed for each member in excess of five in such a manner that the total area admissible to the family does not exceed twice the ceiling limit for a family. The ceiling for a family of five members may be fixed within the range of 10 to 18 acres of perennially irrigated land or irrigated land capable of growing two crops. . . . There should also be an absolute ceiling for a family of five. Exemptions in the existing laws in favour of mechanised farms, wellmanaged forms, etc need to be reviewed. Other exemptions in favour of plantations of tea, coffee, cardamom, rubber, etc will be carefully examined. . . .

The coming into force of the 25th Constitutional Amendment will clear the way for the imposition of ceiling on ownership of urban property, based on the family as a unit. Effective measures will also be taken to prevent racketeering in the purchase and sale of urban lands. . . .

The interests of the minorities will continue to be safeguarded in accordance with the complete and unswerving devotion of the Congress to the tenets of secularism and democracy. . . .

We are determined that India's strength and size shall never become a cause of apprehension to any of our neighbours. We are pledged not to interfere in the internal affairs of our neighbours in any way but to live with all countries in a spirit of coexistence, equality and mutual respect. We reject not only great power chauvinism but also the doctrines of spheres of influence and balance of power.

To the new state of Bangladesh, born out of sacrifice and dedication to freedom, we offer friendship and cooperation. We say to the people of Pakistan that India wishes to live in peace and amity with them. Peace and security can be achieved only through cooperation and not through confrontation. All the nations of our region have one supreme challenge, the eradication of poverty. Let us work together to conquer this common enemy. . . .

The Ten-point Programme (Adopted by the AICC in New Delhi, June 1966)

The All-India Congress Committee desires that the process of implementing the programmes towards the attainment of a socialist democratic society should be accelerated. In this connection the following items call for consideration:

1. Social control of banking institutions;
2. Nationalisation of general insurance;
3. Commoditywise progress in state trading in imports and exports;
4. State trading in foodgrains;
5. Expansion of cooperatives;
6. Regulating growth of monopolies;
7. Provision of minimum needs to the community;
8. Unearned increments in urban land values;
9. Rural works programme, land reforms;
10. Privileges of ex-rulers.

The AICC after careful consideration takes the following decisions:

1. The election manifesto mentioned "it is necessary to bring most of the banking institutions under social control in order to serve the cause of economic growth and fulfil our social purposes more effectively and to make credit available to the producer in all fields where it is needed." The AICC requests the government to take steps to implement this programme.

2. A scheme should be worked out to bring under the public sector general insurance.

3. The AICC is of the view that the export and import trade should be progressively undertaken through state agencies. The government is requested to undertake a commoditywise examination and formulate a phased programme to this end.

4. A national policy of public distribution of foodgrains, particularly to the vulnerable section of the community, should be worked out for this purpose. The Food Corporation of India and cooperative agencies should be utilised to the maximum extent.

5. Consumer cooperatives should be organised to cover urban and rural areas for the supply of the more essential commodities to the community at fair prices. To make this distribution effective, processing and manufacturing industries in

the state and coöperative sectors should be established on an extensive scale.

6.   The AICC welcomes the decision of the government to implement the Monopolies Commission report and hopes effective steps would be taken to curb monopolies and concentration of economic power.

7.   The AICC is of the opinion that positive steps should be taken towards the provision of minimum needs to the entire community by the year 1975. As a first step, the government should promulgate a socialist charter for children which would ensure the provision of high-protein food to children and such other amenities as could be organised and to work out a phased programme for implementation.

8.   The pattern of conspicuous consumption and wasteful display which increasingly characterise some urban areas are out of place in a socialist society. They also constitute a drain on the resources available to the community for productive investment. There is thus a compelling need to impose limitations on urban income and property. Concrete steps should therefore be taken for placing restrictions on individual holdings of urban land for preventing racketeering in land in urban areas.

9.   The AICC desires that a plan for a rural works programme which would give opportunities for employment, especially to the landless, and at the same time help to create overheads in agriculture such as agro-industries, reclamation of land, soil conservation, afforestation, minor irrigation, feeder roads, cattle development and other programmes of area development should be formulated to be implemented.

Laws for tenancy reforms have been enacted in many states. It is obvious that the land reforms have in some respects not been implemented effectively. The implementation should be accelerated.

Credit should be made available to agricultural labour against personal security or assets that are to be created. Minimum wage legislation for agricultural labour should be implemented more effectively.

Drinking water should be provided in all rural areas by a national programme of wells, conservation of water and utilisation of scientific methods.

10.   The privileges and the privy purses enjoyed by the ex-rulers are incongruous to the concept and practice of democracy. The AICC is of the view that the government should ... take steps to remove them.

Mrs Gandhi's Note on Economic Policy (Presented to the AICC in Bangalore, July 1966)

The time has come to restate our economic policy and set the direction in which we have to move to achieve our social goal. This has become all the more necessary in view of doubts that have been raised with regard to our intentions and our willingness to take the hard and difficult steps which are necessary. In respect of many of the items some steps have already been taken but what is important is to intensify our efforts and to keep the social goal all along in the forefront.

Congress has always championed the cause of the weaker sections, minorities and the underprivileged. This should continue to be the policy of the Congress:

a.   Impose ceiling on unproductive expenditure and conspicuous consumption of corporate bodies;

b.   Nationalised financial institutions should introduce a change in creditworthiness criteria in their lending policies, so as to encourage professional and competent persons;

c.   Special efforts should be made to finance new entrepreneurs in less developed regions and a special fund should be provided for provision of assistance to backward regions;

d.   Expeditious appointment of Monopolies Commission manned by persons of integrity;

e.   Public-sector projects should be given more autonomy and manned by young competent persons committed to the project;

f.   Special effort should be made to build up a cadre of public sector projects;

g.   The consumer industries should be reserved wherever possible for development in the cooperative and small-scale sector and entry of big business should be banned in the manufacture of these products;

h.   Special efforts should be made to encourage new talent to provide avenues of employment to the young and educated;

i.   Foreign capital should not be allowed to enter fields in which local technical know-how is available;

j.   Heavy penalties should be imposed on those who indulge in restrictive trade practices.

There are other suggestions which may not fit within the present policy framework. However, I have already asked the Finance Ministry and the Planning Commission to look into the feasibility of imposing ceilings on incomes and holdings of urban properties.

There is strong feeling in the country regarding the nationalisation of private commerical banks. We had taken a decision at an earlier AICC meeting, but perhaps we may review it. Either we can consider the nationalisation of the top five or six banks or issue directions that the resources of banks should be reserved to a larger extent for public purpose. Investments of banks in government securities stood at 24.75 per cent on June 13. This is, of course, a fluctuating figure. During the busy season, banks liquidate their investments in government securities and finance trade and industry. During the slack season, when the funds return, investment in securities is increased. This figure of investment in securities is raised on the average for both slack and busy seasons by about 5 per cent. This will make available about Rs 200 crores for the public sector.

Against this, it may be argued that this will involve denial of credit to trade and industry and will also affect the profitability of the banks. But in times of credit squeeze, private industry somehow adjusts itself. They mobilise deposits on their own, cut their investments or bring in unaccounted money and somehow manage. The question whether banks' investment in government securities should not be raised has to be seriously considered. If necessary, this extra 5 per cent can be invested in special types of securities, proceeds being utilised for quick-yielding schemes like minor irrigation programmes, rural electrification, fisheries.

Even after the new policy of social control and reconstitution of boards of directors, the former industrialist-chairmen of the banks still continue on the board and naturally influence the present chairmen, who had previously been general managers. We may examine whether through legislation or otherwise we can prevent these men from continuing on the boards. The chief executive of the banks will not then feel obliged to the former chairman and may be expected to take an independent line in regard to lendings.

While it may not be practical to nationalise all import and export, can we not consider the nationalisation of the import of raw materials? This would make collective bargaining possible and might get us better prices. The policy of the distribution of such import licences should also be reviewed. We should review the licensing system so that licences are not given only to the bigger houses. Shares could be distributed with more equality.

We have already decided in the cabinet that ministries of the Central Government should first approach the public sector with regard to their requirements before they decide to buy from the private sector or import. I believe some state governments have issued such directions to their ministries, but Congress governments have a special responsibility in this reagrd.

Some thought should be given to profit-sharing in industrial establishments, but alongside this some schemes should be thought of with regard to incentives for greater production as well as the regulation of the work.

I fully realise that overall development is the best and the only reliable way of increasing employment opportunities. However, the situation is so acute in the country that it has become necessary to have some special programmes to give employment in the rural areas as well as to the educated. Naturally, whatever scheme we think of cannot be adequate to meet the situation, but it should give the impression that we are taking a first step and making a genuine effort.

a.   Service cooperatives should be built up in rural areas;

b.   Special assistance should be provided to small agriculturists and form cooperatives to enable them to take processing of agro-based and other industries;

c.   Special attention should be paid to development of minor irrigation projects;

Land reform is no less important. If we do not act urgently, grave political and economic problems will arise. From time to time, suggestions have been made to imporve the lot of the tenant and of landless agricultural labour:

a.   Declare all tenancies non-resumable;

b.   Give the tenants the right to mortgage their interest in land for obtaining credit;

c.   Place restriction on sale of land by scheduled castes and scheduled tribes and backward classes in favour of others;

d.   Enforce ceiling on landholdings energetically;

e.   Draw up a programme for distribution of government wasteland and lands held by panchayats;

f.   Enact legislation to protect tenants, agricultural workers from their house sites.

If these points are agreed to, the following minimum programme is indicated:

a.   A tenant should not be liable for eviction as long as he pays his rent regularly. Provision to this effect exists in tenancy laws of most states, but the law is not enforced effectively. States should be asked to set up special machinery for effective implementation of this measure. Penalties should be suitably enhanced;

b.   There should be a proper record of rights of tenants;

c.   Land ceiling laws already implemented should be enforced;

d.   Restrictions could be placed on purchase of land belonging to scheduled castes and scheduled tribes, but whether similar restrictions could also be placed on land belonging to backward classes is doubtful. The list of backward classes is pretty long in many states.

The suggestion that tenants should be also given the right to hypothecate their interest in land to obtain credit for agricultural development may meet with resistance. There would be no serious objection to credit being made available for short-term purposes, for example, seeds, fertilisers, on the security of the crop. But in regard to long-term loans for such purposes as sinking of wells, installation of pumpsets, landholders may well insist on their consent being obtained.

But if we can at least make a beginning with rigorous and effective enforcement of the existing laws, we would have demonstrated our earnestness and reduced some of the tension in the countryside.

A review of agricultural wages is also called for in the light of increased yields now obtaining. Minimum wages for agricultural labour may have to be prescribed for each tract and enforced. This will enable landless labourers to participate in the fruits of the green revolution.

Mrs Gandhi's Letter to Congressmen (Released on November 8, 1969)

There is a crisis in the Congress and in the nation.

It is not a crisis which has come about all of a sudden. It has been building over a long time.

What we witness today is not a mere clash of personalities, and certainly not a fight for power. It is not as simple as a conflict between the parliamentary and organisational wings.

It is a conflict between two outlooks and attitudes in regard to the objectives of the Congress and the methods in which the Congress itself should function.

It is a conflict between those who are for socialism, for change, and for the fullest internal democracy and debate in the organisation on the one hand, and those who are for the status quo, for conformism, and for less than full discussion inside the Congress.

Even if some people are in the second group, this basic analysis is not affected. An individual here or there, not sharing the outlook of the group does not alter the basic facts of the situation.

The Congress stands for democracy, secularism, socialism and nonalignment in international relations.

The various policymaking units of our organisation, whether the working Committee of the All-India Congress Committee or the delegates' session, have reaffirmed these objectives from time to time. But within the Congress there has been a group which did not have total faith in these objectives. People of this group paid only lip-service to these ideals because they knew that if they openly expressed their reservations they would lose the power and influence they had derived from the party.

This group is not a new phenomenon. It has existed in our party throughout the last 22 years and even before. I know that this group constantly tried to check and frustrate my father's attempt to bring about far-reaching economic and social changes. The Congress was moulded by Mahatma Gandhi and my father to be the prime instrument of social change. The acceptance of office and of responsibilities of government was, after all, to bring about this nonviolent revolution in our society. If this cannot be done, what is the use of Congress or what is the purpose of being in government?

In his last years, my father was greatly concerned that there were people inside the Congress who were offering resistance to change. My own experience even before the fourth general election was that the forces of the status quo, with close links with powerful economic interests, were ranged against me.

While the biggest leaders of the Congress were involved in the tasks of government and administration in the years after freedom, some persons developed a vested interest in power. They began to regard themselves as the Congress, forgetting that they could keep their mandate only through service and only if the Congress had a powerful mass base.

To consolidate their hold and in the name of discipline they pushed out of the Congress many honest and devoted workers, whose loyalty to the organisation and its ideals was beyond question. Their arrogant use of authority made some people resign from the Congress or retire from active work. It also discouraged fresh streams of young workers from flowing into the Congress.

The worker in the field was denied his right to mould the party and the party registers were packed with bogus names. Recently the tendency to acquire factional control of the organisation has become more intense. This is linked up with the desire to control the direction of government policy and economic life in line with the narrow purposes and interests of a limited section.

This is the background to the present crisis. As I recently told the Bombay Pradesh Congress workers, some of those who are now worried about a split remained complacent when the strength of the Congress was being wilfully sacrificed in state after state, and in election after election.

The time has come to bring all this into the open, so that there might be full and free discussion of the problems of the Congress. I do not want a split in our great national organisation, which brought freedom to our country and which has to fulfil its promise by building a new society.

But I want unity which is a unity on principles and on methods of work. To speak of socialism and secularism, to vote for them in meetings, but to have public image of association with those who were opposed to secularism and socialism is no service to the Congress.

The full details of the present crisis are well known to all of you. For your convenience copies of the letters which were exchanged between Shri Nijalingappa and me (and between him and Shri Fakhruddin Ali Ahmed and Shri C. Subramaniam) are attached.

The correspondence fully brings out the background of the requisition which the majority of the All-India Congress Committee members presented to the Congress Working Committee and which was so summarily, unconstitutionally and unwisely turned down.

As you know, certain chief ministers strove to bring about a compromise, but even while they were continuing their efforts, Shri Nijalingappa asked me to explain my "conduct"; even after this notice was served, I met Shri Nijalingappa and discussed with him certain proposals on which Shri K.C. Abraham and Shri

Veerandra Patil had worked.

Since Shri Nijalingappa, for whose personal qualities I have regard, had felt that the requisition was a vote of censure on him, inasmuch as it was confined to the Congress President's election and left out other elections, I suggested that we might have a new election to all elected offices above the PCC level as an interim measure, pending the revision of rolls and new elections at all levels on the basis of rolls which were cleansed of bogus membership

Shri Nijalingappa on the contrary spoke of taking up the whole process of election on the basis of the existing rolls—which is obviously no answer to the crisis since it would retard the remedial action that can still be taken to set things right in the organisation.

Even as regards this proposal, unsatisfactory as it was, Shri Nijalingappa made no firm commitment. He only said that any written proposal which was made to him would be placed before the Working Committee. He did not vouchsafe any information on whether the meeting would be that of the truncated body or of the full body. I did not discuss the show cause notice with him and he did not offer to rescind it. From other reliable sources it was learnt that he had every intention of taking action against me and others.

To go back from these details to the main question of the crisis before the country—outside the narrow confines of our party, great and turbulent changes are taking place in the minds and hearts of our people. There are new trends of thought. There are new aspirations. And there are new tensions apart from some other older tensions. Political consciousness has matured and deepened among the masses and in this process, many ideas, some old and some new, are being canvassed, and a kind of crystallisation has been steadily taking place.

Faced with this change in the national political enviornment, our party has been in danger of losing its orientation—it has been trying to cope with the situation by a ritualistic repetition of the formal positions of the past without making a fresh assessment of the needs of the present and the future in accordance with its own living revolutionary tradition.

There is loss of confidence in ourselves and in the destiny both of our country and our party. There is a tendency to be influenced by the forces of reaction, revivalism and vested interests.

In this situation, it is necessary for the Congress to recognise frankly that it no longer commands in full the loyalty and emotions of the nation as it did in the past. It must also recognise that it cannot discharge the role of leadership unless it redefines its position sharply in relation to the competing points of view in the country—and it can serve as an effective instrument of the national purpose only if it revitalises its membership and its methods of functioning.

The Congress must open its closed doors to winds of change, reestablish its living links with the people in every town and village of India. It must make a fresh effort to forge fresh links with the new generation which has grown since our independence. It must reflect the modern elements in our society. It must draw unto itself the live elements of modern science and technology. It must command the loyalty of our intelligentsia. It must seek to induce amongst the ordinary people a feeling of confidence that we are a party which seeks to serve the people.

In the nature of things, a national debate on the issues at stake and the competing points of view cannot be carried on without some pain and emotional disturbance. But the need for the debate is inescapable. No one can stifle it. Indeed, effective political leadership lies in promoting an orderly, sober, civilised discussion of the issues we have to resolve. We cannot treat a fresh debate as the sign of a revolt against any individual or group. The subversion of free debate constitutes a danger to democracy not only within our party, but in the country.

The basic issue in the conflict must be separated from other issues which, though important, are secondary. The basic issue is whether the democratic process shall prevail or not in the Congress.

There are the legal and constitutional aspects of the conflict. These have been discussed fully in the correspondence that has passed between me and Shri Nijalingappa. The legal and constitutional issues are important. But behind them is the far more important issue whether Congressmen who have built the Congress at great sacrifice are to run it and mould it as they like or whether bosses should run it as they like. There has been always a conflict between bossism and democracy, and it is this conflict which has reached a critical stage.

The aim of the Congress still is to bring about far-reaching social and economic changes amounting to a social revolution. But it has ceased to be a fit instrument of its own aims and is losing its sense of purpose. It has been losing its articulation. its sense of direction and its old confidence. The average Congressman has been denied his voice in it, and the committees at various levels are hardly functioning.

The present conflict, or debate, or whatever else it is called, concerns what the Congress can still do for the people. It is wedded to democratic socialism. Both democracy and socialism are necessary. Without the one, the other cannot exist. Democracy is inevitable in the conditions of the country. So is socialism. The democratic process and the socialist process can go together. The Congress, as the most broadbased organisation, can do it best. That is why it has always to keep its goal of socialism in view and maintain the democratic process within itself.

There is no place for a sectarian approach. Socialism in this country can come about only as the result of an open, broad movement. It cannot come overnight. Both the Government and the people must work for it. The people must be mobilised in support of socialist measures undertaken by the Government. Legislation alone is not enough.

The organisation is important to mobilise the people for socialism. It is not enough for it to come to life only for elections. It must be constantly at work to educate the people regarding our policies and actions. Social power has to be organised in support of political power.

This social power is necessary even to win elections. The organisation cannot afford to become weak in any part. It must be ever-vigilant and active. Even with its recent amendments the Constitution is still inadequate for the fast-changing situation. The desire to immediately change the set-up, even to a limited extent, arises because of the necessity to consider in depth in what manner further radical transformation of the organisation can be brought about. The membership must be real, not artificial. The commitment must be sincere, there must be a sense of urgency.

The government is a part of the organisation. If the organisation is alive, the government will be aware of its responsibility. The state of the organisation is reflected in the legislative parties and the government. There is no conflict between the two wings. The relations between them have often been discussed and are well understood.

The importance of the organisation cannot be minimised. To make it real and alive and to make it work democratically, and dynamically, is the aim of the meeting of the members of the All-India Congress Committee that will be held in Delhi. It can release vast energies, and these energies can take the Congress and the people forward. This is the issue before us—other matters are secondary.

INDEX